The

Second

Fifty

Your Roadmap to Fitness and Healthy Aging

By

Tom Geimeier
and
Jerry Auton

7290 Investment Drive, Unit B
North Charleston, SC 29418

Published under the company name of:
Second Fifty Innovations, LLC.
c/o Tom Geimeier
5936 Vice Lane
Burlington, KY 41005

ISBN: 13: 978-1533237828

10: 1533237824

The author and publisher specifically disclaim all responsibility for any liability or loss, personal or otherwise, which is incurred directly or indirectly of the use and application of any of the contents of this book. The health information in this book is for information only and is not a medical guide.

Before embarking on any fitness program, especially over age 50, it is always advisable to have a thorough physical exam with your family doctor before pursuing any physical training program.

Cover design: Adam Geimeier

Table of Contents

Appendices:

Foreword

By Ray Hughes

I heartily endorse the concept of *The Second Fifty* and especially the uniqueness of utilizing a knowledgeable, well experienced *panel of experts*, who have worn the victory laurels and the battle scars of over 400 years of combined experience. The effort by Tom and Jerry is no meager cut and paste production with little value between the covers. The bios on the *panel* clearly indicate they have earned the right to give the reader the value of their trials, errors and successes.

There are hundreds of books that have been written on fitness for men, women, and active athletes in every possible genre of fitness, athletics and sports competition. These books, whether written by a single person or converted into a TV infomercial are based on the research and success of one possible, self -claimed authority, on fitness. *The Second Fifty* is a virtual powerhouse of information, not from one source, but by a collective group from many disciplines. It is certainly a condensed and valuable knowledge, in one book, by potentially eight authors.

The reader will see a certain consensus of the *panel* on many of the crucial aspects of fitness presented. That consensus should put the reader on the right path to personal success; answer many questions; save the reader valuable time; eliminate needless trial and error; reduce the possibly of injury and keep the participant in the proper frame of mind.

The authors have assembled an outstanding *panel*, with impressive bios, and I am honored to be included in this comprehensive book. I have worked very hard to earn my reputation and have been very conscientious about lending my name to any project, as I have trained, associated and competed with and against, a number of military, United States and world self- defense champions. I will not do or say anything to tarnish what I have worked for over the past 60 years. In the tristate area of greater- Cincinnati I have been instrumental and on the cutting edge of establishing most of the current martial arts clubs and I do not and will not endorse anyone or project I cannot fully support.

The expertise of the *panel* seems valid and I feel confident and regard the contributors as qualified to present this book on physical fitness. I hope the readers will consider this book an excellent knowledge base that will propel them to great personal success and the accomplishment of their *Second Fifty* goals.

Preface

By Tom and Jerry

The Second Fifty is a reflective piece that makes a sincere effort, to help those over 50, avoid the pitfalls that can ruin the quality of the second half of life and eventually the final quarter of your existence. Once you pass the mid- century mark and look into the mirror of truth you might ask yourself what strategies can be utilized to maintain what you have; seek what was lost, if it ever existed; and avoid the outcome of those who throw their fate to the winds.

The major difference between *The Second Fifty* and the dozens of other fitness themed books is the **extensive, cumulative experience** of the authors and contributors who make up our *panel of experts*. Many current publications have researched numerous books and articles to accumulate a presentable, intelligent knowledge base that taps into the experience of so called experts in the field. Many of the authors are young and could not have possibly attained the information presented through their own experiences, but they may sound good in theory. There are also many fitness oriented magazines on the market, but the advertisements usually outnumber the pages of informative text.

The Second Fifty is the real deal with a wealth of cumulative personal knowledge and practical experience to back it up! *The Second Fifty's panel of experts* have over 400 years of personal experience covering the major fields of athletics, nutrition, rehabilitating injuries and an extensive variety of fitness. We present the facts pertaining to each chapter and ask our *panel,* comprising our living bibliography, for their expert advice. We follow-up **the *panel's* comments** with w**hat the research says** incorporating current additional information from the numerous books and articles from the fitness, health, and medical arenas. **What the research says** is followed by **the bottom line** or a summation of the input from all sources. Finally, we offer **the hot tip**, which is a brief parting bit of advice that provides the reader with special, ready to use insight.

We have been very fortunate to have enjoyed a life with numerous experiences and opportunities in athletics and fitness. We have also been very fortunate to have met a variety of quality people, with the same mindset, who we consider experts in their respective fields do to their notoriety and accomplishments. We extend a heartfelt thanks to our contributing *panel* for agreeing to share their knowledge through dozens of interview hours. We can attest that there were no fees exchanged and our *panel* eagerly agreed to participate on a *panel* of their peers because they agreed with the premise of the proposed book. Every member of our *panel* had to meet certain specific qualifications: must be over age 50; have accumulated over 50 years of experience in their respective field; be considered an expert by their peers; and have obtained a solid knowledge base in physical training and numerous exercise systems. Our *panel* consists of: **Terry Collis** (karate / fitness / athletic trainer), **Devorah Dometrich - Herbst** (karate/ kobudo), **Dave Guidugli** (football / boxing/basketball / professional athletic trainer), **Ray Hughes** (judo / fitness), **Lanny Julian** (arm wrestling / fitness), **Roger Riedinger** (track and field / bodybuilding / nutritional consultant / athletic trainer /gym owner). The cumulative experience of our *panel* is truly a treasure trove of real world, hands on knowledge you are not likely to find in any one source or current publication

Ideally, *The Second Fifty* is directed primarily for those over 50, to assist them with a logical fitness path, but it may also prove to be a valuable resource for all ages that have the foresight to think beyond their years. *The Second Fifty* would be a wise investment for those wanting to expedite their progress and who realize that our living *panel* has the knowledge that will assist them in achieving their goals while minimizing the potential pitfalls and setbacks.

How often the young take a pass on the sound advice that should be heeded because they feel immune as though they are wearing that cloak of invincibility. Our main objective is to help the reader avoid needless mistakes and direct them in their pursuit of healthy, more productive life with a goal of making it to that elusive age of triple digits. We are insightful enough to understand many of our over fifty readers have probably had some past injuries and medical problems to overcome, but there are plans and programs in *The Second Fifty*, which can provide benefits for anyone seeking a better outcome. **We are presenting a book we sincerely wish was available for us to read years ago.**

Introduction

By Tom Geimeier and Jerry Auton

Before taking any important journey we usually make numerous plans and develop a roadmap for the success of that venture. Today, most travelers have their trusty GPS devices to take them on their journeys and return them back to their starting points. There is no guaranteed GPS for a journey through life and it is imperative that we make logical and detailed plans for the success of that journey. Maybe, *The Second Fifty* can suffice, as a substitute GPS, for your fitness and health roadmap, in the long life, which we all hope lies ahead?

The Second Fifty begins with an honest assessment of exactly where you are regarding your current health and physical condition. What are your physical limitations and what are your realistic expectations and achievable goals? What is the best path for the reader to follow in order to maintain and realistically enhance their chances for quality aging and greater longevity? Life is a balance of positives and negatives, but the key to good health, aging and longevity is to accentuate the positive and diminish the negative baggage. A good, well thought out roadmap, certainly offers more potential and possible success than trusting your future to the four winds or the hands of fate.

Unfortunately, there are millions of people who will not benefit from reading any book dedicated to fitness and health. Many people are consumed by their professions, careers, and providing stability for their families. Those are fantastic and admirable qualities, but hopefully they will leave time for maintaining their health. It is an old and sad story, often repeated, how someone was consumed by work and neglected their health only to find out catastrophic news shortly after retirement. The quality time with family, friends, hobbies, and the joy of the golden years can suddenly become a time of despair. Please do not think in the short term, but think well ahead and plan for your success accordingly.

It is unbelievable the number of people driving their automobiles with handicapped stickers hanging from their rear view mirrors; parking their cars and entering the restaurants or shopping malls that appear to be very healthy looking people, but looks alone can be deceiving. Reports on health state that America has some of the fattest people on earth, regardless of economics. When you turn 65 and report to your local Social Security Office you will be in for another very big surprise. Those 65 and over are often in the minority because many of the clients present will be in their 20s, 30s 40s, and 50s, with a plethora of real or contrived health ailments. The system is being drained by millions who are sometimes hoping, with pride, to obtain a disability status and a guaranteed monthly check with little regard for their health or longevity. Most of those people are thinking about today and could care less about the future. When the future arrives, often more quickly than expected, there will be no easy solution and turning back the clock may be extremely difficult and probably impossible. The years of neglect may well result in a shortened life span, premature aging and the vaporization of one's hopes and dreams.

A positive state of mind is also crucial as you embark on your journey. There will be ups and downs in life that can potentially derail or even destroy your mind and body. A person must be strong, resilient, in the survivor mode and with a sincere effort to keep their life in balance. There will be times you may bend, but you must will yourself never to break. There will be ailments that come with aging; possible genetic influences; and potential injuries that can be anticipated, but greatly minimized. Yes, one of the most important tools for your success will be your state of mind. Imagine a 70 -year old still trying to do the heavy single or max repetition and whine that his bench press or squat is down from their best efforts at age 35. A good friend, Paul Tipton, age 85, jokingly told us, "The golden years are not for wimps." Setting realistic goals that will avoid injury and prioritize health concerns is part of a good, comprehensive roadmap. The priority of *The Second Fifty* is to provide the reader with a fitness roadmap and program that adhered to, with consistency and a sound nutritional plan, will give them an advantage in that all important *Second Fifty*. There are no guarantees regarding tomorrow or our time on earth, but being proactive is a much better option than simply doing nothing. Crossing your fingers and hoping for the best cannot be substantiated by any research.

Yes, there are certain age related events and problems no one can totally avoid, but can be cautiously anticipated and intelligently planned for. Forewarned is forearmed and a thorough understanding of these age old pitfalls might arm us to do battle with them. You have nothing to lose and so much to gain. Time is elusive and the years will certainly fly by so we encourage the readers to decide if the active approach in the *Second Fifty* is a better option than the passive.

Finally, it is important to remember that there are three things in life you will never get back:

- The sands of **time** wait for no one and your first fifty years are ancient history. Remember that the clock is ticking!
- All the tears in the world will not bring back the missed **opportunities.** We encourage you to take advantage of the 400 years of collective experience in *The Second Fifty*.
- Countless, useless **words** and excuses show failure to commit when this book is a call to action.

Tom Geimeier

About the Authors

Tom Geimeier

I passed the Medicare age milestone, as this book was in the developmental stage, and feel the timing was right to present the information to those entering their *Second Fifty*. My writing credentials, until now, have been limited to writing several published articles for historical magazines. (SAR Magazine, Fall 2013) I attained an Associate Degree in Civil Engineering from the University of Kentucky; a Bachelor's Degree in History and Biology from Northern Kentucky University; two Master's Degrees in Educational Administration from Xavier University, in Cincinnati, and spent a 39 year career in education. A lot of credit goes to Uncle Sam and the GI Bill for making my educational goals more financially achievable after serving four years in the United States Air Force.

My physical fitness interests began around age 14 by observing and learning from local bodybuilders, weightlifters and various martial artists in my neighborhood. I remember at least seven or eight black belts in the various martial arts, as well as, a number of early weightlifters, bodybuilders, and fitness types just within my neighborhood. Many would become the role models that unknowingly planted the mental seeds that fitness, self- defense, and athletics were beneficial and time well spent. I also joined the local YMCA for swimming and basketball and eventually the German Turner Society or local gymnastic Turnverien. The Turner Societies in America started as German based organization that emphasized a strong mind and body philosophy. Like other youth of the baby boomer generation, I was also influenced by reading various fitness magazines; the adventures of the comic heroes and the early TV heroes; but mostly by the role models I personally observed.

My credentials in the physical culture world include: gym owner; bodybuilding and powerlifting competitor; contest promoter; State and National AAU Physique Judge; Kentucky AAU Physique Committee Co-Chairman; founder of the largest one day bodybuilding contest in America (The Northern Kentucky)); martial arts enthusiast for over 25 years (Sin The' instructor in Shaolin Do); semi-pro baseball player (The West Covington Athletics of the Buckeye League in Cincinnati); and typical youth baseball, high school track and field, and basketball. I was also a high school and youth coach in a variety of sports, over a 15- year period.

Unfortunately, my body has paid a very high price for some mistakes and poor decisions regarding the quality of my own well- being. I have never had a serious illness and take no daily medications, but I have wreaked havoc on my skeletal system, especially my joints. Patience was not one of my best attributes and I was always open to taking a risk or dare. I can speak, from personal experience, about injuries you can possibly avoid, as well as, the extensive medical bills and countless hours of physical therapy required for rehabilitation. There was an unavoidable situation in 1987 where I rescued a trapped kindergarten student from underneath the wheel of an automobile driven by his own frantic mother. I was able to lift the right side of the 1970's automobile off the screaming child and by the grace of God he was basically unharmed, but over the next three years that event required five surgeries.

*See the documentation, from the General Assembly of Kentucky, in Appendix B.

Jerry Auton

Co-authoring *The Second Fifty* made me realize that our lives are so often formed by our experiences at a very early age. As one of eight children in our family, with a father who worked very hard as a house painter, I learned early on that I had to carry my own weight and utilized a variety of methods of earning money for school, clothes and establishing a savings account. Shoveling snow in the winter, cutting grass, and caddying at the local golf course in the summer were only a few of the jobs that not only provided money, but taught me real life values and the importance of being strong and in good physical shape. On my thirteenth birthday my dad surprised me with my first set of real weights, a Billard Company110 pound barbell set that included two dumbbell bars and collars. Wow! The plates were gold painted, seemed very heavy and brand new! I could now discard the paint buckets and cans that were filled with hardened concrete, with a broom stick or piece of pipe stuck between them, as a crude, workable handle.

I also worked throughout my high school years to lighten the load for my dad by paying many of my own expenses. A strong work ethic was valued in my family and playing sports was not a priority or the best option. My mom and dad would have supported me if I didn't work while in school, but I preferred earning my own way and have never regretted that decision. I have always taken pride in working hard, being thrifty and saving my money whenever possible. Little did my dad realize that his special birthday gift would set into motion the active mind of a 13- year old and fifty years later his son would still be involved in fitness and have that first set of precious barbells, as a reminder and motivator, from those early years. I learned a lot from those early benchmark events, my education and personal experiences, which I have listed: Bachelor Degree in Health, Education and Physical Education from the University of Kentucky; Certified Trainer (ISSA) Specialist in Senior Fitness; Certified Personal Trainer (DWS) Specialist, Brain, Cognitive Fitness, Older Adults; placed 5th in the Mr. Kentucky Physique Contest at age 22; placed 4th in the Mr. Northern Kentucky Physique Contest (60 and over class) at age 62; (largest one day physique competition in the U.S.) performed best personal max bench press on 40th birthday; competed in and placed in numerous arm wrestling competitions throughout the mid- west; tore in half lengthwise both the Chicago and the Manhattan telephone books, on a local TV show, that measured over 4 inches thick; and have ranked in the top 10 to runners in my weight division for 5 K runs in the Cincinnati area.

Chances are you are reading this bio because you are either at the senior citizen stage of your life; rapidly closing in on it; and hope this book was not a waste of your money. I also hope that you are reading our book to find out how you can improve the quality of your life during your senior years. It is never too late, but there is no easy road or fountain of youth to drink from! Success will always be accomplished through a combination of: hard work, knowledge and enthusiasm.

The choice is yours! I know that if I am going to live through any part of my *Second Fifty* I do not choose to do so in the waiting rooms of doctors' offices or needing the support of a walker for a daily trip to the mailbox. I also do not intend to spend my life-long retirement money on endless medications, hospitalization and depending on the charity of others.

If this book helps just one person increase their lifespan; their quality of living; and the enjoyment of the fruits of their *Second Fifty;* then we have accomplished our objective. Maybe you have a grandchild who you can talk to and convince them to put down their I- Pad, Smart Phone, or I- Phone and join you in a workout. Maybe your positive attitude and actions regarding fitness training could be the mentoring and role modeling that every young person vitally needs. You never know, but the simple, gentle actions of a caring grandparent may set the mind in motion of an eager and impressionable 13- year old. Act now! Please don't wait for tomorrow!

Fit seniors, Jerry and Tammy Auton
The Fit Senior, Customized Fitness Training

Meet the contributing *Panel of Experts*

Terry Clyde Collis

Terry has dedicated over 50 years to the practice of martial arts, more specifically karate. He was one of the original students of William Dometrich, at one time, the highest ranking non-oriental, in the United States, in the Okinawan style of Chito Ryu. Terry is also a certified trainer and works with clients on an individual or group basis. Terry began studying Chito Ryu in 1962 with Sensei, William Dometrich and was promoted to the rank of Black Belt in 1963. Terry founded a Karate Club, at Eastern Kentucky University, in 1963. He also studied Tai Chi Chaun with Mr. Mok Lau and started the study of Shotokan Karate (ISKF) in 1982 with Greer Golden and Teruyuki Okazaki. Terry achieved the rank of second Dan Black Belt in 1985. (Ni-dan) and participated in numerous tournaments throughout the U.S. Terry was honored with a Meritorious Service Award in 1999. Terry achieved the rank of 6th Dan in Chito Ryu in 2010. (Rok kyu-dan) Terry's teaching experience includes the Karate classes at the Tri City YMCA (Florence, KY) from 1983-2005 and current instructor in Chito Ryu at Northern Kentucky University. After the death of Sensei Dometrich, Terry had the prestigious honor of being awarded his belt, from the family, for his dedication to that Karate form and art.

Terry enlisted in the U.S. Army in 1958 where he served in the United States and Korea. After his discharge, Terry enrolled at Eastern Kentucky University where he attained a Bachelor of Science in history and later went on to earn a Master's Degree in the same field.

Terry Collis

After teaching a year of high school in New Miami, Ohio, Terry pursued a career with Cincinnati Bell for the next 22 years, developing and teaching courses for their employees. Today, Terry stays busy in numerous historical organizations that include: Kentucky Society of Sons and Daughters of the Pilgrims; Kentucky Jamestowne Society; the Kentucky Society Sons of the American Revolution; and is a member of the Erlanger Historical Society.

Devorah Dometrich- Herbst

Devorah Dometrich- Herbst retired several years ago from the Covington, Kentucky Police Department and is currently working for the Grant County, Kentucky Sheriff's Office. Devorah has a dojo in her home and conducts classes on Kobudo, or martial arts weapons, through Skype to over 40 locations worldwide. She is considered one of the top Kobudo experts in the world for men or women. Devorah won the U.S. Women's Black Belt Karate Championship, in 1965-66, as a 15- year old, at the U.S. Armory in Washington, D.C. where she had to fight in 21 two minute matches throughout the day to reach the final match. It was an amazing feat considering that she had not yet attained the rank of brown belt. She received her trophy alongside the male grand champion, the famed Joe Lewis, who went on to martial arts fame, as one of the greatest karate practitioners in American history.

Sensei Dometrich-Herbst joined the U.S. Air Force in 1972 and was stationed in Okinawa from 1974-77 where she was able to pursue her advanced weapons training. In 1974 Devorah won the National Karate Championship once again, through the Shotokan National Japan Karate Association. (SNJKA) Devorah is also a pioneer in female law enforcement fitness standards and in 1974 was asked to perform a fitness demonstration, for the Los Angeles Police Department, while at the national competition. The Los Angeles Police Department did not have a female who could do a single pull up and wanted to witness what Devorah and female officers were actually capable of. After performing 10 pull ups in strict fashion and demonstrating other advanced fitness skills a new standard or baseline was set for the females on the LA Police Department that quickly expanded to others throughout the country.

Devorah was paid a special compliment, for her martial arts skills, by Master Akamine, while stationed with the Air Force in Okinawa. Several Okinawan women wanted to take up martial arts and were told, "Go home, marry and raise children." The women answered, "You have an American woman who trains with the men. Why can't we?" Master Akamine stated, "Because she has the skills of a man and is only disguised as a woman." While stationed in Okinawa, Devorah also entered a Kobudo Tournament that included men and placed second overall. (2nd

Grand Champion) She placed 2nd in the Nunchuka, Sai, and Bo competitions. Devorah currently travels the United States, Europe and Asia demonstrating her skills and instructing various groups in the arts of Kobudo and Karate. In 1997 she became the first woman in the world to attain the rank of 7th Dan, in Kobuto.

Devorah Dometrich-Herbst

Dave Guidugli

Dave's athletic resume includes: track and field; basketball; football; boxing and professional fitness consultant. Dave played football for about 15 years, as a defensive end, in a semi-professional league in Cincinnati (Stroh's Lions). Dave started serious boxing in his late twenties and placed in the final four of the World's Tough Man Championship, a precursor to the Pride, Bellitor, Strike Force, Glory and the UFC contests you see on TV today. Dave was also a high school coach and originated one of the first fitness camps that have continued for the past 25 years.

The camp, or *Next Level Academy*, concentrates on blue chip high school and college athletes, although all comers are welcome. Dave's camp is known as the Speed, Quickness, Stamina and Special Skills Camp. Dave conducts personal training sessions as "The Guru of Fitness" with professional football, basketball and baseball athletes. Dave frequently receives calls from NFL and NBA coaches who want their draftees toughened up to face the rigors of pro competition before reporting to training camps. (Bob Huggins, Don Nelson etc.) Dave assisted Dave Cowens, as the assistant coach for the Boston Celtics Continental League team known as the Boston Bay Bombardiers. Dave has been endorsed by numerous professional athletes and coaches for his ability to take already talented players to a higher level.

A certified special education teacher with a Masters from the University of Cincinnati Dave has also volunteered a number of years as the Special Olympics trainer, coach and manager. Dave is certified as a pro Trainer by the International Sports Sciences Association (ISSA); a Consultant for Hammer Strength Conditioning Equipment; member of the Northern Kentucky Sports Hall of Fame; and a keynote motivational speaker. Dave's trainees and contacts include professional athletes: Dave Cowens, Larry Bird, Oscar Robertson, Danny Fortson, Zeke Reynolds, Bruce Kozerski, Eric Glaser, Doug Pelfrey, Joe Walter, Tyrone Hill, Hal Morris, Aaron Pryor, Tony Tubbs and Shawn Alexander. Coach Bob Huggins once commented, "When it comes to developing speed, agility and quickness, Dave is the #1 guy in the country." Shaun Alexander stated, "Dave Guidugli is the world's greatest trainer." Dave is also a close friend with former basketball coach Joe B. Hall of the University of Kentucky and Coach Hall once made a comment that he probably should have hired Dave as his full time strength coach for the Wildcats.

Dave Guidugli

Ray Hughes

Ray was on a United States Military Championship Judo team while serving in the U.S. Air Force in the 1950s that included several national and world champions. Ray has taken that special skill to new heights and is currently a 6th Dan black belt in the art. Ray, along with two of his friends, John Purvis and Harvey Eubanks, founded the majority of the Judo clubs in the greater Cincinnati, Northern Kentucky and Dayton, Ohio areas. Ray has also been involved with other martial arts clubs through his good friend and protégé, William Dometrich. Ray has been interested in physical fitness from his early years and he continues to work out at the Central YMCA, in Cincinnati, where he has belonged since age 10.

In 1960 Bill Dometrich, Harvey Eubanks, and Ray opened the first Judo and Karate self- defense clubs in the Cincinnati area. During this period Ray spent much of his time in a club that operated in Hamilton, Ohio. A product of this club and head

John Purvis and Ray Hughes, along with Harvey Eubanks
and Bill Dometrich, had a hand in founding most of the martial
arts clubs in the greater Cincinnati, tristate area

The 1960 United States Air Force Championship Judo Team
Back: George Harris (world champion), Ron Hubbard, Tosh Seino
(world champion), Ray Hughes; Front: Aubrey Mize, Samuel Boone, T.
Stephens

instructor John Purvis was Kayla Harrison, the 2010 World
Champion and also 2012 Olympic Champion, in the 78 kg
division. Harvey Eubanks went on to become the head instructor
for the Los Angeles Police Department and some of his holds led

to the Supreme Court decision outlawing various judo choke holds, as practiced in Judo. Bill Dometrich went on to become Asst. Police Chief of Covington, Kentucky and founded the nationally known Chito Ryu Karate Association. Ray feels it was a great honor to be associated with Bill, John and Harvey at the genesis of Judo and Karate in this tri-state area.

Ray first joined the Cincinnati YMCA in 1949, at age 10, in a special program for poor inner city Cincinnati kids and he worked out there until he joined the U.S. Air Force in 1956 and returned shortly after his discharge. The YMCA was a hotbed of fitness activity, but Ray primarily utilized weights with power lifting and body building exercises. He tried boxing under Frank Carino, a well- known trainer at the time, and later Dick Harbors. They trained at the St. Sheriff's Club at Liberty and Vine Streets. Later they moved under the PAL Boxing Club, at the Police station, in Price Hill. Ray commented, "I was never that good at boxing and in retrospect was probably used as a punching bag for Frank Carino's up and comers.

While in the Air Force, Ray was transferred to Strategic Air Command (SAC) and began training in Judo and self- defense, at Pease AFB, in New Hampshire. Ray competed in the 180- pound weight class and won the brown belt 180 pound 8th Air Force championship, in 1959. He was promoted to Shodan or 1st degree black belt in 1960 and won or placed 1st, 2nd or 3rd in the following tournaments: 8th Air Force Strategic Air Command, All Air Force, and USAF championship National Team. Ray's team mates were George Harris Pan American Champion; Ed Mede, Pan Am Champion; Phil Porter, US Champ and instructor at the Air Force Academy. Tosh Seino, (Mr. Uchimata) World and US Champ; and Robey Reed, Air Force Champ. They were

17

trained by Mike O'Conner, former All-American judo athlete. The last tournaments Ray participated in and won were: New England Judo Championships, and the Ohio AAU Championships. Ray's current rank is Rokyudan (6th Dan)

Lanny Julian

Lanny is a former world class arm wrestler who participated in over 125 tournaments from 1969-1981 and included the following accomplishments: 111 first place finishes; five North American titles; 1973 World Champion; 1974, 75, 76 United States Champion and runner-up on several occasions to World Champion legends Larry Pacifico (Ohio) and Steve Stanaway (Virginia). Lanny's expertise and competitiveness allowed him to move from the 185 pound and 200 pound classes to challenge the larger heavyweights of the sport.

Lanny began training in the late 1950s and early sixties in the typical home gym fashion. Lanny developed a unique style of training that focused on tremendous finger, hand, wrist, forearm, biceps and shoulder strength. He mentioned, in our interview, that no competitor was ever able to slip from his grip once locked in place. He designed his own specialized equipment and exercises that helped him achieve his arm wrestling goals. Lanny is one of the most skilled and respected arm wrestlers who has ever participated in the sport and has uncanny insight into the skills, strength, timing, and technique that takes years to master. He was recently inducted into the Northern Kentucky Sports Hall of Fame for his dominance in this sport. That was a great tribute and recognition because the Sports Halls of Fame is dominated by the typical football, basketball and baseball players.

Denny Dase's place in Cincinnati

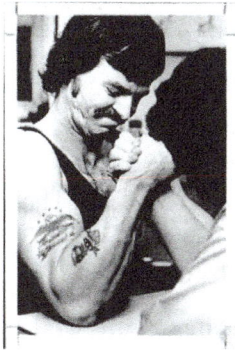

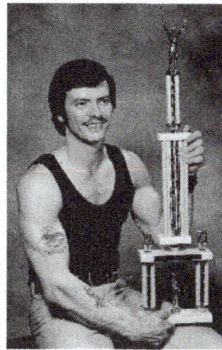

(left) At the 1974 Eastern USA and (right) Lanny's
first World Championship, in 1973

Lanny once mentioned that he regularly did wrist and forearms curls / rolls with a bucket attached to a rope and handle filled with 200 pounds of weight. He was also able to do chin ups by pinch gripping the rafters in his basement instead of using a standard chin bar. Lanny still makes fitness his number one priority and is also involved, with his wife, in the Masonic Eastern Star Organization. We asked Lanny how he handled the unofficial challenges that came his way and he responded, "I usually extended my hand for a handshake and once they felt my grip that was usually enough."

Roger Riedinger

Roger is a former high school and college track and field athlete. Roger was a field event man and former Kentucky State high school Champion in the discus and threw the discus, at the University of Cincinnati, on an athletic scholarship. Roger earned a degree in education and started that career as a middle school math teacher. He eventually obtained several graduate degrees and spent a large portion of his career in educational administration.

Roger won a number of local and regional trophies in bodybuilding with the prestigious Masters Mr. USA the pinnacle of his victories. Roger has been a high school coach, personal trainer, gym owner, writer for national fitness magazines, national physique judge, physique committee co-chairman, and promoter of numerous bodybuilding competitions. The Northern Kentucky contest, founded in 1979 and promoted by Beverly International, eventually became the largest one- day bodybuilding event in the United States with well over 300 contestants.

Roger retired as a school administrator in 1990 and with his wife, Sandy, purchased Beverly International Health Foods and Supplements, which has been a premier company since 1967. Roger and his wife, Sandy, are known as the "Gurus of Nutrition and Bodybuilding Preparation" for their sound advice sought out by aspiring bodybuilders, athletes, and health conscious people across the nation. Roger and Sandy are honest, extremely hard working and sincere in every aspect of their business. Think back to the old *Iron Man Magazine* and the dedication demonstrated by Perry and Mabel Rader. Roger and Sandy are the embodiment, although a much younger version of that same spirit, dedication legitimate concern and expertise.

Roger Riedinger

Jerry Auton

Jerry learned early in life the value of hard work, persistence, and developing the total individual. Jerry's sports participation was limited as a youth, but eventually played baseball on the semi-professional level being the home run champion during one particular season. He started on a path of self- improvement in his early teens that would see him compete in power lifting, bodybuilding, arm wrestling, tumbling and fencing. He has won trophies in every endeavor and was also Kentucky's first state fencing champion with only a few lessons under his belt. Jerry's career has included a number of sales positions and has been deemed a national and world champion on several occasions, for his achievements. Jerry belongs to a local Toastmasters group and has given numerous motivational speeches in the Cincinnati area over the past 20 years.

Tom Geimeier

Tom retired as a school administrator, after 39 years, with an extensive teaching and coaching background. Tom won a *Golden Apple* in 1987, for teacher excellence and was

Kentucky's School Administrator of the Year in 2000. Tom opened a neighborhood gym in 1967 and through the years has participated and promoted competitions that included: bodybuilding, powerlifting, karate and semi-pro baseball. Tom tried arm wrestling because of his arm strength, but drew world champion, Steve Stanaway, in his first match, which was a huge mistake. Tom spends numerous volunteer hours working with the VA, local historic organizations and doing genealogical research. His life philosophy can be summed up as: always try to exceed yourself; do the right thing; you never get a second chance to make that first impression and no one wants to be involved with a half ass or poorly run organization.

The Interview Questions

Each member of our *panel of experts* was asked to respond to the same set of questions so we had a uniform database to compare their responses for possible consensus on methodology, as well as, the specific differences. Those questions were:

- ❖ Why is your form of exercise or fitness the best?

- ❖ How long have you been active in your special area of fitness?

- ❖ What benefits have you gained from your fitness training?

- ❖ List your priorities in training

- ❖ What do you look for when selecting a gym?

❖ What advice would you give to a young person starting out?

❖ What advice would you give to the over 50 age person?

❖ What are some of the mistakes you have observed in the gyms and dojos?

❖ What are the leading causes of injury in adult trainees?

❖ What injuries have you personally observed in the over 50 crowd?

❖ What injuries have you experienced, the causes and final outcomes?

❖ Your best advice on rehabbing injuries and surgeries?

❖ What special advice and comments can you make regarding females over 50?

❖ Are the priorities for women different than for men?

❖ Give us some insight about your beliefs on nutrition

❖ Comment on the use of nutritional supplements.

❖ What has motivated you to continue training and maintaining your PMA or positive mental attitude for over 50 years?

❖ List any personal mentors who helped you develop your fitness concepts and training philosophy?

❖ List any other fitness role models you think are worthy to mention?

❖ Add any other information that may have value?

* Appendix A contains the full interviews with the *panel*

** We would also like to mention that the *panel* interviews were recorded and written exactly as stated, with very little grammatical editing by the authors. We feel that this technique maintains the authenticity of the *panel* member's voice and may give some insight into that contributor's personality. Each member of the *panel* is an expert in their preferred area of expertise, but they have also attained extensive knowledge in fitness and various training methods through their half century of competitiveness.

Chapter 1

The Mirror of Reality

"There is only one truth. Take another look into the mirror of reality and separate reality from your imagination"

Imagination and reality are often at the opposite ends of the spectrum when taking a personal assessment of our physical fitness or condition. It is very difficult to take an honest look and not see the past, what used to be, or in a distorted mind what never was. When you look into the mirror of reality you may see a person who has neglected their health and body for a number of years; a person who is overcoming serious injuries from a work related incident; possibly an automobile accident; a person who has faced serious health problems; the former athlete; or a person who has maintained a reasonably sound physical condition and sensible diet; and finally the physical phenom who has never strayed far from exercise with good cardio, flexibility, agility and dietary habits.   That ideal scenario will rarely be the case regarding those over 50!

We remember our early heroes, as youngsters, and have a very good visual image of what physical traits they had. The original TV Superman was an average guy and certainly did not resemble the muscular heroes depicted in today's comics. Many were big baseball fans and recognized the greats like Al Kaline, Frank Robinson, Roberto Clemente, Carl Yaztremski, and Hank Aaron were certainly not muscular marvels in appearance. The thick, boxy, Mickey Mantle probably displayed more muscle mass, as a natural mid-western farm boy, than most athletes of the 1950s through the 1980s. The same physical template could also be applied to football, basketball, boxing and the other major sports. Any professional athlete with extreme muscularity was the exception rather than the rule in the 1950s, 60s, 70s and would have very easily stood out in a crowd. Regardless of your favorite sport, the major athletes of your era; the heroes of the comics; the men and women in the bodybuilding magazines; and maybe the Charles Atlas ads had a definite influence on the goals, aspirations and expectations of several generations of youth. Sadly, youth has passed by and the men and women today who are over 50 must live in the present and with the reality of what it takes to stay fit. The immediate goal is to understand what it takes to maintain a quality and productive life now and hopefully, fight off aging and seek the longevity we all desire.

"Before embarking on any fitness program, especially over age 50, it is always advisable to have a thorough physical exam with your family doctor before pursuing any physical training program. The over age 50 trainee should also schedule yearly physical exams / wellness visits and adhere to all necessary screenings and vaccinations. To avoid that starting point would be very foolish and ill advised!" [1] The

---

[1] Mayo Clinic Staff (11 March 2014) Exercise: When to check with your doctor first, Retrieved from mayoclinic.org/healthy/lifestyle/fitness/in-depth-exercise/art-20047414

[1] Dr. Nary, Dot (5 Feb 2014) Warning Exercise May Be ~~Hazardous~~ Essential to Your Health, Retrieved

next logical step would be to meet with a knowledgeable trainer who could assist you in formulating the best possible workout plan to achieve your goals. Remember, that your goals may be long term and will not happen overnight, especially if you have neglected your health for years. Modifying your diet will also be a key if your plans are to eventually reach the level of success you are hoping for. Many of the top name athletes have often stated that their success or performance edge was attributed to as much as 80 percent diet and nutrition. The human body is a delicate machine that must be properly fueled for optimum performance. Likewise, negative results and malfunctions will eventually result from the reverse.

You will need to find a place to exercise and a specific time to make your program successful. The best advice we can give is to check out the site before signing any contracts. Gym memberships can be expensive and you probably want a gym with a variety of equipment; qualified trainers on site; flexible hours; easily accessible; clean; and probably not a specific haven for competing power lifters or bodybuilders. Gyms are in business to make money and they like the clients who come in to work out, shower and leave. Many gyms have rules about types of clothing, screaming, grunting, and throwing the weights around for the staff to pick up. There are gyms for the more competitive type, but that is not the place for you! That is also not the clientele that will boost gym memberships and as a matter of fact can destroy a gym's atmosphere or eventually run it out

---

nchpad.org/585/2528/warning~exercise!may~bc~hazardous~tessential~to~ your~health

of business. Please realize that you are the only person who knows and controls your commitment to a fitness program. You must look over your current schedule of responsibilities and prioritize how often you can train and the length or duration of each session. The best bet is to lock in specific days and times so your body will become accustomed. Many insurance companies today offer free gym memberships like *Silver Sneakers* ® for their clients over 65, as an incentive to maintain your health and hopefully, reduce overall future health costs. Check with your gym to see if they participate in these programs before paying any fees. The *Silver Sneakers*®[2] programs are offered at over 13,000 locations worldwide and by 65 major health plans.

Are your immediate goals to lose weight, gain weight, improve your cardio, firm up what you have or add strength and stamina? Check your weight against the charts and determine what would be your ideal bodyweight. It is essential that you consult a knowledgeable, certified trainer or a qualified friend who really knows the business. Don't be impressed with a trainer's resume and numerous certifications. There have been many instances where trainees have been injured with exercises that common sense would dictate to stay away from. "Research says we lose from 3-8% of our muscle mass every decade past 30 and that amount is accelerated after 70." [3] That can be a scary thought!

---

[2] Healthways Silver Sneakers Staff (17 June 2015) Why should your health plan offer Silver Sneakers®? Retrieved from https://www.silversneakers.com/partners/health-plans/

[3] Webb MD Staff (3 Aug 2014) Sarcopenia with Aging or How Much Muscle Loss Per Decade, Retrieved from webbmd.com/healthy-aging/sarcopenia-with-aging/

What if you never had a lot of muscle mass or have lost the majority through inactivity over the years? You may want to add some muscle or maintain what you have with muscle toning while cutting back on your overall body fat. Assess your bone structure. Remember, there are three basic bone structures: ectomorph, endomorph and mesomorph. These basically represent light, medium and heavy boned skeletal systems. They indicate how much weight a person should ideally carry and how heavily muscled a person can potentially become. You cannot change your bone structure, which will be the final judge, in how much weight your body can lose or gain safely. My advice to anyone with large hips / pelvis or thighs is *you cannot reduce any further than bone!* Do the best you can with what you have to work with. Forget about measurements as they apply only to the person with an ideal build or frame. Some fictional, ideal measurements on a very tall girl or man would make them look skinny and on a short person's frame too large. Bone structure can be determined with measurements at the hips or the various joints such as the wrists, ankles, elbow and knees. The buzz word or acronym today is BMI or body mass index. That basically is a calculation or comparison of your body fat and muscle mass. Don't be surprised if doctors use this index in the future to determine what medical procedures can be paid for by your insurance company! Doctor's offices are already compiling this statistic as part of a database that may determine your future medical options.

The legendary Steve Reeves who starred in the old Hercules movies was said to have one of the most symmetrical and perfect muscular bodies often compared to Michelangelo's statue of David. The ideal measurements for perfection stated that the measurement of the neck, upper arms and calves should be the same. (Reeves measured all three at 18") The classic chest measurement was said to be about 16-18 inches larger than the waist and the thighs four to five inches smaller than the waist. (Reeves 32", 48" and 28 inches) In the old days, many of the over 50 generation read the available muscle magazines: *Muscular Development* (Bob Hoffman); *Mr. America and Muscle Builder* (Joe and Ben Weider); *Iron Man* (Perry and Mabel Rader; and *Muscle Training Illustrated.* (Dan Lurie) Many of us thought we could reach the same results by adhering to the routines we found in those pages each month. Many dedicated trainees did find a measure of success, but the routines were too severe for the average person. Pumping out 20 super sets of arm work could often lead to a decrease in size unless you were on those "special supplements."

Our opinion is that *Iron Man* had the best overall approach and most sensible training routines. Perry and Mabel Rader also included the amateurs and the professional articles or in those days the AAU and the IFBB information. *Iron Man* also had the latest results on powerlifting and Olympic weightlifting. *Iron Man* was a very comprehensive and non- political magazine with few advertisements. The next time you are at the newsstand take a look at the magazines and you will be shocked. Huge, high priced magazines with too many ads; bodybuilders featured (men and women) who look like cartoon characters that make the heroes of Justice League America look like skinny wimps. I don't think it is any revelation that those featured monsters are not the result of a healthy diet and pumping iron. That same theory would also apply to some of the overly developed professional athletes of the basketball, football and occasionally baseball world. We will address that in a later chapter, but that should not apply to our audience if you are truly interested in health, fitness and longevity.

The American Heart Association, *Life is Why*, suggests the best type of exercise for an older adult is anything that makes the muscles work more than usual.[4] The older you become the more muscle strength, mass and flexibility you can expect to lose with each new decade. The quality of life that potentially lies ahead is the struggle to maintain your highest level of health and total functionality. Many people frequently ask us, "Which is the best type of exercise for me?" An article on *Tech times.com* indicated that five minutes of walking was required to reverse the damage to the arteries in the legs, for every hour spent sitting. The article created by the Centers for Disease Control and Prevention, Division of Nutrition, Physical Activity and Obesity discussed various types of exercise and concluded that there is an endless array of workouts tailored for different levels of ability. Many of those experts surveyed mentioned walking as an excellent basic fitness program. The article warned against *actively sedentary* people or those who work out an hour or so a day, but sit or are inactive the rest. [5] There was an interesting comment, on the

---

[4] American Heart Assoc. *Life is Why* staff (22 June 2015) What Type of Physical Activity is Best?

[5] Keating, Lauren (29 Sept 2014) What is the best form of exercise? Retrieved from Techtimes.com/articles/10732/20140929/what-best-form-exercise-experts-walk.htm

Website philly.com Sports Doc about what is the best type of exercise for you. Their answer was, "Any type of exercise you will do!" [6] Finding an exercise program that you truly enjoy and look forward to will always be your best option.

Certified Amateur Athletic Union (AAU) judges were and National Physique Committee (NPC) bodybuilding judges are currently tested on their expertise of the muscular system so they can evaluate and correctly place contestants in competitions. **The *panel* recommends that every trainee familiarize themselves with the basic muscles of the body and understand their function.** We have included two outstanding charts for your reference. * The AAU no longer includes bodybuilding, as one of the 34 sports /activities, promoted under their jurisdiction. We thought it was too confusing to add dozens of arrows to pinpoint the various muscles on the charts, as if you were taking an anatomy class. We think it is more productive and less confusing to see the basic location, shape, attachments and relation to other areas of the body.

Specific muscles of the human body often have two or three sections, heads or sub groups that must be worked with a variety of different exercises. ex. The deltoids of the shoulders have three heads and usually require three different exercises for complete development. The biceps have two heads and the triceps three.

---

[66] Moore, Heather, PT, DPT, CKTP (3 July 2013) What is the best type of exercise? Retrieved from philly.com/philly/blogs/sportsdoc/which –type-of-exercise-is-best-your-favorite.html

Anterior and Posterior Views (Male)

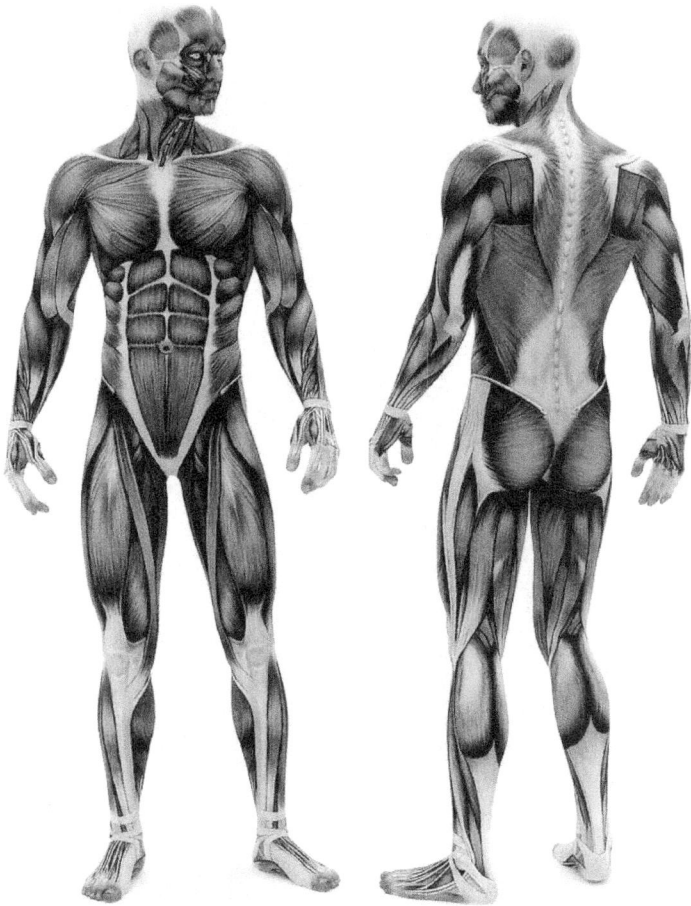

Shutterstock image[7]

---

[7] Shutterstock, Inc., 350 Fifth Avenue, 21st Floor, New York, NY 10118

Anterior and Posterior Views (Female)

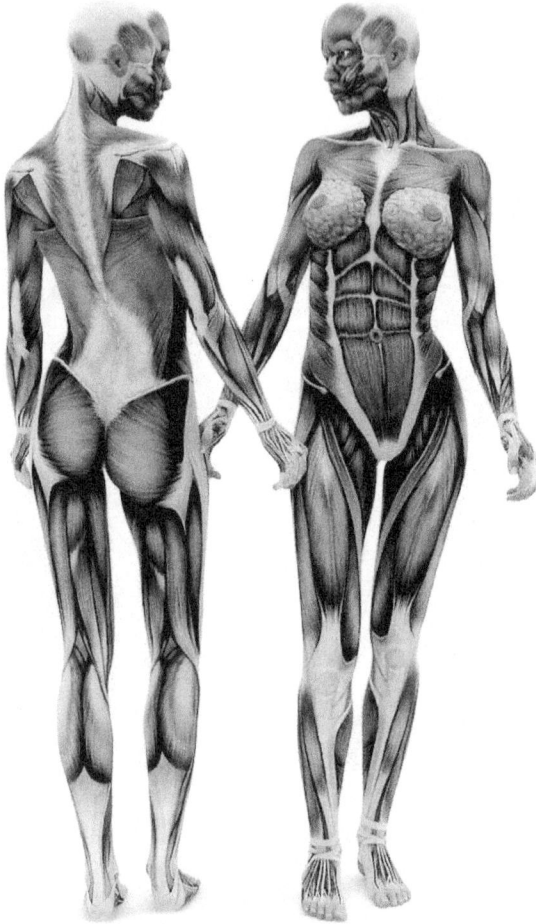

Shutterstock image

Somatotypes (Body Shapes) for Females

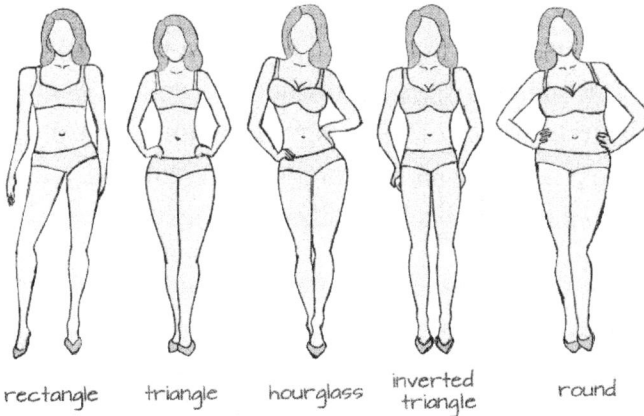

rectangle   triangle   hourglass   inverted triangle   round

Somatotypes, as mentioned previously, are body types that apply to all men and women. They are based on a person's natural skeletal frame or bone structure and determine how much muscle and bodyweight can be carried safely. Your physician can determine your somatotype at your next exam or your trainer can assess this with a few measurements at the joints. (wrists, elbows, knees and ankles) The proportion of body fat versus muscle mass will determine your BMI or "body mass index" and that number should be in the mid twenty range for a person over 65 who is in good shape. BMI scores are currently calculated on the patient printouts from their Wellness Visits and scores over 30 indicate an overweight condition or possibly obesity.

Ectomorph – this body type appears lean or slender, with longer arms, legs and narrowness at the chest and shoulders. They carry a very low percentage of body fat with long, thin muscles and development that is very evident. The ectomorph's thyroids are very active, which increases the metabolism and allows them to consume a large number of calories, just to maintain their weight. They may be prone to kyphosis, lordosis and scoliosis due to lack of strength in the lower back muscles. (spinae erector muscles)

Mesomorph – they tend to have greater muscularity with larger bones and thicker joints that are often accompanied by more strength than the other body types. They have a larger shoulder structure, chest area and smaller waistline. The extremities may exhibit well developed calves, forearms and upper arms. The largest proportion of mesomorphs would be men. Mesomorphs need to be active and can be quite successful in athletics, except for the endurance events, which favors the ectomorph. Moderate training will allow this body type to maintain their athletic shape, but overeating will cause eventual weight problems.

Endomorph – this type tends to have a softer, smoother musculature and will tend to be on the chubby side, due to excess fat storage. Characteristics may include a short neck, rounded face, wider hips and sometimes a thick, potbellied look. Endomorphs tend to have a lazy thyroid with a slower metabolism. They rarely have back problems, but are suspect to knee problems. Maintaining an ideal shape for this group requires a strict diet with a regular training program.

Recent changes in the female somatotypes have generally favored using the five body shapes shown above rather than the strictness of the standard ectomorph, mesomorph and endomorph. The majority of males and females would probably be a combination of two of the somatotypes and show varying characteristics of each. You can actually Google "body shapes or somatotypes" and take a quick test to determine which characteristics you have to work with.

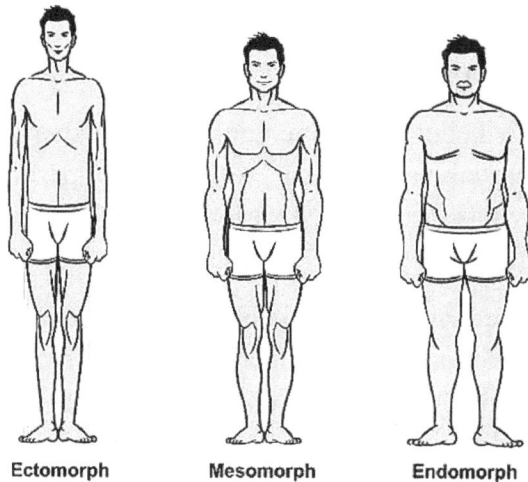

| Ectomorph | Mesomorph | Endomorph |

By Granito Diaz (own work), CreativeCommons.org [8]

SEE YOUR PHYSICIAN
Before beginning any exercise program or changing your physical activity patterns, you should always consult with your doctor or physician, particularly if you have been inactive, are overweight, have or suspect any sort of medical condition that might be worsened by exercise.

---

[8] Diaz, Granito (own work), Retrieved from
https://upload.wikimedia.org/wikipedia/commons/a/ab/Bodytypes.jpg

Panel of Experts ... Question #1

The answers are purposely kept brief and in an outline form, to make it easier for the reader to follow and utilize. The panel's comments are also in their own words and with very little editing. We feel this maintains the authenticity.

Why is your form of exercise the best?

The *panel's* comments ....

Terry Collis believes in a complete exercise program that combines martial arts training with other types of physical fitness. Terry has incorporated various martial arts and physical conditioning into his personal program.

Devorah Dometrich-Herbst believes strongly in the internal value of her martial arts and Kobudo training. Her system builds confidence and also has great physical value. Sensei Devorah commented, "I have learned more in a dojo than at church." She also stated she doesn't need a gym or equipment because her gym is basically her body.

Dave Guidugli feels his system is all encompassing and does not focus on any one aspect. Dave's system is a five-point system that gears exercises to speed, flexibility, cardio, strength building, and specific performance skills. He incorporates a variety of training methods and uses boxing training to bolster mental toughness.

Ray Hughes has incorporated a variety of training techniques, throughout his life, but has always favored weight training to gain strength and muscle mass. At age 76, Ray has changed his philosophy and believes that barbells and dumbbells are not really needed to get into shape. A good instructor will know other methods and technique is also very important. Judo and other martial arts have provided the mental aspects and confidence building that he feels are the keys to success.

Lanny Julian believes in whole body conditioning with light weight, high repetitions and very little, if any, maxing out. Lanny incorporates specific exercises to strengthen his hands, wrist, forearms and shoulders for his competitive arm wrestling matches.

Roger Riedinger feels that progressive resistance training is the key and it provides the over 50 trainees with maintenance of muscle mass; prevention of osteoporosis; and can lead to better self-discipline and goal setting, which are crucial for success in other areas.

Jerry Auton states that his system of weight training, with his emphasis on cardio, is the most practical due to thousands of hours he has spent on researching fitness and the various workouts he has experienced during his lifetime.

Tom Geimeier believes the best form of exercise is what contributes best to an individual's maximum health. Total fitness should be the key and that form will change with time and age.

What the research says ....

The answer may never be known! There are literally dozens of systems on the market each claiming to be the best for you with endless ads in the magazines and the infomercials on TV. They all offer great and fantastic results if you complete their program and we're sure they all have some value. They basically all combine strength building, endurance, flexibility, and balance or agility exercises in various proportions. Research suggests that the best results occur when you adapt and persist with a system that suits your particular goals; provides personal enjoyment and also appeals to your common sense.

The bottom line ….

Most programs or types of physical conditioning have value to the human body. It's true that some have more options than others such as the comments regarding the specific skills with martial arts. The fact is that dedicating yourself to achieving realistic personal goals and being consistent are the keys to success! Collis, Guidugli, Hughes, Julian, and Auton all agreed on the added benefits of a more complete holistic program of fitness. Riedinger stayed true to his belief in resistance training and Geimeier mentioned that time and age required changes with new priorities in a training regime. It would seem logical to incorporate some sort of physical conditioning that also pays dual dividends such as the added benefit of attaining self- defense or sport specific skills. One comment that stands out was from Dometrich-Herbst that stated," I don't need specific equipment because my body is my gym." She also stated that," I learned more in a dojo than I did in church." This alludes to the discipline, organization, goal setting and the added confidence that comes from martial arts or any fitness program. When the mind is in the game the body will usually follow. There was absolute consensus from the *panel* on this issue. Many athletes today have common ground in that they participated in a variety of youth sports and have taken some form of martial arts instruction. When talking about increasing longevity and the chances of making it to triple digits then a balanced program of resistance training, with the implementation of some cardio and flexibility certainly enhances that expectation.

The hot tip ....

Remember that there are many areas of fitness that you will have to choose from. **To each their own!** Many trainees may prefer to train in the confines and comfort of their own homes. Fitness centers and gyms offer a variety of machines for resistance training, as well as, Pilates, Yoga, Spinning, Power Walking, dance, calisthenics, martial arts, and many other systems. Age, physical limitations and common sense may dictate the exercise program that is best for you. **Keep an open mind and find a system that appears custom made for you!**

Chapter 2

Setting Goals, the beginning of any successful venture

"I don't know where I'm going or how to get there, but here we go"

This book was written with special consideration for the priorities of the over 50 adults. Many of the current publications today cater to a specific type of athlete such as: the avid golfer; Iron Men and Iron Women competitors; hunters; swimmers; Cross Fit; bikers; MMA fighters; spinners, dancers; bodybuilders; power lifters; American Ninja Warriors and various martial arts programs forming an almost endless list. How many publications even attempt to deal with the over 50 athlete or to some the geriatric, baby boomer set, which actually makes up the largest segment of today's population? That's what makes our book unique. Before we read any book we do a little research on the authors and find out if they are an actual authority on their subject or trying to get by with a few buzz words and fitness phrases from various sources. **What is their credibility?** In *The Second Fifty* you have input and guidance from those who have actually walked the path for over 50 years; accomplished some really amazing feats; have heavy duty resumes; and have often paid a high price in regard to the wear and tear on their bodies. This can be valuable advice, especially when an obvious consensus of opinion is reached among the *panel* members on the various topics addressed.

We believe the first step, after receiving the go ahead or clearance from your doctor is to ask yourself, *"What do I want to achieve and what am I still capable of accomplishing?"* Many people will say they want to maintain a high energy level with some good muscle tone and a high functioning cardio system. For others it might be to lose some weight and feel physically mobile with an interest in travel and just looking presentable in their clothes. There are of course others who have been able to maintain a very high standard of physical fitness without any significant injuries and want to continue training like they did 10 years earlier. A warning must be issued here about injury prevention. Your training regime must constantly adapt to your age and abilities. That doesn't mean settling for second best, but becoming wiser as a few gray hairs settle in. Don't forget the person who has suffered through a serious disease or illness and just wants to regain a part of what was lost. Finally, there are the extreme models who still want to compete at some level. There are a number of athletic competitions for those over 50, in an array of categories. That can become an obsession or manifestation of prior habits and our congratulations go out to that unique group.

Many early fitness buffs were just kids who wanted to wear a tight muscle shirt; tank top; have some pectoral muscles and a set of arms that might draw some attention; and inspire a good feeling about their self. No more the Mr. Bones look or the target of getting laughed at or having the proverbial sand kicked in your face. The basic goal was to look and feel better about their personal appearance while feeling more confident in any undertaking. Confidence can certainly take you a long way! A lot of guys in the neighborhoods had the same basic goal and that was to put on some muscle, get bigger, faster and stronger, regardless of any specific athletic goals.

Goal setting is as easy as mapping out a vacation and taking a drive across the country. Merely jumping into your car, without any regard to planning, is almost a guarantee that you will encounter problems along the way. You may encounter so many problems that you give up the trip, turn around, and return home to where you started. Your valuable time and money wasted, but more importantly, you become discouraged that the opportunity to accomplish that specific goal was not achieved.

What if you checked your resources for a map; charted a sensible route; and had your vehicle checked out to be sure all parts and systems were prepared for the long drive to your destination. Do you think that it might also be a good idea to plan stops along the way to see historic and scenic places and to check on your progress? Do you think proper planning would be more worry free and enjoyable than forsaking the necessary initial preparation? We feel most people would agree that preparation is essential whether planning a trip or a pathway to fitness and better health. Setting your goals for your health and fitness is extremely important for the over 50 crowd because the wise use of your time is imperative. 50 years of your life have somehow pasted by and it is truly now or possibly never! Regardless of whether you have never engaged in any type of fitness or have been inactive for many years please get yourself checked out by your doctor. A personal physical assessment is absolutely necessary for you to understand your limitations, especially if you are hiring a personal trainer. Any personal limitations can then be communicated to your trainer and they should know what exercises may pose the risk of injury.

Another key question to consider is, "What is your final destination or goal?" Never be ashamed or embarrassed that your starting point may be simply to walk for just 10 minutes, at a slow pace. Acquiring a better state of fitness is a gradual or progressive process so that 10- minute walk will soon become 20 minutes, 30 minutes or more, with time and consistency. "How long does it take to eat an elephant"? "One bite at a time."

A qualified and experienced personal trainer can guide you over the necessary hurdles through progressive training techniques that are safe and successful when properly followed. Rome was not built in a day and there are no quick fixes. You do not need to risk injury or become so sore that getting out of bed or tying your shoes is agonizing. The best trainers are those who have been properly trained and have the necessary certifications to prove it! Examples would be: the ISSA or the International Sports Sciences Association or the Exercise Etc Incorporated.[9] They offer certifications for Senior Fitness, with complimentary course work in osteoporosis, knee problems and cognitive fitness. Your main goal is always to make strides and hit bench marks in your progress that are safe and sound! Goals can be short term like weekly or long term as quarterly or yearly. Charting your progress and keeping a journal, along that fitness

---

[9] Knopf, Karl, EdD (2010) Senior Fitness Handbook, Carpenteria, CA: International Sports Sciences Association

path, is another great way to reflect on your accomplishments and to look ahead.

Remember that a long healthy life, with the possibility of off-setting many of the effects of aging, is a key objective desired by most people. We feel that your spare time should be quality time and not spent in doctor's offices, treatment centers and hospitals. That isn't living, but sounds a lot more like a life of depression and misery. We believe the best option is to have the energy and functionality to spend time with your family, grandchildren, hobbies and social organizations, which is a much better way to live a quality life. You must have your priorities in order; the best resources available; and be mentally committed to the task. Commit now and don't take the chance of missing out on those extra weeks and years that may contain some of the best and most beautiful experiences of your life.

Another key to your success is to write your goals down where you can see and review them daily. The power of your own handwriting can have amazing results and that daily reminder can be the boost that keeps you on track. Make sure that your goals are attainable and that you know where you've been and where you are going. Another key is to confide in a good friend or spouse about your plans, as they may want to join you in this adventure, or can help you persevere when you feel like slacking off. Also, think about providing yourself with small rewards for achieving goals and that will serve as reinforcement for future challenges.

Finally, remember that many of us have been in situations where we had to break a bad habit. The bad habit of years

of physical inactivity and ill- advised dietary habits will not be easy ones to break. Think positive! **Bad habits and good habits are equally difficult to break!** The so called life- long health advocates that dedicated years maintaining their fitness levels probably developed those good habits early in life and they have accordingly become an integral part of their daily routines. The decision is in your hands and the same opportunity can be yours!

Panel of Experts …Questions # 2 and 3

How long have you been active in your special area of fitness and what benefits have you gained?

The *panel's* comments ….

Terry Collis – I have been active in martial arts for over 58 years. My interest began by writing an English class thesis on Judo, while in high school, in 1957. I followed up this early interest by taking some Judo lessons in Hamilton, Ohio. Each type of self-defense and fitness has a different flavor for the practitioner. Shotokan Karate is a more fighting oriented style, of Japanese origin, with emphasis on blocking, kicking, and punching movements. My preferred style is Chito Ryu, which is an Okinawin style, with more emphasis on self- defense. That style also incorporates some Ju Jitsu techniques. One old Karate Master described the specialized martial art of Aikido as just a form of Karate. I have gained expertise that allows me to teach and maintain my physical condition well above the average person's.

Devorah Dometrich – Herbst - I started at 12 years old and at 65 that gives me over 50 years of training in kata, kumite, and Kobudo. My gym or dojo is wherever I am. I don't need expensive equipment or a special place to work out. My bodyweight and inner motivation are all I need to be successful. Recent physical exams and tests indicate I still have the bone density of a person 30 years old. I have traveled all over the world to compete and showcase my skills. I also conduct classes worldwide in martial arts that is very lucrative for me.

Dave Guidugli – I developed my program in 1979 while living in Boston and working with Dave Cowens and some of the Boston Celtics. I have met and worked with a huge network of athletes from the Special Olympics to the professional level. I have made contacts from the East Coast to the West Coast and was nicknamed the "Guru of Fitness" by several sports writers. My system develops athleticism in competitive athletes and leads to a better conditioned and more confidence in the regular trainee. I have great cardio; still work side by side with the athletes I train privately and at my camps; but have devoted my last few years to working with an inner city Golden Gloves boxing program sponsored by local Cincinnati restaurateur Buddy LaRosa. I have been active in fitness since 1965 and today have great cardio and a resisting pulse rate of about 48.

Ray Hughes – I have been active in physical conditioning since age 10, which was in 1949. The local YMCA offered free memberships to inner city youth and I was fortunate to be able to take advantage of this great program. This was at the Downtown YMCA in Cincinnati, Ohio. I began Judo at 17, while in the Air Force, and have practiced for over 57 years. Judo with the required grappling is a great self confidence builder. The mental aspects of any sport or area of fitness cannot be overlooked! While a member of the U.S. Air Force Strategic Air Command (SAC) Judo Team we practiced three times per day, with sessions each morning, afternoon and evening. I remember the endurance builder we did several times a day: walk a minute; jog a minute; and run a minute were the toughest workouts I ever had. Today, I like the use of free weights because of their versatility. I also use a few machines, but my priority is to train for endurance and durability. I consider myself in very good shape and train almost daily at the same YMCA.

Lanny Julian – I started training with my homemade dumbbells in the late 1950s and early 60s. I entered the U.S. Army in 1963 and resumed my weight training after my enlistment was up. I started entering local Cincinnati arm wrestling contests in 1969 and competed until 1981. I still advise many arm wrestlers and my son, Dom, (age 48) who is also an active participant. I have been able to maintain a healthy lifestyle and good physical condition, with very few injures, for over 50 years. I have also learned the importance of good training partners and the power of "self- talk" or focusing my mind for world class competition.

Roger Riedinger – I started weight training regularly at age 14 and am now in my 53rd year of weight training. The self-discipline and principle of systemized progress has been a big part in creating my Beverly International health food business. Health, strength, vitality, skin tone, and appearance are all benefits of progressive weight training when properly applied. I feel I have reaped the benefits of a life- long, sound fitness and nutritional program. The knowledge I gained has helped me, as a competitor, gym owner, trainer, promoter, judge and as a business owner. I still train regularly and feel very positive about my current physical condition.

Jerry Auton - I have been active for fifty-two years. I've competed as a powerlifter, bodybuilder, arm wrestler, physical fitness trainer, and at one time was the Lexington, Kentucky fencing champion. Endless benefits! I have been able to be free of any prescription drugs and other medications that most men my age are required to take. I can still compete in the 60 and over class of men's bodybuilding; run solid times in 5 km road races; and have the resting heart rate in the low 40s. I feel that I project an aura of personal fitness and take pride in my conditioning. My health care professionals seem very complimentary of my fitness level after taking and reviewing my vitals.

Tom Geimeier - My father bought me a YMCA membership in 1956 when I was 8 and dropped me off every Saturday to swim and learn the basics of other sports. Like many other early teenagers, I bought a Joe Weider course when I was about 14 and also watched Jack LaLanne on TV. At age 17 I joined a local Turner's Gymnastic Club and did some gymnastics and tumbling. I started baseball at 12 and kept playing until about 40. I picked up martial arts in college and continued in the military, along with competitive powerlifting representing the U.S. Air Force. I coached track for 15 years and practiced every event, but the hurdles. I'm not a purebred athlete in any specific sport, but I consider myself a type of hybrid. The type of training I focused on added to my self- confidence and the ability to relax physically and re-charge mentally. I still train regularly, with sensible modifications that compensate for past injuries, and am not dependent on any type of medications or treatments.

What the research says ....

There is no mystical fountain of youth, but everyone would like to find that silver bullet that would extend their life; turn back the aging process and give them more quality years than their predecessors. The Mayo Clinic, *Healthy Lifestyle Fitness* advocates seven benefits of regular exercise based on their research which correlates with the thinking of our *panel*. We advise reading that entire article for greater detail. [10] That article elaborated on the following benefits:

- Controlling your weight; improving overall health and combating age related diseases; improving mood and self- confidence; increasing energy; more efficient sleep; improvements in sex life; and looking better, which can lead to better nutritional habits.

Federal Fitness Guidelines advocate 150 minutes of moderate intensity aerobic exercise weekly or 75 minutes of vigorous exercise. The statistics support that only 51.6% of adults meet this standard. A minimum of two muscle strengthening activities are recommended each week, but a disappointing 29.3% meet this guideline. Only 20.3% of adults meet both guidelines, which

---

[10] Mayo Clinic Staff (Nov 2014) 7 Benefits of Exercise, Retrieved from http://www.mayoclinic.org/healthy-lifestyle/fitness/in-depth/exercise/art-20048389, p.2

are very minimal.[11] This American Time Use Study (ATUS) also indicated that 71% of those surveyed as active in the 25-54 age group preferred yoga and 60% said they liked cardio vascular equipment. Cycling and aerobics were tied for third place with 59% followed by weightlifting at 57%. The over 55 statistics listed the top five physical activities as: walking 48%, golfing 39%, cardio equipment 29%, aerobics 29% and dancing 28%. [12]

How do you utilize your 24- hour day? The chart below is based on a survey of typical Americans.

By the numbers:
AVERAGE HOURS PER DAY AMERICANS SPEND

Sleeping	Working	Watching television	Participating in sports, exercise and recreation
8.75	7.55	3.49	1.60

Source: 2013 American Time Use Survey, Bureau of Labor Statistics

The bottom line ....

The reader will obviously conclude that the members of the *panel* have 50 years of experience in a variety of fitness models and are still active today. A common thread that formed a consensus among the panel was those all important benefits of confidence

---

[11] Centers for disease control and Prevention Staff (3 May 2013) Federal Fitness Guidelines, Retrieved from cdc.gov/physicalactivity/basics/older_adults/

[12] Bureau of Labor Statistics (18 June 2014) American Time Use Study, U.S. Department of Labor, Bureau of Labor Statistics, http://bis.gov/tvs/charts/leisure.htm

and feeling better about one's self. There was also a dedication to their early endeavors and many members have made a very successful addition to their personal income and careers. It is obviously an advantage to start early and make it a lifelong habit, but never too early to start regardless of age or gender. The *panel* members also reported that their latest Wellness visits, to their doctors, indicated they have been able to maintain a quality physical condition well ahead of expectations for their age. There is an underlying importance for the commitment and regularity of whatever program the reader embarks on.

The hot tip ....

A U.S. Census Bureau, Statistical Abstract of the United States in 2012 indicated that physical fitness definitely contributes to overall wellness, but taking time to enjoy leisure activities is also an important factor for well- being. According to the study the top five leisure activities of Americans were: dining out, entertaining friends or relatives at home, reading, barbecuing, and going to the beach. [13]

---

[13] U.S. Census Bureau Staff, (August 2013) Top Five Leisure activities of Americans, Retrieved from
http://www.census/gov/library/publications/2013
/compendia/statab131ed/arts_1243recreation -travel.html

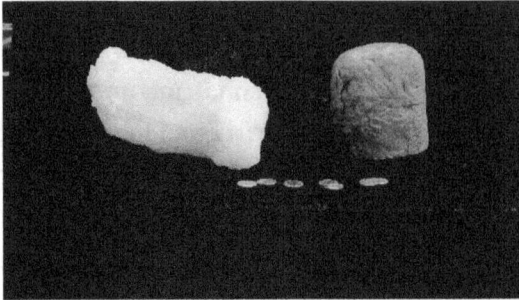

Five pounds of fat versus five pounds of muscle

The photo above depicts, in actual size, five pounds of body fat (left) as compared to five pounds of muscle. (right) A handful of quarters had been placed in the foreground for an additional perspective. Once fat cells are established they may be reduced in size through diet and exercise, but can never be totally eliminated without a medical procedure, while muscle cells may dissipate with age and lack of activity. Many athletes have attributed their high level performances, to as much as 80%, from well thought out diets and nutritional strategies.

The only exception we can think of where sheer size and weight might be an advantage could be applied to the sumo wrestler where sheer bulk is mandatory. The down side is how this massiveness would affect their overall health and longevity? Today, many college and pro football lineman carry weight in excess of 300 pounds that correlates to much higher than usual body fat percentages when compared to athletes of lighter weights. The more athletic linemen weigh less; do heavy weight training to achieve the same strength; have the advantage of being quicker with greater endurance for that crucial fourth quarter and probably much healthier.

Chapter 3

Logical and Appropriate Training Priorities

"Common sense and expert advice should not be ignored"

How often do you see a member of the over 50 set seemingly maxing out on the bench press, deadlift, or squat at every opportunity? Once again, there is nothing wrong with setting high expectations, but do you really need to max out on every piece of gym equipment to feel good about yourself? Twenty years ago the minimum age for the *masters'* category concerning athletic contests was 35, but the times have certainly changed. Today, there are *masters'* competitions for over 40, over 50 and now the over 60 athletes who still have the urge to compete. We have heard rumors that over 70 competitions may be on the horizon! My co-author Jerry Auton has been in several over 60 bodybuilding shows, but they seldom have more than five to six entries and some contestants seemed to have entered the show on a dare. The fact that many physical fitness competitions are adding *masters'* classes for the over 50 groups is a credit to the perseverance and dedication to fitness by this older group. Life is precious and enjoying a long life is everyone's dream, but living a long and quality life, with optimum health is the very best option. The priority and motivation to train for some individuals may be an actual level of competition. That's great and more power to them. Most of that senior age group, however, will be happy to find the time to train on a pain free, consistent basis, just trying to offset the ravages of father time.

Jack LaLanne, of TV fame, was an early idol for many of us and we certainly enjoyed reading about his feats of strength and endurance. Jack's yearly swim, handcuffed in San Francisco Bay, was always an event that made the newspapers and numerous talk shows. We think Jack was living proof that sound nutrition combined with sensible training was the perfect combination to keep you healthy and active well into your 80s. **Jack was an endurance master and the feats he performed are legendary with many still unbeaten**. Jack was still in his trade mark sweat suit selling his juice machines on TV even as he approached the age of 90. It would be an interesting study to see his health history and any injuries he suffered during his lifetime.

Another person who comes to mind was a man from Cincinnati named Louie Roth. Louie was a physical education teacher in the Cincinnati Public Schools who also taught gymnastics at the Cincinnati, Ohio and Covington, Kentucky Turner Societies, (Vereins) or Clubs. These were versions of the Turnvereins from Germany that were found in many cities with large German populations. Louie and his wife Mitzi never owned an automobile and they rode bicycles everywhere they went, until their deaths, well into their late 80s. Louie was the instructor and Mitzi played the piano, which was in the gymnasium, while her husband tapped out a cadence for warm up calisthenics with a large wooden stick. The gymnastics instruction then commenced on the various pieces of equipment. They concentrated on a healthy diet and continued to exercise regularly themselves. Once again, the combination of sensible exercise and good nutrition gave Louie and Mitzi a long and healthy life with very few limitations. We all know similar stories and characters who exemplified what healthy aging or quality longevity is all about. Maybe the best longevity advice a person will ever receive are the examples of the success stories they have witnessed with their own eyes!

"We do not stop exercising because we grow old, we grow old because we stop exercising." This quote by the famed doctor of medicine, Dr. Kenneth Cooper, who introduced the concept of aerobics, in 1968, says it all![14] We have all experienced some sort of setback in our lives that prevented us from continuing our regular workout programs. Some of these setbacks resulted in long layoffs and most, hopefully, were of a much shorter length. The key to getting back on track sooner, rather than later, or not at all, comes from your individual determination. It is a simple fact that a shoulder injury should not keep you from your regular cardio workouts. A lower extremity injury like a knee, calf or foot injury is not going to keep you from a multitude of upper body workouts. You can be lazy or take some time off for a short period of time, just don't stop completely! Allowing an injury or unfortunate situation to end or derail your long term health is the primary excuse that the weak of spirit have been using since time began. We're sure you've experienced meeting the former star high school athlete at the class reunion, or grocery store and hardly recognized them

---

[14] Cooper, Kenneth Dr. (1982) The New Aerobics, Retrieved from cooperaerobics.com/health-tips/prevention plus/your-prescription-for-good-health.aspx

because they are now so far out of shape as to be almost unrecognizable. **That person became the victim of hypo-kinetic disease (aka: couch potato syndrome). Did you know that those categorized as unfit people will experience a decline in physiological performance of about two percent per year? Multiply that over 40 years and your body may be well past the point of return!** [15] So far we have covered only the surface benefits of regular exercise. The benefits of proper nutrition and exercise, as little as two hours per week, can make a remarkable difference over the long run. A commitment to continued mobility, with improvements in nutrition, and regular exercise are the keys to warding off many of the expected aspects of aging and the potential for age related diseases that plague seniors.

We want to emphasize that sensible exercise and a quality diet will improve the quality of life, at any age! We don't know of any seniors who want to exist in the survival mode bound to the easy chair and so frail they may be afraid to leave their own homes. We believe there is true meaning to the term "golden years" being a time to enjoy life and possibly experience all the things that have been put on the back burner while families and careers have previously taken top priority. Many seniors may have worked two jobs to support their families and started at the bottom of their career ladder, with very little regard for their personal health. Our wish for all seniors is to see them enjoy

---

[15] Senior Fitness Handbook (2010 Second Edition) Chapter 1, Introduction, p.3, Carpenteria, CA: International Sports Sciences Association

those well- deserved senior years and at 85 have the fitness level of the average 50- year old. Why not!

Jack LaLanne lived to the age of 96 and was still doing his two hour per day workout until he was 95. **Now that is what we call growing well, not growing old!** Jack had a well- documented life with many feats of strength and physical endurance recognized by individual honors too numerous to list. Known as "The Godfather of Fitness," Jack practiced what he preached and every one of our experts on the *panel,* in *The Second Fifty,* are well aware of his tremendous legacy in the fitness world. Some of Jack's one liners from 50 years ago still hold true today and are worth repeating:

"Exercise is king and nutrition is queen- together you have your ideal kingdom."
"People work at dying, they don't work at living."
"If it tastes good, spit it out."
"Would you feed your dog a cup of coffee and a donut in the morning?"

According to Jack's family, he had performed his usual, two-hour daily workout routine, just the day before his death. [16]

Unfortunately, from the very minute we enter this life we also begin our slow march toward our ultimate death. The reader must realize that it is never too late to turn your physical health around, but that life changing decision, to strive for better health and a better life, is only in the hands of one person. The prodding by

---

[16] Lalanne, Jack (2015) Retrieved from http://www.jacklalanne.com

your spouse, the tears of your children, input of friends and family will never do it. You must have the personal pride, spirit, intrinsic drive, determination and come to the realization that you will not be spending your golden years in the doctors' waiting rooms, with limited mobility, and taking an endless array of prescription medications. **Every day that you let pass by and don't work at LIVING is another day working at DYING.**

Find a person who knows the fitness game and can show you the true path. Avoid the years of trial and error and trying to duplicate the professional routines in the popular magazines. Your best bet is to find someone who has been properly schooled and whose physical condition may be the proof that their approach actually works. Luckily, our *panel of experts* was fortunate enough to have crossed paths with such mentors, in their early neighborhoods, or on life's pathway that were willing to take on a few eager novices. Those early mentors allowed the *panel* members to build a sound foundation and eventually they were able to exceed expectations, while expanding their horizons. Once your progress becomes visible, you may want to proceed to a higher level so you search for new mentors in your areas, various clubs, colleges or the military. In some cases, that fitness fever may allow you to live the dream of surpassing the exploits established by many of your original mentors and in other cases the fitness bar may have been originally set so high it became a life-long fitness motivation. Hopefully, that motivation will carry you through *The Second Fifty* years of training!

One of the first gathering places for your authors was a club called the Sons of Samson established by Kenny and Ronnie Brewer in Covington, Kentucky. The Brewers had converted the second floor of their house into a well- equipped gym and young guys from all over the city trained there on a regular basis with many others appearing occasionally. One of the early trainees was a guy named Bill *Snipe* Landrum. *Snipe* was a name his friends could call him and hope to get away with it. He was the typical 95 pounds weakling and looked destined to possibly become a jockey. His first barbell was a broomstick with a couple of five pound weights on each end because he could not lift the 25- pound metal bar. *Snipe* never missed a workout and his form and technique was meticulous. Over a period of three years his weight went to a muscular 123 and his strength was amazing, in any pound for pound comparison, with other lifters. An example of his strength was the bench press, which was 265-270 pounds, with a two second pause on the chest.

Snipe eventually became a competitive, world class, power lifter and surpassed, in training, the then existing world record of about 275 pounds held by Enrique Hernandez. Bill would achieve a lift of 275, but the world record would move to 280 and so on until he eventually maxed out at a 290 bench press. Remember, that's at a weight of 123 with a two second pause and no extra boost from the spring loaded super shirts, super wraps or the pharmaceutical labs! Bill was also able to perform endless chins behind the neck and parallel bar dips, with 45 pound plates attached to his waist. His other lifts were equally impressive and pound for pound our friend who started training with basically nothing was able to evolve into one of the strongest lifters in the country. He was also listed in the pages of *Iron Man Magazine,* for a number of years, as one of the top power lifters in the country. *Snipe* won a number of overall best lifter awards, using the old Hoffman Formula, which was used to determine who was the best when comparing lifters of different weight classes. We can emphatically state with certainty that the guys we trained with used absolutely zero performance enhancing drugs. (PEDs) Most trainees in the mid-west didn't even know Dianabol, Winstrol, Maxibolin, Durabolin and the other steroid drugs existed until they heard rumors or worked out with a few athletes who had access to them through various sources. Our first knowledge came from several track and field athletes we trained with at a state university we attended. We will present a more detailed discussion about that negative and life shortening aspect of training in Chapter 14.

The untimely death of Bill *Snipe* Landrum was a blow to everyone he knew. He inspired us to achieve more than we ever thought capable. One night while doing bench presses, at his friend, Bill Schwartz's home gym, he sat up on the bench; took a deep breath and fell back to the bench in quiet silence. No one knew he had a genetic heart defect like his father, uncle and brother before him. A priest from the local hospital called everyone on a phone list *Snipe* had kept in his wallet and said we should come to the hospital as soon as possible. We said, "We'll be right there." The priest answered back, "There is no need to hurry." What a sad ending for a 40- year old man just entering the prime of life. We also believe that *Snipe* was an example of the amazing things that can be achieved with conviction, desire and dedication. **Also, remember the earlier comments about a very thorough physical before you attempt your new pathway to fitness!**

Panel of Experts ... Questions # 4 and 5

List you training priorities and what you look for when selecting a gym?

The *panel's* comments ....

Terry Collis – I look for all white gis or uniforms, with no black or red, because the white gis reflect the old system of humility and the true Buddhist philosophy. Besides the amenities that provide the martial arts atmosphere, I also consider the gym monthly charges, dues, and type of credit card system used. I like to see a disciplined approach, especially with the younger students and of course a high level of instruction for all ranks or color of belts.

Devorah Dometrich – Herbst - The knowledge of the martial artists there, but I will state again that I don't need a specific gym or facility. My gym or dojo is anywhere I chose.

Dave Guidugli – My priorities are always the same ...cardio, core work, increase energy, staying mentally sharp, staying flexible with a full range of motion. My personal concern is monitoring my blood pressure. I look for a training environment that allows me the flexibility, space and resources to implement my program. I need an area open for speed and quickness drills; a variety of machines for resistance / strength training; boxing equipment and hopefully, a ring.

Ray Hughes - Cleanliness is first on my list and then the variety of the equipment that is available. I still like to train every day, in my old neighborhood, even though that means a longer commute. I like to mix my workout with free weights, machines and add in some cardio with the treadmill. My training philosophy has changed over the past two years. I decided to focus on more core exercises and much lighter weight for my strength training. I also like to finish off with a sauna, steam or a dip in the pool.

Lanny Julian – Training is a gradual process and achieving your personal goals will come with time. My philosophy has always been to train with light weight with high reps, which I believe is the key to long term success. Consistency is crucial, but be proactive and train to avoid injury. My wife and I have trained in many gyms including all of the popular fitness chains. The modern fitness centers have every possible type of equipment, but my major concern is still cleanliness. There is no excuse for not wiping down the machines and maintaining high sanitary standards. I would advise anyone using a fitness club or center to take their own bottle of spray to wipe down the machines before and after.

Roger Riedinger – A full range of movement while, maintain strength and flexibility, maintain muscle tissue. I'd look for a gym that includes a mixture of free weights and machines. More importantly, I'd look for a gym that is managed by an experienced weight trainer who can identify the good in each new fitness fad, but who also has a solid grounding in the fundamentals of progressive weight training.

Jerry Auton - Always plan your workouts ahead on a weekly schedule. It is imperative for maximum results to workout with an experienced partner or spend the money and hire a qualified and certified personal trainer. My highest priority is cleanliness. I go the gym and dedicate myself to maintaining my health and condition. I don't expect to bring home infectious germs or staph. The second priority is to find a gym with a variety of strength and cardio machines.

Tom Geimeier - I've always been proud of my flexibility and have tried to maintain that edge. My early training concentrated on gaining strength and utilizing power lifting type workouts. Today my priorities are: do nothing to aggravate old injuries; be moderate and sensible; do a cardio warm up first followed by resistance exercise; be consistent in training and try to maintain a sound mind and positive outlook. Like the other members of the *panel*, I've belonged to a number of gyms since age 12, from the back alleys to the deluxe, and can tell very quickly if the gym has what I need. I like a variety of machines for each muscle group because that gives me the option of selecting machines that do not give me pain while exercising. Cleanliness is a key in the exercise room and locker room. Finally, a gym where people know how to use the machines properly and the staff makes an attempt to keep everything in working order.

What the research says ....

There are a vast array of options and locations when it comes to selecting a gym or fitness center that you feel comfortable with and look forward to working out in. We feel that decision is very important and will have a tremendous impact on your future successes. Our *panel* has considered the significance of that decision and we have listed their priorities below:

- Cleanliness of the facility including the workout areas, saunas, locker rooms, water fountains, bathrooms and equipment

- The variety of equipment and options for each muscle group

- The hours of operation and meeting the needs of your personal schedule

- Knowledgeable and courteous staff who also enforce the rules

- Ample equipment so there is very little wait time (a friend's wife told us she enrolled in a new fitness club and had to wait in line to use the bathroom facilities)

- A safe environment with no slip and trip hazards in all areas

- Ongoing program of equipment maintenance

- A fair and competitive price

- Multiple class offerings beyond the use of free weights and weight machines

- The clientele in proper dress and attire

Unfortunately, we cannot personally select a gym's clientele so you have to put on the blinders and ignore some of the rampant stupidity that just should not happen. Large gyms have hundreds of men and women that make up their memberships. Many are aware of the etiquette, but there are always those who don't have a clue. The high school after hour's programs and locker room behavior doesn't belong in a fitness establishment. The best thing a gym chain could do to save maintenance repairs and complaints would be to hire a roving instructor to correct improper equipment use. They have staff members who should be assigned to this duty when they aren't on phone membership duty. If the staff see a piece of equipment being used improperly, someone throwing the weights or refusing to rack them, they could intervene on the spot. A novice using too much weight or using a machine improperly could also receive some training advice, which may avoid a potential personal injury and damaged equipment. Being a member of a large gym, with hundreds of members, will require some tolerance for the experienced trainee. The best option for others is to train at home, but that can be a lonely venture, unless you have a spouse, dedicated friend or older children to partner with.

First and foremost, you will want to select a gym that offers a variety of equipment, classes, ease of access and flexible hours. You also want a gym or fitness center that will work with you on the contract, maintains their equipment and has a staff that keeps the place clean and sanitary. Is the broken equipment repaired in a timely manner and do you see staff regularly cleaning the workout areas? Needless to say the restrooms, showers, changing areas, and water fountains need to be sanitary and inspected often. It is simple logic that the larger the gym and membership the more frequently those areas must be inspected and cleaned.

What about the clientele that comprises most of the members? If you hear screaming, grunting, weights being tossed around and the floor cluttered with free weights you are probably not in the best atmosphere. How are the members dressed? Remember that an effective gym trying to make a profit will have a variety of ages and as many women as men. Members should be appropriately dressed in tee shirts, sweats, tank tops with the sides still in place, shorts or sweatpants. Men should not be shirtless, dressed in street clothes or dirty work clothes. The women also have a dress code and they should also be dressed in the workout mode. How often have you seen a young woman trying to work out fully armed with maximum makeup and a pair of daisy duke shorts a few sizes too small? There are other places better suited for socializing or finding a date.

An idealistic set of rules we would like to post in every gym:

- ❖ Dress appropriately
- ❖ Wipe off the machines before and after using.
- ❖ Don't invade someone's personal space when they are using a piece of equipment.
- ❖ Rack or replace any piece of equipment that is not part of a machine.
- ❖ Do not ogle eye or stare at the ladies or the men.
- ❖ Casual conversation is okay, but the gym is not the place to corner your prey.
- ❖ Nobody cares about your conversation. Keep it private.
- ❖ Ask if someone is still using a machine before you jump on it.
- ❖ Avoid the use of profanity.
- ❖ Use proper hygiene in the workout area, locker room and while using all gym amenities.

❖ Shower before using the sauna, whirlpool, or swimming pool. These can be incubators for germs.

The bottom line ....

A survey of the *panel* indicated a main priority was a variety of exercise equipment that included free weights and an assortment of machines. Another issue addressed was the cleanliness of the facility and proper sanitation by those who used the equipment. Lanny Julian mentioned he even carried his own spray bottle to wipe the equipment down. Devorah Dometrich –Herbst emphasized that she does not need a gym because her body is her gym and that is really all she needs. Her gym goes wherever she goes, which solves the potential situations of sharing gym equipment. Roger Riedinger mentioned a qualified trainer was essential as well as the training staff, which was also seconded by Jerry Auton, Tom Geimeier, Devorah Dometrich-Herbst and Terry Collis. Dave Guidugli prioritized the need for space because of his specific type of training. His regime requires a boxing ring, which cannot be found in the usual chain fitness centers. Ray Hughes felt more comfortable in his old YMCA neighborhood gym where he had been a member for 65 years. He was also concerned about additional amenities like the pool, sauna and steam room. Terry Collis was concerned about selecting a dojo that offered instruction that was true to the martial arts philosophy, atmosphere and the discipline found there.

The hot tip ....

Make sure to visit several gyms and ask each for a trial workout. A quality business should have nothing to hide. Those few visits will give you time to size up the atmosphere, staff and clientele. If you are over 65 make sure to ask if they participate in insurance sponsored programs like the *Silver Sneakers* ®. You know better than anyone else your personal limitations and equipment needs. Use your common sense and past experience to select a facility that is best for you! We have listed a few scenarios you might encounter while attending or visiting a gym. Our point for the readers is to stay focused on a common sense path of fitness that does not jeopardize your progress with un-needed setbacks.

The best case scenario will always be to stay focused on yourself and other likeminded members will do the same. The key with any exercise, martial art, free weights or exercise machines is to utilize perfect form. Proper technique will enhance results, and help avoid injuries. Performing your exercises should never be a struggle! Those who are prone to use too much weight on their exercises and sacrifice proper technique can be seen and heard around the gym as the weight stacks or dumbbells come crashing to a halt. We understand the mentality of wanting to appear stronger than one looks, but that training philosophy is rather foolish. It takes discipline to use the appropriate weights when everyone around you may be using more weight. The key to fitness or athletic success, as the *panel* has emphasized, is a gradual progression with a selection of exercises and equipment based strictly on your personal needs. To be perfectly blunt, no one in the gym is really interested in what you are doing. Anyone who appears to be interested probably wants the machine you're using, after you are finished.

A final bit of advice regarding the training staff that most gyms employ to assist members for an additional fee. When was the last time you saw an experienced trainer that you would accept training advice from? Beware and be very cautious about who you accept advice from. What are the credentials of the designated instructors and what is the depth of their experience? We have seen trainers working with their clients, during their hourly sessions, literally put their charges into cardiac arrest. Most of the clients that encounter that experience will probably never return, which costs the trainers future business and the fitness center bad PR.

One of the biggest concerns of our *panel* on selecting a gym was cleanliness, sanitation and the upkeep of the facility. There is no excuse for anyone to be sitting in the sauna with their street or sweaty gym clothes on, including their shoes. The approximate 115- degree temperature of the sauna can make it a virtual incubator for germs. The same applies to the communal whirlpool. Showers should be taken before using either, but don't be surprised by what you actually witness. We also wonder about foot problems when many locker rooms are carpeted and those carpets are known to harbor a lot of mold and fungus.

Photos by Geimeier
Left -typical dumbbell rack in the "free weight" area
Right - Bill *Snipe* Landrum
Bill chased the world record, in the 123- pound weight class, for over 20 years.

Chapter 4

Age Appropriate Training Routines

"High expectations are a must and attainable. Don't accept what fate has in store for you"

In the 1950s and early 60s you may have been motivated to play a certain sport because you saw professional athletes that you idolized for various reasons. Maybe you read a bodybuilding magazine or fitness magazine and saw muscles the ordinary person did not have and never would. Ego can be a powerful motivator to begin training and everyone likes to be admired whether they say it or not. Men in the neighborhood coming home from basic training, in the military, were often in the best shape of their lives. Even the muscular arms of a construction, concrete, or slaughterhouse worker may have been enough to inspire a young kid. I'm sure there were examples in every neighborhood that motivated someone to improve their physical abilities; want to add some muscle to their frame or drop some baby fat for a more positive appearance.

Maybe your early goals were to purchase a set of weights or barbells and work towards packing on the muscle for a better self-image and self- confidence. It is basic human nature. Most kids in our neighborhood wanted to have muscular arms, broader shoulders and be able to handle themselves physically. Every kid had a pair of boxing gloves and wrestled in someone's yard as a frequent activity. Nobody we knew wanted to be the neighborhood punching bag and afraid to come out of their house or apartment. There were numerous kids in our neighborhood who eventually began lifting some weights with the basic bench presses, curls, power cleans, deadlifts and all the exercises they saw their role models perform in some dingy basement or cellar. There were YMCA's, Boys Clubs, and in some locations neighbors with garages or basements that had basic fitness equipment and initial training opportunities.

One of the key mistakes made by the early fitness buffs was to try and duplicate the training routines that appeared in the popular magazines. Imagine a young novice trying to do 15-20 sets of arm work because he saw a Mr. America or Mr. Universe swearing by that training method. Guidance and experienced mentors would have been the best solution, but that option was not always available. Most young kids found success in small leaps, strictly by trial and error, or by finding a workout location with people who had found a more sensible, result producing system and a sincere interest in helping others.

Once you developed a more common sense approach to training and were driven by your personal motivation the desired results would soon begin to follow. That same philosophy also applies to improving the skill levels in any sport, but the trial and error method can be a hard teacher, with lots of frustration and possibly very little success. Parents or older siblings may have been your first coaches teaching you the basics of early sports endeavors. You may have received a ball glove for your birthday or Christmas and soon learned how to catch, throw, field ground balls, and swing the bat correctly. You signed up for a Knothole or a Little League baseball team; a Pee Wee Football team, or possibly a basketball program at the local YMCA. Your early coaches and mentors assuredly had various skill levels, but all should be commended for putting in their valuable time to see you succeed. As your skill level developed, you moved on to different teams and levels of play with new opportunities to develop your full potential. The more competitive the sport became the more important your level of fitness. Reaching the top in any sport or athletic competition is really a survival of the fittest.

We have a shared belief about physical maturity and make a crucial statement here that cannot be supported by any current research we've found. We've often stated that the best high school athletes will obviously be those with the best skill level and possibly the best genetics. **Our un-founded, x -factor personal belief is that the best athletes in high school will almost always be those who have reached physical maturity first**. That is why many parents hold their child back a grade (red shirt) or falsify their birth certificates. Tom remembers working at a high school that won a state high school football championship in the mid -1970s and most of the key players were men, not boys. If those guys didn't shave in the morning, then by late afternoon there were a lot of five o'clock shadows. There were also several key players whose parents had red shirted them in elementary school to give them another year of athletic eligibility. It's unfortunate we don't take the same philosophy towards academic performance! There were age limitations to play and also a limit to how many years a student could be in high school, but according to many state laws a parent has the right to "red shirt" or hold their child back one year, for any reason. (grades, maturity, behavior, personal preference) Maturity and age were certainly key components for early success, but had one negative aspect. **We believe that those who mature the earliest also will see the effects of aging the earliest.** Look at the high school star athletes at your 30, 40 or 50 year reunions. You might be utterly amazed!

Your days of youth have already been spent and hopefully you have made gains in knowledge, maturity and what your appropriate goals should be. The passage of time will dictate your physical limitations and that will change from year to year and decade to decade. I'm sure every reader has made some significant achievements in their lives and those are wonderful reflections, but the truth is you must be concerned with the **here and now**. We believe that the best path to follow will be the one that leads to the greatest functionality and fewest physical limitations of the human body. The wise trainee will incorporate some sort of resistance training to maintain and prevent as much muscle loss as possible, while also reducing the loss of your bone density. A sensible, well designed diet will assist in offsetting the needless accumulation of body fat, which will eventually lead to a variety of ailments including heart disease. Cardio can often be overdone, but some cardio is a smart strategy to keep the veins and arteries clear of plaque buildup. Research has proven that very excessive running can wreak havoc on the joints and you can actually reach a point where the positive dividends go into the negative. Flexibility is one of the basic keys to later life functionality and we feel the martial artists have a huge edge here. The martial artists do a variety of crucial stretching and warm up activities that are frequently given the lowest priority by those strictly dependent on resistance training or "pumping iron."

Parents were not as driven in the 50s and 60s, as today, for their child to be a super star and dream of all their glorious exploits that were expected to come. It has often been said that," It is too bad youth is wasted on the young." If we could only turn back the hands of time with maintaining the knowledge that comes with maturity and a realistic appreciation of our health and fitness. Since turning back the hands of time is an impossibility and that, *if and but* mentality being detrimental to progress, we have no option but to focus on the opportunities and possibilities of the present.

If you were born between the years 1946 and 1964 you are known as a "baby boomer," which distinguishes you from other age groups like the younger "millennials." You are in good company and will not grow old alone because that prestigious group of "baby boomer" seniors has **10,000 new members admitted to the club every day.** [17] What does that mean to "boomers?" Unless you are homeless or are living under a rock, you will start receiving junk mail, of all sorts, by the handfuls. Your information can be found in various databases that allow insurance companies, retirement communities, hearing aid companies, and dozens of other agencies free reign on your mailbox. The unsolicited flyers found in your mail will remind you on a regular basis of problems to anticipate like: osteoporosis, arthritis, Alzheimer's disease, depression, incontinence, hair replacement, sexual function, plastic surgery and hormone replacement to name a few.

---

[17] Population Reference Bureau Staff (2002) Baby Boomer Population, http://www.prb.org/publications/article/2002

Technology today has allowed these things to happen, so why not use this new technology to your benefit? We now have the opportunity to make the most of this great era of easy access information. Today, we have the knowledge and resources the last generation could never dream of that affords us much healthier choices than our parents had. It is very difficult for us to imagine our parents sitting with their I-Pads looking up the most available vegan diet or workout programs. Why you might ask? Our society has been slowly acclimated and recently propelled into the everyday use of the available technology. The idea of living longer through proper nutrition and exercise did not just show up yesterday. It was not long ago that older adults were discouraged from exercise and told to play it safe and stay in the rocking chairs. Within our lifetime almost everything we were taught about aging has been disproved or completely reversed. We are in the midst of an exciting time when medical doctors, exercise pathologists and gerontologists are redefining the aging process. The next ten years of scientific research and breakthroughs may well lead to some breathtaking discoveries that will extend our longevity. Those golden years ahead are starting to show a beautiful sunset on that distant horizon.

Hopefully, you are starting to realize the necessary motivation to make the most out of your senior years. A good motivation may come daily as you sort through your daily or weekly junk mail. The desperation of those mailers is starting to show. Those companies now realize that their primary target customers are moving targets and once on the move will cause them to lose money! They are doing everything possible to instill negative thoughts into your psyche. Don't fall victim to that ploy. Stay positive in your outlook and if your motivation fails seek out a qualified personal trainer who can help you. You don't really want to spend your hard earned retirement savings on doctors, medicine and nursing homes.

A good example of this progress is exemplified by the Northern Kentucky bodybuilding competition. In recent years this 37- year old contest has evolved into the largest one- day physical culture event in the United States. In past years there has been a men's *masters* 60 and over category. New competition classes are expected, as the younger 50 and over group, is now bulging with competitors. Look around at the number of seniors that are participating in jogging, cycling, entering 5K, 10K and marathon races. The Senior Olympics and various state senior games have also continued to expand their offerings to meet the demand. This is indeed a new era we are fortunate to live in today. Twenty years ago we were in our forties and the thought of competing athletes over 60 was given very little attention. Don't be left behind! The wheelchairs and walkers are for the seriously injured or impaired or possibly the unmotivated and non-believers. If you want a little extra motivation, use the new era of technology called the Internet and Google 'Team Hoyt.' [18]

The best advice to begin any training is to know how to use the equipment and the machines. Learn which exercises work the various muscle groups and how many sets and repetitions to perform. Knowing a variety of exercises and having different machines to select from will avoid boredom and keep your

---

[18] Hoyt, Dick (23 August 2014) Yes, You Can Retrieved from
http://teamhoyt.com/

training fresh and something to look forward to. When we were tested as certified AAU Kentucky and National AAU physique judges we were required to name every possible competition pose and every single muscle in the body. The muscle knowledge was actually a written test before you could even sit at a judges table.

Learning the anatomy of the human body would also be very advisable to the fitness enthusiast. The test was administered by a professor, at the University of Louisville, who was the Chairman of the National AAU Judging Committee. The AAU was a power name in bodybuilding before the **NPC and the earlier IFBB**. The AAU was also the controlling organization regarding power lifting, weight lifting and 35 other sports. [19]

Once you know something about the anatomy of the human body, your basic bone structure, the condition of your present health, the exercises and any physical limitations you have it is time to find the perfect system for you. There are hundreds of systems you see at any gym, fitness center or on the TV. Pick the one that you actually enjoy and seems the perfect fit for you. There is also an advantage to finding a regular training partner, with the same basic goals, to motivate and keep each other on track.

The Insanity is Over

Have you observed the new training priorities in the gyms and fitness centers? Take a look at the trend in working the deltoids, traps, back, abs and arms. In the old days the so called "gym rats'

---

[19] WIlklpedia (2015) IFBB and AAU Organizations, retrieved from wiklkipedia.org/wiki/amateur-athletic-union

could not wait to hit the gym and focus on bench presses and endless arm exercises. Flat, incline, decline, barbell or dumbbell benches were the mainstay exercises for those key show muscle groups, but have given way to a more balanced and sensible approach. Very few people were working their legs; working their "core" or achieving those melon- like deltoids. A good set of pecs, muscular arms and a tight fitting tee shirt were in vogue. The legs were often neglected, unless you were a powerlifter, and the number one question was usually how much you could bench. Many of the younger group training hard today seem to be taking a more balanced approach and should be congratulated on that aspect.

Today, the first priority seems to be the deltoids or "delts," but still with a good set of biceps and triceps to go with it. Those are the show muscles of today. Take a look at the college basketball and NBA players and you will see the emphasis their strength coaches have also put on this muscle group. The young trainees today seem to have more knowledge and a better attitude towards balanced training. The only flaw we see is that the young guys still have poor technique and that can mean trouble when compounded with handling weight that is often heavier than needed. The form is often so poor that you have to turn our heads away. Another key muscle group worked in tandem with the deltoids is usually the traps. That is a logical approach, but once again we often see people doing shrugs with 400 plus pounds and the benefits could be more efficient with much less weight and better form.

We also see a lot of young guys in the gym with a regular routine of deadlifts and squats. There has been a definite paradigm shift in training. The new kids on the block also want power and somehow they have learned that comes from king squat, deadlifting and power cleans. Maybe that new mentality has been instilled by the improvement in knowledge of their high school and college strength coaches, which was severely lacking and almost bordered on incompetence for several decades.

Panel of Experts ... Questions # 6 and 7

What advice would you give to a young person starting versus the advice to the over 50 crowd? *(our panel would like the over 50 readers to see the difference in priorities that should exist between the younger person and those over 50)*

The *panel's* comments ....

Terry Collis –Expect gradual progress, take it easy. The body and the mind need time to adjust. Practice, learn the basics, build a proper foundation, stick with it thru the initial stages and give it a fair chance. Basically, that same approach applies to any sport. Realize your physical limitations. Stretch, warmup, and the instructor will determine the intensity. Stay within yourself. You can't come back to the same level of fitness or competition after years of layoff. The over 50s may try to do things the same as when they were teenagers. They get discouraged after one or two training sessions. They also need to stay within themselves. Work the special katas 4-5 times per day & do a lot of routine stretches. The shoulders and hips especially need to be stretched & associative muscles. Some advanced members push the new students to do exercises their body is not accustomed to. Ex. The

Makawara Board and heavy bag where the young guys injure fingers & knuckles because they think they must have big calloused knuckles. The same applies to the feet and these extremity injuries can become arthritic in later years.

Devorah Dometrich – Herbst – Both groups can benefit from the same advice. Find your passion and pursue it. That gives the person a solid foundation from which to set realistic personal goals. Regardless of what you want to do listen to your body. Start with realistic goals; build a strong base and evaluate yourself and build from there. Find a trainer your own age that has the experience and knowledge to guide you to your goals without injuring you. Set realistic goals and be patient with yourself or forget it! Moderation is the key and nothing extreme is required. There is no need or benefit from spending two hours doing kicks or punches. Diversify your training and work different areas of the body and different techniques. Many people torture their bodies and don't know how it will affect them until later years. The Martial Arts philosophy is about your opponent getting hurt ...not you!

Dave Guidugli – "Rome wasn't built in a day." Expect gradual improvement as you work on stretching, toning, core, and especially cardio. Evaluate yourself to establish a realistic baseline. This would include: speed, strength, flexibility, explosion, and mental toughness. Your weak areas become your priorities and no matter what has happened the night before you never miss your workouts. Fitness must become your lifestyle and an extension of yourself. Also, try not to get bored by keeping variety in your training sessions. Joining a gym that does not meet your needs is a huge mistake so select a location that offers you the opportunity to work on your total health. Think about your heart, blood pressure, and hormone levels. It's too bad you can't find a gym with everyone your same age. That would be the ideal situation. Lifting more than you are capable of to impress someone or get a false reading about your progress only increases your chances of injury. Improper warm ups and not stretching the tendons and ligaments to stabilize them before beginning will increase your chances of injury.

Ray Hughes - Find a good mentor and don't pay any attention to what others are doing in the gym or dojo. Stay within yourself and expect progress to be incremental. Come into the gym with the proper mental attitude and be sure to warm up properly before beginning your workout. Remember that you don't have to prove anything and be smart enough to realize that you cannot perform at the same level you did years earlier. This applies to all age groups and especially after a long layoff! Continue to warm up, stretch and add in cardio, but if you have been inactive, start slowly and try to workout at least three to four days per week. I used to enjoy the physical aspects of judo that included: grappling techniques and throws, but I don't need that bone breaking risk at age 76. Two years ago I had an intense workout with a group of 20- year old athletes that almost killed me. I was relatively strong and could still bench close to 300, but let my ego get in the way. That brutal workout caused me to take a several month layoff and re-think my entire exercise philosophy. I still walk and jog every day, but came to the realization that proper technique is the most important and the amount of weight secondary. I work core with a variety of exercises and have adopted a much lighter weight with higher repetition format.

Lanny Julian – The advice is the same regardless of age. See your doctor first. I like to have a physical twice a year with blood work included to monitor my body's key functions. Use your head, start slow, and use common sense! "You cannot do what you did years ago or when you were younger." Start light and work your way up. Your personal goals may take years of commitment and dedication to accomplish. Also, be sure to see your doctor first to make sure you have their approval. Don't forget to enjoy your training sessions. I was in a particular arm wrestling tournament and had five or six long pulls that left me tired. (a quick match might be four seconds and a long pull 20 seconds to a minute) My last match went a minute and there was a loud "pop," which resulted in a torn ligament in my forearm. Proper rest and recuperation is also a key to progress without injury. I also have a problem with many of the trainers I see in the gyms. They seem to have everyone on the same program regardless of gender, age or ability.

Roger Riedinger – Not that they would listen, but start well within your current ability and gradually increase each week. Start with a classic weight training program, not with one that you read in a muscle magazine or where you do bench and arms every workout day. It's never too late! Start with very basic goals. If you are inactive, start with a basic walk of 50 steps there and back, three days a week and make incremental increases, as your body becomes acclimated. Soon you'll be walking a mile, then two. Act like you're 16 and start lifting weights with just the bar adding a small amount each week. Don't make your goals too hard to or impossible to achieve. They must be realistic lifetime goals and ideally broken down into yearly, quarterly, monthly, and even weekly sub goals. For example: your lifetime goal may be to clean and jerk your bodyweight. **A starting point may be 65 pounds while your bodyweight is 165. Your first 1- week goal would be 67.5lbs. Year 1 goal might be 115 lbs. (just 1 lb. per week increase). 1st 3- month goal is 2.5 lbs. per week, 2nd 3- month goal is 2.5 lbs. every other week – that gets you to your 1st year goal with 6 months to spare. It's usually better at this point to drop back about 10%** and start again with the same progression. Another round of the above progression will take you to 135 at the end of year one and you still have a lifetime to go to add just 30 more pounds. Never try to increase strength or endurance too quickly!

Jerry Auton – The two most common mistakes are actually direct opposites. Train too hard; too fast; too often and you become discouraged with extreme soreness and possible injury. The opposite fault is training too light, being afraid to challenge yourself by increasing the weight; and training infrequently. That also results in discouragement due to little improvement for both age groups. The key is to find the happy medium. A certified trainer is a must in this situation, especially if it has been years since you last regular sessions. Take the time to think about what you actually want to accomplish on a particular workout day. Again, plan, warm-up, stretch and seek professional, experienced assistance. All ages are prone to poor technique and trying to lift more weight than can be properly handled. Poor technique alone can result in injury, but combined with too much weight is a recipe for disaster. Muscles, tendons, and ligaments that are torn can have an adverse effect on your training for a lifetime. Be smart, cautious and don't be afraid to ask for help.

Tom Geimeier – A good mentor can set you on the right path, motivate you and save you years of mistakes and lack of improvement. Too many people I know have learned, but often paid the price, through trial and error. A good mentor can also serve as a life- long role model and building a good foundation because a house built on sand cannot stand. Find a type of fitness that you enjoy and use it with regularity. Make sure the benefits include: cardio, flexibility, and resistance training for muscle tone. The training must have a low risk of injury and also be convenient. Have a thorough physical before you begin and set sensible goals. A good motto or mantra would be to know thyself and your personal limitations. A quality program that enhances and can excel your progress must be more than mere exercise. Fine tune your diet or nutritional plan and include some techniques on relaxation for mental health reasons. Finally, you will need an ideal place to train and commit yourself to life habits that will propel you toward that elusive triple digits or century mark.

What the research says ....

Special considerations for *The Second Fifty* age group

If we were trying to motivate or counsel a friend, co-worker, neighbor or relative about starting an overall plan for better health we might start with a few key points the bulk of research will substantiate.

- Any positive steps you take at any age regarding exercise, activity or improved nutrition are wise choices in the long term.

- What your parents and grandparents told you or did in their daily lives may not be the best option for you.
- A sound nutritional plan has the ability to energize you, keep the internal organs in good working order and make you feel a lot better about yourself.
- A personalized fitness program that takes into account your limitations and abilities can improve balance, coordination, muscle tone, bone density, and everyday functionality.
- The gyms and fitness centers of today are full of the over 50's. There are a lot of customized group classes and your age group may be in the majority.
- Many insurance providers offer the *Silver Sneakers®* program, which gives you a free membership if you are over 65 and on Medicare. Home training is always an option, but you lose the atmosphere and the socialization benefits.

There are tremendous benefits of exercise that should be very appealing to everyone who is interested in healthy aging and greater longevity. Exercise of any type is a wise and productive use of time and a positive alternative to doing nothing and taking your chances. A regular exercise program has been proven to improve sleep, improve mood, inspire greater self -confidence, increase your ability to focus on tasks, improve the ability to relax and distress, improve flexibility, balance, improve body functions, control weight, maintain muscle mass, and improve or maintain bone density.

The bottom line ....

There is an absolute consensus of the *panel* on the advice given, to the young person starting out and the over 50 trainees, possibly re-entering their fitness pursuits after years of very little activity. The consensus advice was to always begin slowly and methodically with reasonable and periodically achievable goals. The *panel* indicated that progressive improvement and results would be the wisest path to follow. Another common denominator was utilizing a mentor, trainer, role model or instructor who had the expertise of taking you through the various techniques that enabled you to achieve your goals in the shortest time.

Another common thread was to know your limitations or you could possibly pay a price in later years. Terry Collis, Devorah Dometrich-Herbst, Dave Guidugli, Lanny Julian and Roger Riedinger mentioned to expect gradual progress, knowing your limitations and avoiding extreme exercises that may cause you problems in later years. Ray Hughes advocated never try to prove anything. An ideal program should be customized to your needs and realize that nobody in the gym cares what you are doing. Dave Guidugli made a good point with his phrase that "Rome wasn't built in a day." Dave and Devorah also mentioned it was too bad everyone in the gym or dojo were not the same age. Jerry Auton mentioned that starting gradual is key, but don't be afraid to challenge yourself. Lanny Julian and Tom Geimeier mentioned some other key factors for progress and hitting bench marks like incorporating ample recuperation time, upgrading nutrition and relaxation. The interviews also revealed another consensus and concern regarding proper technique. The *panel*, regardless of area of expertise, stated emphatically that good technique enhances progress whereas poor technique will eventually lead to injury and potential limitations later in life.

The hot tip ....

Make sure you have a wellness assessment yearly or as often as your health insurance will permit. Know your limitations and plan accordingly. Find a gym that will allow you to meet these needs. A qualified trainer or workout partner can save you time and make your goals more achievable. Dedicate yourself and make sure you find true enjoyment in your chosen activity.

Age	18-25	26-35	36-45	46-55	56-65	65+
Athlete	49-55	49-54	50-56	50-57	51-56	50-55
Excellent	56-61	55-61	57-62	58-63	57-61	56-61
Good	62-65	62-65	63-66	64-67	62-67	62-65
Above Average	66-69	66-70	67-70	68-71	68-71	66-69
Average	70-73	71-74	71-75	72-76	72-75	70-73
Below Average	74-81	75-81	76-82	77-83	76-81	74-79
Poor	82+	82+	83+	84+	82+	80+

Resting Heart Rate Chart [20]

Your resting and exercise heart rate can be taken at the wrist or the carotid artery on the neck. Count the beats for 10 seconds and multiple by 6 to find your one- minute total. Your exercise rate should never exceed 200 minus your age.

---

[20] American Heart Association.com

Chapter 5

Training Routines by the *Panel*

We asked each member of the *panel* to design and contribute a workout routine, from their area of expertise, that would have benefits for someone over 50. Some routines are more detailed than others and several address the needs from the beginner to the moderate trainee and beyond. The variations in the suggested routines certainly cover a wide spectrum and provide the reader with a thorough overview of the possibilities that may align with one's personal goals and abilities.

The *panel's* comments ....

Roger Riedinger

Roger suggested a basic progressive resistance routine that would apply equally for the young beginner or the **over 50** making their return or just beginning. We have outlined that program below with some additional comments from Roger. Roger stated it over and over again in the previous questions regarding progressive resistance that you should take it slow and steady like the tortoise. You will beat the hare in the end and be much stronger, healthier, and injury free. He further recommends a basic program with realistic goals; sticking with your program; progressing slowly and eventually accomplishing your personal goals. Then you'll have to set new ones, adding years to your life and a better life to your years.

*York Barbell Course No. 1 (this is a basic course from the famed York Barbell Company, in York, Pennsylvania directed by the famed Bob Hoffman and legendary John Grimek)

This basic program includes exercises designed to:
- Build muscle and strength
- Build vital force, improve circulation, strengthen internal organs, develop both power and endurance of the lungs
- Increase speed and prevent stiffness
- Increase flexibility with stretching exercises
- Develop timing, coordination and balance.

This frequent used system of progression begins with just 6 repetitions of each exercise. **Every 3ʳᵈ day add one repetition** and when you are able to perform **12 strict repetitions** increase the weight by a **small amount** and return to the starting point of 6 repetitions. Repeat that sequence as your new goals are met. All exercises must be performed in **strict form with proper technique and controlled breathing**. Strict form does not involve speed, but means slow and controlled, with concentration on the muscle groups being worked.

Barbell Curl - (biceps) keep the elbows near your sides and **slowly** lower to full extension and return.

Two Arm Press – (deltoids, upper back and triceps) start at your chest/ clavicle area and press to arm's length over your head and return. Do not jerk the weight or allow your body to sway.

Squat (full) – (thighs, hips and lower back) **A safety rack is required** and all gyms will have a variety of these. Keep you back flat and head up with eyes focused ahead and upward.

Breathing Pullover – (chest, lats /upper back and rib cage) this exercise follows the squats because the squats will increase your breathing and immediately doing stiff arm pullovers will stretch your rib box and chest. Lie on a bench with arms directly overhead and slowly take a very light bar or dumbbell over your head concentrating on stretching the rib box. **Concentrate on the stretch, not the weight!**

Straight Leg Dead Lift – (lower back, hamstrings, hips, abs, and traps) bend over, grab the bar with a reverse grip, back flat, head and eyes slightly focused upward and stand up to the erect position and slowly lower to the floor. **Never look at the floor or lift with a humped or round back!**

Bench Press – (chest, triceps, and frontal deltoids) take the bar off the rack and slowly lower to the nipple area of the chest and push to arm's length. You can use a machine for this or utilize a spotter. The *Smith Machine* can replace a spotter.

Side Bend – (waist, especially the oblique muscles) place a dumbbell in each hand and alternate bending from one side to the other. These can also be performed on a pulley machine.

Dave Guidugli

Dave designed a routine that utilizes typical boxing training methods that focuses heavily on aerobic conditioning, strength, balance, coordination and flexibility benefits. **Dave mentioned, "All strength training does not have to come from lifting weights or resistance machines."** Dave is a firm believer that his methods will produce and maintain better tendon, ligament and joint strength that will reduce the chances of future injuries. Boxing and other types of self- defense also have the extra benefit of confidence building and the ability to handle physical confrontations. The confidence building is not a priority for those over 50, but Dave's methodology has great benefits for seniors when approached realistically. Dave also feels strongly that the average person dependent only on weight lifting does not warm up the ligaments, tendons or joints before jumping into strenuous workouts. The proposed workout below should be about 45 -55 minutes three times per week. *** A word of caution before attempting Dave's routines. Dave is used to working with "blue chip" college and professional athletes and older athletes who are in very good condition.** Dave at 6'2 and 230 pounds has a resting pulse rate of about 46 and the cardio of a cross country runner. **Dave can easily modify or customize his training sessions by reducing the number of exercises, sets, time and the rest intervals.** Famed NFL running back, Shaun Alexander, mentioned that, "Dave would make me feel as if I was going to be the strongest, fastest, toughest, and the smartest player there ever was." **Dave, at age 68, uses these same routines with modification for his training. * Note – Dave was possibly the first trainer in the country, 30 years ago, to incorporate his system for women and seniors as part of a regular fitness program.** He probably should have Trademarked that concept?

Walk or jog the track – warm-up by walking around the track or in the gym for specific times and dependent on physical limitations.

Stairs – walking up and down a set of stairs with an 8- pound medicine ball (cardio)

Heavy bag – 1 minute rounds with resting intervals between rounds (for strength)

Speed bag – 1 minute rounds with resting intervals between rounds (hand-eye coordination)

Double end bag – 1 minute rounds with resting intervals between rounds

Agility and Balance – step ups on a bench, vertical jumps, and two legged jumps

Flexibility – with knees to the ground, slowly lean back as far as possible and hold for 15 seconds

Rope jumping – as ability and condition permits

Medicine ball – wall throws for 10 to 15 repetitions

Barge rope – 30 seconds with an up and down motion and a side to side motion (rest intervals to be determined)

Cool down – walking and various stretches

Jerry Auton

Jerry recommends that the first two steps should be: **talk with the trainee and complete a full physical assessment to understand limitations; and make sure they have a doctor's approval.** Jerry's method, for those starting a **fitness program over 50, would be to use a combination of rubber bands /tubing, exercise balls, stretching and light dumbbells** to achieve results **in strength, balance, flexibility and cardio.** The starting point is very basic and considers that the trainee may have been inactive for many years. The program can be easily modified depending on the fitness level of the participant.

Warm-ups – 8-10 minutes of light movements of the joints which may include: arm rotations at the sides, trunk twisting side to side, ceiling stretches, lunges, back stretches (rockers) and half knee bends. Each exercise is held for 5-20 seconds with no bouncing. Jerry believes it is important to warm up the knees, hips, ankles and upper body joints before moving on to other exercises. This is not the approach Jerry used in his early years as a bodybuilder and power lifter, but has come to embrace with the knowledge from his senior training certificate classes. The rubber resistance bands or tubing mentioned comes in different colors, which specifies different levels of tension.

Strength building- (these exercises are performed with rubber bands or tubing) three sets of chest pulls from a door; three sets of triceps pushdowns; three sets of curls with elbows against sides and three sets of wrist curls. The bands have an attachment that can be placed inside the top, middle or bottom of the door.

Aerobic-cardio - a one mile walk outside or in the gym; 8-10 minutes on the treadmill and 8-10 minutes on a recumbent or elliptical bicycle.

Stretching / flexibility – 10 minutes of various stretches for the calves, hamstrings and quads followed by hanging stretches

Exercise ball - utilizes a variety of core exercises to work the upper and lower "core" area (abs, oblique muscles) These exercises would include: crunches, knee ups and forms of leg lifts.

Tom Geimeier

How do you design a routine for someone you have never met, which would equate to nothing but a shot in the dark? You need to know your clientele and that can only happen from an accurate physical assessment, before training begins or as a priority, on the first few sessions of training. This approach is the safest, most sensible and will protect you and your client. We have all seen the novice who tries to duplicate the monster routine of his athletic and possibly professional idol. That motivated novice may actually torture himself into doing a massive amount of exercise that has the opposite desired effect and a negative impact on any progress. Likewise, **the older possibly former jock, hits the gym with the same vengeance he had 20 years older** and is berated by his wife for stupidity as they leave the emergency room. **Common sense must always reign supreme!**

Warm-up – Your cardio warm-up prepares your body and is essential for every training session. Your cardio workout should be at least 15 minutes and could include: walking, jogging, spinning, or work on a treadmill. I don't recommend a stair stepper, especially if you have experienced knee surgery.

Calisthenics - I recommend a basic get the kinks out program that would incorporate at least four sessions per week lasting 35 - 40 minutes each for **three weeks**. Each exercise would be performed for two sets of 12 the first week; 3 sets of 12 the second and 4 sets of 12 the third. **The exercises in order would be: pushups, chins between chairs, dips, bicep curls, squats, lat stretches, lunges, toe touches (hamstring stretches) and abdominal crunches** with no more than two minute's rest between exercises. If you are unable to do regular pushups, then try pushups **on your knees or with a ball under your chest** for control. Your strength will gradually improve. A homemade method for chins is to lie on the floor between two chairs and place a bar across the chairs. You can chin with your palms facing you or away. The dips can be performed by standing and leaning against the two chairs and lowering yourself downward a few inches. The bicep curls are done slowly with a light set of dumbbells. Perform your squats with your hands on your hips or with your back against a wall if you need more support. You can also place an exercise ball between your back and the wall while squatting. The "lat" stretches can be performed by grabbing a vertical pole or object with both hands and legs slightly bent; slowly pull to and fro concentrating on stretching the back muscles. The lunges are good for hip flexibility, balance and the inner thighs and glutes. You can do these while walking around a track or your house.

Cool down - the toe touches (hamstring stretches) and crunches should be done slowly. The crunches are more effective than the old style sit-ups. With your knees up and hands behind your head, move your head slowly toward your elevated knees. The hamstring stretches are performed by bending over, grabbing the lower leg and concentrating on a full stretch of the hamstrings. A good finish is to walk several laps around the track. **Don't forget to drink as much water as possible!**

A **moderate program** or transition would be to **shift training, after the initial three weeks, to a free weight or resistance machine format.** The machines are the best option because they **do not require a spotter** to assist you. I suggest a four day a week program. The routine would be for one hour four days per week. It is important to move through the routine with a good pace or intensity to reap the maximum aerobic and muscle toning or anaerobic benefits. Start with two sets of each exercise for 12 repetitions. **Add one set per exercise every two weeks until you reach four.**

Warm-up – spinning for 20 minutes or walking the track

Legs – seated leg press machine or squats on the *Smith Machine*

Chest – seated bench press on one of the pectoral machines

Back (2)– Nautilus Machine pullovers and seated rowing machines

Shoulders – light dumbbells or a pulley machine using the front, side (lateral) and rear positions

Biceps – barbell curls, which can also be performed on several different machines

Triceps - triceps dip machine or triceps pushdowns using a pulley type machine

If you want to add a little variety to your workout and feel up to it try adding the calisthenics work to begin or end your moderate training session. You also have the option of working each body part to completion or rotating from one exercise to another in what is called a "circuit training" fashion. The problem with "circuit training" in a fitness center is the possible wait time for use of the machines you need. If you feel the need to exercise each day don't forget the benefits and two or three hours in the garden, taking a long hike, a yoga class, Tai Chi, a punching bag, or participating in an athletic activity. The ultimate goal is to tone muscle, keep muscle mass and burn fat. Muscle protects the body and has a certain contour or shape while fat is fluid, infiltrates the muscles, adds thickness to the skin and has no shape. Your mind, memory, mood, and posture will take a turn for the better.

Cool down – walk the track for 10 minutes or stretch in one of the available rooms

Small successes will eventually create a greater success. You are taking positive steps to develop a life time habit and consistency in training will have the added benefit of developing a desire for better eating habits and more positive relationships with your family.

Ray Hughes

Ray had a wake- up call, at age 74, that he refers to as 'hitting the wall." His heavy weight style lifting, with fast paced high intensity training, put him out of commission for nearly 12 months when he attempted a hard core routine with a couple of 20 year olds. Ray's **new mode of thinking believes the ideal routine for a 50- year old would be one with possibly few or no weights.** That is a complete shift from his previous 65 years of training! Ray's ideal training routine would include a number of exercises for the "core" or abdominal area like abdominal crunches and leg lifts with light resistance training and stretching.

- Ab crunches on an adjustable incline bench – 3 sets of 50

- Leg raises holding onto a chin bar – 3 sets of 12

- Lunges with no weight – 3 sets of 20

- Bench presses – 3 sets of 25 with a **very light weight**

- Squats **(free hand)** – 3 sets of 20

- Cardio work that alternates between the treadmill, spinning / cycling or a cardio /endurance builder that has the trainee walk a minute, jog a minute and run a minute. All three exercises are continued for 15 minutes.

- Basic judo skills (depends on the age and fitness level) *The reason for the Judo is this is my area of expertise.

Your instructor or mentor must be very knowledgeable in the proper technique and how to maximize the use of any equipment. Ray would incorporate some of my judo background skills in the form of grabbling and throwing for the 50- year old. **"A 70 plus year old does not need to risk injury, regardless of the skill level."** Ray believes that judo is harder on the body than other forms of martial arts because of the constant combat and physical demands. The goal is to be working out 10 years from now with his bodyweight still under control. Ray **enjoys walking, hiking and doing the things he enjoys and will do nothing that may limit those interests in the future.** Ray sums us his new training philosophy as, **"I no longer have an interest in trying to whip the world!"**

Terry Collis

Terry likes to stay **true to his martial arts philosophy and incorporates all aspects of his training to support the objective of achieving greater martial arts proficiency**. His ideal program would start with a number of basic stretches to warm up the body that also provides benefits to all ages and fitness levels.

Warm –up - these may include: butterfly and hurdler stretches to warm up the hamstrings, quads and groin area; free hand squats, one legged squats, crunches, several types of leg raises, side twists, neck rotations and leg spreads.

Stance demonstration – next would be a demonstration, by Terry, of the two basic stances followed by specific punches, blocks and kicks. The students or trainees, regardless of age, would then duplicate each of those techniques, under Terry's supervision, completing each technique 10 times on the right side and 10 times on the left.

Kata practice - the students will work on performing their katas in strict form and utilizing the proper technique. To add an aerobic effect, the students will complete their kata sessions by gradually increasing the speed, while maintaining proper technique.

Sparring or kumite - to be determined by instructor based on age and ability. **This would not be a priority for older adults training for conditioning!**

Cool down – basic stretching.

Devorah Dometrich-Herbst

Devorah is a true martial arts advocate and relies on her early dojo methodology. She knows the stretches and warm-ups that prepare her body for the katas that she consistently practices to maintain her precision. She is concerned with the proper stances, body positions, grips and the flow of the movements. Devorah frequently demonstrates weapons katas, through Skype, to as many as 40 international dojos at one time and her reputation demands that her presentations are accurate and performed with precision. The unique aspect that made Devorah a United States women's two- time black belt champion and a world famed Kobudo expert is her mental toughness. This is an intrinsic value and very hard to teach.

Lanny Julian

Schedule a visit with your family doctor first, especially if you are unsure of your physical limitations. Talk with someone who has experience working out and is knowledgeable. Your beginning fitness workout program should not be more than two to three times per week with a concentration on working the major body parts and muscle groups such as the: chest, back, arms, legs and "core." Select a few exercises for each muscle group and do two sets of each for 12 repetitions. Start light so your form and technique will be correct. Once you can perform 15 reps easily, add a little weight and start the process over.

Weight training of any kind will add muscle tone, strength and reduce the effects of osteoporosis. Be sure to include cardio or aerobic training at least five times per week. The aerobic exercise might be walking, swimming or trips up and down the stairs in your home. It is a good idea to have someone to walk with, but if that is not possible, you can always take your pet for a walk a couple of times per day. I would suggest you cut back on sugar, which will reduce the waistline and drink at least six to eight, eight ounce glasses of water daily. Eat more fibrous foods, which includes fruits and veggies and definitely cut out the fast, junk foods.

Over 50 Training – Another Perspective

By: Roger Riedinger, (Copied, in part, from *No Nonsense Magazine*, Volume 18, issue 3)

*Editors' note- Roger is a former Master's Mr. USA bodybuilder and he has been able to maintain unusual high levels of strength due to his training regime. This has worked great for Roger, despite some significant injuries, but his Program #2 may be too challenging for many.

I would like to share some personal thoughts on the best system of training for the mature adult. By bodybuilder, **I mean anyone who is trying to develop muscle and strength**, not just those training to enter an athletic contest. This article is targeted, at those **over 50,** who have some previous experience with weight training, but he may have experienced a long lay - off or just want to try something different from what they've been doing for years.[21]

To start, let's agree that the over 50 adult basic concerns are very much the same as fitness enthusiasts of any age. That objective is to develop an above average degree of fitness, muscle, and strength. For the over 50 age group, let's add to look and act younger than your actual age.

Here is an outline of notes I've taken, over the years, regarding myself specifically, and the aging fitness buff in general. I started training pretty regularly in 1963, so these comments are based on over 50 years of training experience.

CHALLENGES FOR THE OVER 50 BODYBUILDER

#1- Negative factors of aging

---

[21] Riedinger, Roger (March 2014) Over 50 Training, Another Perspective, No Nonsense Magazine, Vol 18 (3) pgs. 2-4

- Males typically lose ½ pound of muscle per year once they hit their late 30's or early 40's.
- Fast -twitch muscles decline and testosterone production is reduced as aging or the years go by.
- An extended "layoff" or "years off" will result in the accumulation of excess fat. In addition, our metabolism slows down as we age.
- Training time is often limited because of work and family obligations. However, this may be a good thing. You are less likely to over train by training too often or with too many sets and reps.
- Injuries – anyone who has been training for most of their life has accumulated various injuries that will interfere with their workouts. My personal list includes lower back and elbow injuries for years, which are now pretty much ok. Current issues include arthritic knees, shoulders (including a complete shoulder replacement of my left shoulder) and wrist (which currently is my most limiting), along with varying degrees of tendinitis. But, injuries, like limited time to train can actually be a blessing. You may have to cut way back on the amount of weight that you use in certain exercises. The reason this is good is that you can really concentrate on **developing perfect form and slowly progress** for a very long period of time before you hit a plateau.

Note: We can counter those negative effects with targeted supplementation. Beverly International offers specific products which will help you overcome these negative factors of aging.

*More information can be found on these recommended products at **www.beverlyinternational.com**

#2 - Positives for the over 50 bodybuilder

- **Self-Discipline** – This often improves with age. We've had to use it throughout our lives and not only in our workouts, but, perhaps in college, the military and building our own business. In fact; any goal we've achieved has had self–discipline as a vital component.
- **Patience** – The older bodybuilder is no longer looking for a quick fix because they know that anything worth achieving takes time and effort.
- **Knowledge** - How the body works and feels; which exercises they can do and which must be modified or avoided.
- **Realistic expectations** – Realizing personal strengths, but also personal limitations. Goals are essential for the over 50-bodybuilder, but unlike many younger bodybuilders they usually have a more practical approach.

Questions

1. *Should I train like I used to or be content with a milder version?* Be cautious, but don't let caution keep you from progressing. Any strength or muscle building routine, to be effective, must include some overloading in the form of progression.

2. *Can I still do certain exercises?* It is more important than ever to focus on the best exercises? These are core exercises for the

shoulder girdle, back, and legs. Try the harder exercises such as: squats, dead lifts, and military presses even if you quit doing those years ago. Give them another chance! Often, you just need to reduce the weight on the bar and improve your flexibility to start doing these exercises safely and productively. **If an exercise is beneficial to a younger athlete, it can be useful to an older one.** Don't build limitations into your routine simply because of your age.

3. *Can I really expect any gains at my age?* Absolutely, the older body responds to strength training exactly as a younger one, but at a slower pace (this could be good for it helps you avoid injury and overwork). You must adhere to the basic principles of strength development.

Realistic Goals

1. *Forget the old numbers.* Don't become fixated on how strong you used to be. You'll lose focus on what you are currently trying to accomplish, and become discouraged. One of the keys to the routines that follow is small, steady strength increases over the long haul. It is important that you set realistic goals based on your current condition. **What you used to do is ancient history!** It's how you look and feel today that really matters. Don't set goals based on your previous best lifts (for some of you that would take you back to your 20's and 30's), but do set goals for your current age. Set new personal records, but base them on where you are now in life.

Sample Schedules

Here are a couple of sample workout schedules. Program #1 is for the over 50 male trainees who is just beginning training or possibly starting back after a prolonged lay off. Program #2 is for **anyone** who is looking for an alternative workout that will save time yet optimize the chances of building strength and muscle.

Program #1

1. Objectives

    a. Acquaint or reacquaint yourself to the basics – perfect your form on the best exercises.

    b. Slowly build or rebuild your strength on the basic exercises.

    c. Halt and reverse age related muscle loss.

    d. Improve body composition – more muscle, less fat.

2. Scheduling - 2 or 3 weight training sessions per week. Alternate workouts A and B, with at least one day's rest and possibly two day's rest, between workouts. Do not over train.

3. Warming up and stretching

    a. Five to ten minutes of a general body warm–up is very important. You can use an air–dyne or elliptical exerciser to warm–up everything at once. Or just go through the various movements you'll be using in your workout with little or no weight.

    b. Next, continue to stretch between sets and exercises, as flexibility is a priority for the older bodybuilder. Your workout should be: Lift, stretch, lift, stretch then leave.

4. Progression – The amount of weight you lift will not be your priority because the smartest strategy is to think in the long term. Start with a weight 70% or less than what you are currently capable of using. Concentrate on training consistency and proper form. We want to progress very slowly over a prolonged period of time. If you add 5 lbs. to an exercise every other week for 3 months, you'll have added more than 30 pounds to each exercise.

a. On the exercises which have a 10–12 rep range, add weight the following workout for exercises where you got 12 good reps on at least two of the sets.

b. For those with a 6–8 rep goal, add weight when you can perform 8 reps in perfect form on one or more of the sets.

5. Keys - Consistency, correct technique and slow, sustained poundage progression. Your weight increases should be as small as possible.

Workout A

Squats: 3 sets of 10 – 12 repetitions

Bench Presses: 3 x 6 - 8

Barbell Rows: 3 x 6 - 8

Dumbbell Shoulder Presses: 3 x 10 - 12

Dumbbell Curls: 3 x 10 - 12

Abs / Calves: One exercise for each, 3x15 or 2x20 per exercise

Workout B

Deadlifts: 3 sets of 6 – 8 repetitions

Incline Dumbbell Presses: 3 x 10 – 12

Pulldowns (using chin grip with palms facing you): 3 x 10 - 12

Barbell Presses: 3 x 6 - 8

Barbell Curls: 3 x 6 - 8

Abs / Calves: One exercise for each, 3 x15 or 2 x 20 per exercise

Program #2

1. Objectives - This workout is for anyone who needs a change from their current program. It is terrific for the 50+ trainee who has been training regularly, but is at a standstill regarding improvements in strength.

2. Objections - Many of you will think this program is not enough, but that may be just the reason your progress has stalled – you've been doing too much. Most assume higher reps are best for the 50 and older bodybuilding, but this is not necessarily the case. If your goal is to regain or continue to gain as much strength as you can that means adding additional sets and lowering the repetitions for the core exercise. (ex. 4-6 sets of 4–6 reps)

3. Advantages - You'll start building (or at the least, regaining) strength and since the workouts are shorter, you'll have more time for recuperation (and a real life).

4. Time Tested - This routine is based on time tested strength building basics. Give it at least a good three months. Personally, I've been using variations of this program for two years and am still making gains (at 68 years of age).

5. Warming up... and stretching - should be the same as **Program #1**.

The Effectiveness of Calisthenics and Remembering Military Basic Training

Calisthenics when done properly can be very effective for strength building, maintaining muscle tone, flexibility, working the core muscles, improving balance and aerobic

conditioning. There is no need for an often expensive gym membership and the only equipment needed is your body. As Devorah Dometrich –Herbst stated earlier, her gym is her body and it goes wherever she goes. Think back to your days in school physical education classes, athletics or your time training with Uncle Sam, in the United States military. Remember your teacher or PT instructor saying, "Look to the front for the demonstration of the exercise." The command, "Exercise begin," to a specific cadence, and after the required number of repetitions, "Exercise halt." The schedule of calisthenics was usually accompanied with some additional aerobic exercises such as a timed 400 meter, half mile or mile run and a trip to the obstacle course.

The annual President's Physical Fitness Test program is also based on this type of non-equipment exercise. A calisthenics program can be performed daily, in the confines of your own home, doing various combinations of exercises and a variety of sets and repetitions. The individual will always dictate the pace or intensity of the workout. The exercises can be done within a home fitness dedicated area, in front of the TV, on your patio or in the backyard. Many trainees can reflect back and agree that they were in the best shape of their lives after completing military basic training and the additional advanced infantry training programs.

Common Exercises

Lunges

This is a great exercise for the hips, inner thighs, quads, balance and flexibility. Stand with the hands on your hips and take a slight over stride with one leg aiming for a medium stretch. You can step back to the starting position and alternate legs for 10 reps with each or continue walking in a straight line, if you have the space.

Squat jumps

Begin in a half squatting position and jump as high as possible returning to the half squat position always striving for excellent and controlled form. Good for quads, gluts and aerobic effect.

Knee -ins

The starting position is lying on the floor with the legs extended. Alternate bringing each knee up towards your chest so you can touch the knee with your hands. This exercise works the lower abs.

Crunches

Good for the upper abs and better than outdated old style sit ups. Lie on the floor with your legs bent toward you. Raise your upper body up so you can touch each knee with your elbows. A variation would be to use a slight twist and placing the opposite elbow on each knee. This would work the side core area known as the oblique muscles.

Push-ups

An all-time favorite for building the chest, triceps, frontal deltoids and upper back. Place the hands on the floor with your body extended and feet firmly in place. Lower yourself to the floor, with chest touching the floor, and push upward until the arms are fully extended. A narrow hand placement will place more stress on the triceps and deltoids, while a wider hand placement will tend to work the chest, pectoral muscles. It might be fun, occasionally, to see how many you can do in a minute to judge your progress. Fitness guru, Jack LaLanne, claimed to have completed over 1000 in 23 minutes. If you are unable to do very few or zero pushups, then begin your training doing pushups from the knee position or by placing an exercise ball under your chest for support.

Pull-ups and Chin-ups

Another great upper body exercise using a standard metal chin-up bar or other **sturdy piece of apparatus**. There are bars that can be purchased that attach to door frames, but use caution and make sure the bar easily holds your weight and is attached securely. The chin-up is performed by placing the hands overhead on the bar with palms facing away. Pull yourself up to the bar with chin touching or slightly over the bar and slowly lower yourself to arms- length. This works the upper back, arms and rear deltoids. The pull-up is performed by gripping the bar with the palms facing and the grip somewhat narrower. Pull up until chin is at the bar and slowly lower. This variation works the biceps and inner part of the upper back. When this exercise becomes too easy and a little boring you can add a 5 or 10 weight plate around your waist. Many gyms have a pull-up /chin-up bar that will offset your body weight so you can benefit from these exercises, regardless of strength level.

Squats

Begin in the standing position, with the legs spread slightly apart, (24 inches) and your hands either clasped behind your head or placed on your hips. (placement on the hips will give you better stability) Squat down until your thighs and hips are slightly below parallel. An excellent exercise to work the quads, hamstrings, glutes and stretch the calves. If this exercise is too difficult you can place an exercise ball against the wall and lean on the ball as you squat up and down with the wall as extra support.

Calf-raises

The calves are the most underworked muscle in the fitness industry. They are comprised of two basic muscles and the basic facts indicate that large, well defined calves are probably more of a genetic factor. Improvement can be achieved by placing the toes on a board or 2 x 4 and slowly rising up and lowering yourself down. Walking up and down a set of stairs with emphasis on pushing off the big toe will work the calves and a variation would be to add a weighted exercise ball. **Caution is to be used if you have experienced an Achilles injury or surgery. A doctor's clearance would be strongly advised!**

Dips

One of the all- time best exercises for building the triceps, deltoid and pectoral muscles, but be very cautious if you have experienced shoulder surgery. All gyms will have a standard set of dipping bars and some are modified to reduce your body weight. Dipping bars are basically a set of parallel bars. You can use two kitchen chairs spaced about 24-30 inches apart. Place one hand on the seat of each chair or on each side bar of the dipping bars; lower yourself down about 6 inches and push or extend back to the original position. A closer grip tends to work the triceps, while a wider grip, will place more stress on the pectoral muscle group.

The All Time Favorite Basic Exercises

Chest- the bench press and the incline bench press still reign supreme whether with a barbell or dumbbells. *Flyes* better known as lateral arm spreads, on the bench, are also an old time favorite.

Back – power cleans and bent over rows for the upper back and dead lifts, end of bar rows or hyperextensions for the lower back. Chin ups will never go out of style.

Legs – many successful bodybuilders always credit the squat for strength and body mass with front squats a close second. Every gym will have an assortment of options like hack squat, leg press, leg curl and leg extension machines. Leg lunges will also produce good leg development. Orthopedic surgeons will tell you to avoid the leg extensions! Many people use too much weight, which forces bad form and will erode the lining of the knee. Never lock out your knees and use a more moderate weight rotating your quads during each rep.

Chest / ribcage / thickness – bent arm and stiff arm pullovers enlarge the rib box and tie in the lat muscles

Calves – pray for good genetics, but most gyms have a seated or standing calf machine.

Shoulders / Deltoids – presses behind the neck with side, rear and front laterals to attack all three heads of the deltoid. The standard presses are very good, but we recommend with dumbbells.

Trapezius – some form of shoulder shrugs or upright rows.

Biceps – strict barbell and dumbbell curls, standing and seated, are the basic exercises. There are variations like the preacher bench, reverse curls, concentration or cable machine curls. Remember to lower the weight slowly, as that is half of the exercise.

Triceps – the king is doing medium to narrow grip parallel bar dips for mass with lying triceps extensions, often called skull busters, with the elbows close to the body. Pushdowns on the cable machine add shape and can also be used in the overhead position. Close grip pushups are another triceps standby and sometimes used to finish off or pump up the triceps.

Forearms – the reverse curl for the extensors and the wrist curl for the flexors. There are wrist rollers and hand squeezers to work these muscle groups and rope climbing can also help.

The above exercises were the ones you probably concentrated on as an under 50 weight training advocate. They added the strength and muscle most endomorphs and mesomorphs were looking for. These were also the exercises that most athletic coaches had their male and female athletes concentrate on because they hit the large muscle groups and could be easily completed with the time and equipment available in many gyms. The major muscle groups remain the same, but the priority for you today is not on building mass and super strength. The common sense priorities today, which we have previously emphasized, should be on; maintaining a high level cardiovascular system; improving flexibility and joint movement; and finally muscle toning the key muscle groups.

Other training options
Yoga

Yoga is a way of life, an integrated system of education for the body, mind, and inner spirit. This art of right living was perfected and practiced in India thousands of years ago, but since Yoga deals with universal truths its teachings are as valid today as they were in ancient times. Yoga is a practical aid, not a religion, and its techniques may be practiced by anyone regardless of religious preference. Yoga is a system that offers benefits to all comers. Yoga is a lifestyle and an exercise form based on the tenets of simple living and high thinking. To the ancients the body was seen as a vehicle for the soul and thus the body had certain needs to function effectively. Regular Yoga classes are part of every fitness centers regular schedule of activities.

The body's needs are classified as: proper exercise known as the Asanas; Yogic breathing referred to as the Pranayama which strengthens the seven Chakras well known in holistic medicine; relaxation; vegetarian diet; and positive thinking and meditation. The physical benefits of Yoga practiced with regularity encourage all parts of the body to work more effectively together. The mental benefits include relief of stress, anxiety, and the ability to expand the mind's ability to meditate. The body's energy levels are elevated which allows for a more energy driven and active senior adult.

Yoga can be practiced by anyone regardless of age. **It is an excellent system for those over 50, especially those who like a more relaxed environment and a low impact system**. The health benefits for the over 50 crowd also include increased flexibility, which is key to the many joint problems that can arise as we add a few more gray hairs. Yoga is taught in many locations across the United States, but it is always wise to find out the credentials of the instructor so you can confidently participant under the tutelage of an expert.

Tai Chi

Tai Chi or Tai Chi Chaun is one of the most ancient forms of martial arts. The initial forms were taught by devoted, secluded Taoist monks, on the Wu Dang Mountain range in China. The name actually refers to the supreme ultimate fist. Today, Tai Chi is practiced by many followers across the planet from the exclusive martial arts schools to health related classes in health centers and hospitals. There have been a number of changes in the initial Tai Chi which has resulted in the evolution of numerous styles, but all with the same basic benefits. Those benefits include: improvement in overall health; posture; confidence; mental focus, relaxation; spiritual development and the added bonus of unique self-defense skills.

Tai Chi is part of the Chinese tradition of *chi kung*, which is a system of exercises that encourage: "chi energy" to flow freely around the body. Chi is the belief that the body has an energy force that travels around pathways known as meridians to every fiber and all organs. Regular practice of Tai Chi enhances the speed that this "chi energy" flows through the body, which has an impact on a person's overall health and wellness. Initially, Tai Chi was a series of postures known as the "Hand Form" that were performed in slow, smooth, rhythmic manner in a time period ranging from several to over 20 minutes. The flowing postures were influenced by imitating various animals and were originally used for self-defense the same as early forms of Chinese Kung Fu styles. There are also weapon forms of Tai Chi the same as in the Kung Fu styles of martial arts.

One of the best known symbols in martial arts, the Yin and Yang, is also a center piece for the study and mastery of Tai Chi. The Yin and the Yang represents opposites in nature and the formula for success is that neither dominates the other, but work best in complete harmony. Some of the various styles you may encounter when evaluating possible classes are: Chen, Yang, Yang Chen Fu, Wu Hao, Sun and many others. The many styles indicate that there has been substantial growth in the way the art form is practiced and there has been a cross fertilization with other systems of exercise. A final note would be to find a legitimate instructor who understands the origin and adheres to the basic principles of the art.

The Ten Most Popular Martial Arts

The origin of the various martial arts is a combination of styles from many countries that have contributed to many styles of self-defense. [22] The correlation with the theme of our book is that the various forms of the martial arts offer physical and emotional aspects to those seeking self-improvement.

- Kray Maga
- Kung Fu
- Mixed Martial Arts (MMA)
- Muay Thai
- Tae Kwon Do
- Tang Soo Do
- Aikido
- Brazilian Ju-Jitsu
- Judo
- Karate (encompasses many styles)

Fitness Boot Camps

Fitness Boot camps offer an opportunity to build strength and endurance. There is an **obvious word of caution** for those over 50 and we advise you think back to your time in the military. This type of exercise is demanding and not recommended for the over 50 crowd, unless you are in decent shape and very committed. These workouts are based on real life military boot camp routines. There may be better options for you! These camps usually employ a combination of calisthenics, strength and

---

[22] Wikipedia (2015) Top 10 Most Popular Martial Arts, Retrieved from www.blackbeltwiki.com/martial-arts-styles

endurance building, with possibly some self -defense skills thrown in with some aggressive motivation. These workouts can be intense and if still interested you better receive your doctor's okay and show your spouse where to find your life insurance policy.

Pilates

Pilates is an exercise system that tries to remain true to the origin in the 1920s. Pilates was devised by physical trainer Joseph Pilates as an effective way to rehabilitate soldiers returning from WW I, as well as professional dancers. The focus is on improving flexibility, strength, and body awareness, but without the priority of building muscle mass. Pilates is resistance based and not aerobic in nature. The two key components of a Pilates workout focus on core (spine, abdomen, pelvis, hips, and accompanying muscles) muscle strength and spinal alignment. Fitness centers usually do floor work versus the machine option. Concentration and proper breathing are constantly encouraged to coordinate the mind, body and spirit. (former members of the YMCAs will also remember those attributes) The history of Pilates mentions that originally there were 34 key exercises.

Aqua Fit

This is a nice option if your fitness center or gym has access to a lap pool or regular swimming pool. A 50- minute workout in the water can improve strength and cardio without the damaging impact on your joints. **These water workouts are a great rehabbing tool after joint injuries and surgeries. A certified physical therapist will be needed to supervise those in that category.** Your body and the desire to improve are all that are needed to participate in these workouts. Other offerings include: water Yoga, aqua Tai Chi, pre and post- natal, duplication of sports movements with the added benefit of positive effects on internal organs and the lymph system.

Zumba etc.

Everybody has seen the huge classes on the TV ads. Hundreds of followers working out with a mix of low and high intensity moves for an interval style, super calorie burning, dance off. A choreographer leads the class and a point to remember is that Zumba Fitness does not charge any licensing fees to gyms or fitness centers. It has been estimated that 15 million participate each week in thousands of locations in over 180 countries. The benefits include a good cardio, muscle conditioning, balance and flexibility workout.

Spinning, Cycling, Biking

These one hour classes can be held in a spinning room with high tech bikes that have you cycling to a course on a large TV screen and the driving voice of a high energy instructor. This can be a vigorous workout, but the participants have the option of controlling the tension and effort on their bikes. This allows you to stay in the class, but at your own level. Each session is a great way to burn the calories and keep the legs in shape. After the hour is up you will feel the burn and like walking on a cloud. The good news is you can sweat it out in the gym environment and not face the hazards of the actual roads and highways. The gyms will also offer other biking options that are not in a supervised class. (treadmills, elliptical bikes, stair steppers, lower level bikes)

Photo by Geimeier
A typical spinning, cycling room

Isometrics or Dynamic Tension

A system of exercise that requires tensing various muscle groups against immovable objects. You might push against a wall with both hands, while tensing your pectoral muscles, for 5-6 seconds, which would equal one repetition for the chest. You would perform various exercises for each muscle group. Many people built isometric racks in their basements in the 1960s -70s to include this concept in their workout regime. The rack would have two vertical sides with a number of parallel holes in each. The user would slide a bar through the sides and simulate bench presses, curls, deadlifts, presses, and other exercises. If you couldn't afford a lot of gym equipment you only needed a piece of pipe and a few two by fours. Charles Atlas designed his famous Dynamic Tension system on this same principle. Another similar term is isotonic, which is similar, but with some give or movement. Flexing in the mirror after a workout is another form of isometrics.

What the research says ….

The Mayo Clinic, Healthy Lifestyle Fitness Internet article titled *Weight training: Improve your muscular fitness* stated that benefits can be obtained, with two to three workouts per week, lasting 20-30 minutes each. The article further stated that one set of 12 repetitions may be as effective as three sets for each muscle group. That same advice also met the recommendations, on senior fitness, from the Department of Health and Human Services. [23]

An article in Everyday Health was written by Chris Iliades, MD and reviewed given a medical review by Pat F. Bass III, MD, MPH mentioned the benefits of weight training for seniors that included: heart health, balance, strength, muscle tone, increased bone density, managing weight /metabolism, looking better and feeling better. The article emphasized that lifting weights or resistance training was not just about bodybuilders lifting big weights in the gym. The article elaborated on preventing the percentage of bone loss and muscle strength that occurs after puberty. An unusual statement was that **resistance training may be as effective as medications in offsetting certain age related diseases.** Additional benefits to mood would also be affected by the elevation of endorphins. Both articles stressed the importance

---

[23] Mayo Clinic Staff (November 2015) Weight training: Improve your muscular fitness, Retrieved from http:/www.mayoclinic.org/healthy-lifestyle/fitness/in-depth/weight-training/art

of a proper warm up, after workout cool down, with adequate rest and recuperation. [24] Lifestrong.com presented several interesting articles that supported weight training. The first, written by Frank Yemi, discussed: _What Are the Dangers of Lifting Weights?_ The article detailed the possibility of muscle strains, bone fractures, soreness and how to avoid those negative effects. A summary of that article suggested many people try to lift weights that are too heavy thus sacrificing proper technique; perform too many exercises for the same muscle group and do not get enough recuperation time. The author suggested training on machines before proceeding to "free weights" and consulting a doctor and professional trainer before beginning. [25]

The International Sports Science Association (ISSA) recommends that you do not hold your breath during exercise because this elevates the blood pressure and the danger of fainting. They also issued a warning about isometric exercise raising the blood pressure, for those over 35, and advised exercise using full ranges of motion. Any type of hopping or jumping causes impact stress to the joints and may also damage the bones of the inner ear or cause stress incontinence. [26]

---

[24] Iliades, Chris,MD, MPH (October 2014) Which Weightlifting Routine is Best? Retrieved from http://www.everydayhealth.com/fitness/add-strength

[25] Yemi, Frank (November 2014) What are the dangers of lifting weights? Retrieved from http://www. Lifestrong.com/article 274669

[26] Senior Fitness Handbook (2010) Holding Your Breath, Carpenteria, CA International Sports Sciences Handbook

The bottom line ....

The expertise of the *panel* encompasses approximately 400 years of condensed knowledge. The *panel's* individual training methods certainly met or exceeded their expectations and produced some very remarkable accomplishments. Think about who is giving you the wisdom of that advice! We asked each member of the *panel* to design a routine they would suggest a 50-year old begin with. Some members obviously started very basic, while others offered moderate routines and sound advice, that will serve the reader, as they work up the ladder of difficulty and more demanding workouts. Also, remember that each *panel* member's advice is coming from their own special discipline. A commitment to any of those routines will allow your bodies to become more receptive and your fitness levels will progressively elevate. An interesting Website known as Fit Montclair Blog, sponsored by Advanced Fitness Concepts, recently presented information, by reputed physical therapists, on 13 bad exercises. These 13 exercises were prone to poor technique which could result in a substantial injury and were recommended to be eliminated from your program. Some of the 13 included were: leg extensions (most orthopedic doctors would agree, especially after a knee surgery), upright rows, bench dips, round backed deadlifts, presses behind the neck, step ups on too high benches and kettle bells. Refer to the article's URL for the full extent of the article.[27] I think the reader will notice our *panel* did not

---

[27] Fit Montclair Blog (31 Oct 2010) 13 Terrifying Gym Exercises and the Horrific Injuries They Cause, Retrieved from

advocate or elaborate on any of those exercises for senior conditioning programs.

The hot tip ....

The *panel* reached consensus during their interviews that whatever path of fitness you pursue should be something that you enjoy and can commit to. Look over the routines, think about the background of those designed and try one out. We have also offered some group type classes that are very popular and easily accessible, at most fitness centers. Many trainees will like the concept of exercising in a group, under the constant leadership and motivation of a head instructor. A final thought is that calisthenics and a few minimal pieces of equipment can be easily utilized as an excellent prelude for your actual exercise program.

Every gym and fitness center offers a variety of exercise machines, which have advantages over the free weight areas.

https://fitmontclair.wordpress.com/2010/10/13/13-terrifying-gym-exercises-the-horrific-injuries-they-cause/

Chapter 6

The Evolution of Fitness Equipment and the Early Influences

A quick course in the evolution or history of fitness equipment may be a good place to begin to demonstrate the array of apparatus that can be used to achieve your goals. The fitness equipment companies have certainly improved the equipment and thus the availability of the gyms and centers offering their use.

In the 1960s many of the old style gyms were remnants of the 1940s and 50 models. The old Turner Clubs or Vereins (German fitness clubs) offered thorough gymnastic programs with calisthenics and even a closet full of the old Indian Clubs left over from the late 1800s and early 1900s. The **Indian clubs** or **Meels** were a type of exercise equipment, which originated in

Edward B. Warman (1847-) Spaulding Red Cover Series, Athletic Handbooks, No. 22R

---

[20] Warman, Edward B., (1913) Spaulding Red Cover Series, Athletic Handbooks, American Sports Publishing Company

the near east, and were used for developing strength, especially the shoulders, forearms, grip strength, core strength and improved coordination. The original Indian clubs were comprised of bowling pin shaped wooden clubs of varying sizes and weights, which were swung in certain patterns, as part of the exercise program. They were used in group classes similar to our modern day aerobics classes. The "clubs" came to the United States, with the waves of the German immigrants, in the middle of the 19th century. (1850s -1860s). American soldiers utilized the "clubs," as part of their basic training, in World War I and they were periodically used by the military until the 1930s. There has been a recent revival of the clubs and the **Clubbell Company** currently produces a modern version.

The early city gyms in the Midwest were also very basic and not much better. We're sure the west coast and some east coast gyms were well ahead of the rest of the country, as they have always been a fitness hotbed of new ideas and concepts. We have both lived, worked or trained in Kentucky, Ohio, Pennsylvania, Virginia, Indiana, and Texas. I think that gives us a much broader knowledge of what was formerly available than the average individual. We remember some of our first experiences in a few old gyms with old worn plank wooden floors, poor lighting, basic apparatus, and minimal restroom facilities. By minimal, we mean a few racks of dumbbells, half dozen benches of different designs that could have used re-upholstering. There were always a few Olympic bars and a rack or two of barbells standing vertically, with a progression of weights and the welded on collars that kept you from constantly changing the plates. There were a few crude, homemade pulley type machines used for lat pull downs and triceps pushdowns; a set of dipping bars; a crude squat rack possibly made from welding pipe and old tire rims together. Add a wall full of mirrors; the stale smell of sweat; old photos of bodybuilding idols tacked up on the walls; an all business atmosphere; a few beefy lifters chugging down a quart of milk and there was little else. In retrospect that was a pretty good environment to begin a fitness path and you met some great and informative people along the way. Simple and basic, but very often effective!

It is also important to point out once again that you can work out at home with basic programs and achieve success with the basic equipment of barbells, dumbbells and a few other pieces. **You will need a spotter or training partner if working out in your home gym** with weights is the preferred option and a **safety rack is also strongly recommended**. There are numerous injuries reported each year in home gym injuries, from attempting to train alone and pushing the weight limits beyond common sense. **Caution is strongly advised! Make sure your equipment is safe** and the exercises you employ utilize proper technique and the weight is reasonable. Remember that the fully equipped fitness centers add the attractiveness of convenience and gym prices can usually be negotiated. **A good tip is to negotiate your gym membership at the end of the month when staff quotas and bonuses are at stake.**

Before 1970 the largest piece of equipment in any gym may have been the Universal Machine usually occupying center stage in the training room. That first piece of multi- use fitness equipment being credited to Harold Zinkin. [29] The machine offered a number of stations based on the price the establishment was willing to pay. Stations may have included: bench press, lat / triceps, curl, leg curl / extension, and press. Each station had an individual weight stack that could be adjusted by inserting a pin and four or five people could be on the machine at the same time. It became the centerpiece in numerous gyms across the country and still occupies a prominent position in gyms today. In the 1970s, Arthur Jones started an equipment revolution with the advent of the Nautilus type machines. Arthur used former Mr. America, Casey Viator, as his poster boy and prototype of what his machines and exercise system could do for you. In just a few years there were exclusive Nautilus Club franchises world-wide that offered a variety of individual machines along with an optional free weight training area. Every gym offered at least a few of the machines. The Nautilus machines were heavy duty, very durable and each machine was designed to work one specific muscle group.

The use of the Nautilus machines made it easier for the trainee. No more loading up the bars and putting the weights away or in many cases leaving them all over the floor. No more returning the dumbbells back to the rack. Just select your machine, insert the pin, and do your exercise. After you worked one muscle group you moved on to another machine. Most lifters still supplemented their training with the use of the old "free weights," as the barbells and dumbbells were called. They still

---

[29] Wikipedia (2015) Harold Zinken reference, Wikipedia.org/wiki/universal gym_equipment

reigned as king! The newer machines basically duplicated the same exercises that were accomplished with the free weights, but with better results. The machines were more convenient; had a better range of motion and made it almost impossible to cheat or use more weight than you should.

Photo by Geimeier
The stair steppers and exercise bikes show the high
end of cardio equipment offered.

Time progressed and we found the smaller gyms going out of business with the big chains dominating the business. Names like World Gym, Fitworks, Golds, Urban Active, Planet Fitness, Crunch and LA Fitness took over the lion's share of the fitness industry. Gyms became huge operations occupying square footage that rivaled that of the big super market chains. New generations of machines were developed and still continue to dot the landscape. The line of Techno Gym; Human Sport multi-purpose machines; Life Fitness, the new generation of the Universal Machine; Hoist, ride oriented exercise machines; Strive individual muscle machines; Free Motion pulley systems; the heavy duty Hammer Strength machines; and the Pre Cor heavy duty leg press, squat and hack squat machines that are typically found in the expanded free weight areas.

The huge gyms not only offer a variety of machines to suit individual needs and body types, but also offer cardio classes, kick boxing, martial arts, Yoga, Pilates, and calisthenics oriented group workouts. Group classes may also have Tai Chi, Tai Bo ®, Insanity ®, PX 90 ®, Body Beast ®, Zumba, Aqua Fit, Boot Camp, exercise balls, resistance tubes / bands, dance classes, and spinning to appeal to an even wider generation of fitness buffs. The clientele who focus more on cardio and flexibility will find an array of treadmills, stationary bikes, stair steppers, abdominal and flexibility machines. The cost of the equipment to set up a large gym is enormous and the maintenance costs are an added, ongoing expense. Because hundreds of people will be using the same equipment daily there should also be rules in place for gym sanitation and etiquette. Wiping down machines, after use and keeping the locker rooms, shower areas, saunas and other areas sanitary is basic respect for your fellow human beings. Recent findings indicate that the bars on the free weights are actually more unhygienic than the machines. Nobody wipes those down.

With all the fitness centers available today there should be no reason or excuses for anyone to neglect their personal level of fitness. The resources at your door step are innumerable. There are also some good deals on the gym memberships if you wait for the special offers like the two years for one periodically offered. If you are at the 65 age mark many gyms offer the *Silver Sneakers* ® program, as previously mentioned, at no cost to you. (Humana, United Health Care Insurance) The insurance carriers support the program in the hopes that the beneficial aspects of a regular exercise program will mean a savings for them and you in the long run.

We also guarantee that within or very close to any large gym will be several health food stores with every nutritional supplement known to mankind. Chapter 10 will deal with nutrition and is written by Roger and Sandy Riedinger, owners of Beverly International Nutrition. Do your research and consult your physician about what the over 50 crowd should be adding to their diets. Think about your goals and possibly check out a number of books from the library to improve your knowledge base. 30 years ago protein and food supplements were in the crude stage. Today, we know that there are 22 amino acids that make up protein with 10 being essential, and in the last 10 years those amino acids have been isolated and specifically identified as to how they contribute and specifically function in the human body. The same can be said of how finite the knowledge of vitamins and minerals has become. The large health food store chains are accessible in every neighborhood and carry a wide range of fruits, vegetables, juices, yogurts, and other healthy choices.

We have recently read newspaper articles mentioning so called "food deserts" that are said to exist in some inner city neighborhoods and make it difficult to find fresh produce. They could exist in some sparsely populated states in the west, or maybe Alaska, but not in any populated areas we know of. Most large cities have chain super markets within walking distance and some sort of "open air" markets that specialize in fruits and vegetables. We can relate to the Cincinnati area and they have the largest market in the city, called the Finley Market, in a region they call Over the Rhine. The Kroger Company, one of the largest supermarket chains in the country, also has a stores within a few blocks of every neighborhood.

Our first physical culture influences

Most of our early role models of physical fitness began their path to success by experimenting with a variety of systems that were probably not readily accepted by the general public. Excessive physical training, especially weight training was believed to cause the participants to become muscle bound, disrupt coordination and balance, cause heart attacks and lessen sex drive. Our early role models challenged the known beliefs and found systems that made sense, produced results and then used their entrepreneurial skills to promote. Many of the early role models started as teens and young men determined to build the proverbial *better mousetrap*. They became the guinea pigs of those early years and then expanded their operations using that same success template into selling millions of training courses, numerous publications, nutritional supplements, promoting contests and creating specialized training equipment that ultimately revolutionized the entire physical culture industry.

Think back to your early years and I'm sure we can all remember a friend or parent warning you of becoming too strong or muscle bound. Tom remembers his mother cautioning him how a cousin was sent home from the military because he was muscle bound. We're sure his service record would reveal something else. We felt it was important and nostalgic to include some of those major influences on physical culture that may have influenced and inspired us. That would be a snapshot of the physical culture world from the 1930s until the present. We've included a few others to create a more complete scenario.

Bernarr Macfadden was known as the "Father of Physical Culture." He was born in 1868 and published the first English fitness magazine known as *Physical Culture* in 1899. Bernarr Mcfadden had health problems as a child, but became motivated to strengthen his body through boxing, wrestling and gymnastics after reading articles in the old *Police Gazette Magazine.* Macfadden's philosophy was considered eccentric by many during his lifetime, but his passion created a publishing empire that eventually encompassed over 35 million readers and made him a multi- millionaire. He also created exercise equipment; recuperative centers that helped you release your inner emotions and various physical culture or bodybuilding contests. One of his most famous contest winners (1921, 22) was the famed Charles Atlas. Macfadden promoted natural foods, with no tea, coffee, alcohol, tobacco, meat or white bread; fitness, outdoor exercise, and nudity. Macfadden typically walked barefooted the 13 miles to work each day, to Manhattan, while carrying a 40- pound bag of sand. He also created the magazines titled: *True Story, True Romance and True Detective Mystery.* Another device invented by Macfadden and currently prescribed by urologists, for men recovering from prostate surgery, was the vacuum pump. [30] Bernarr MacFadden, born as Bernard Adolphus MacFadden, shown on the opposite page photos doing the classic "David"

---

[30] Editors of Encyclopedia Britannica (November 2015) Bernarr MacFadden, Retrieved from http://www.britannica.com/biography/bernarr-macfadden

pose, circa 1890, and many years later in Warm Springs, Georgia with President Franklin D. Roosevelt.

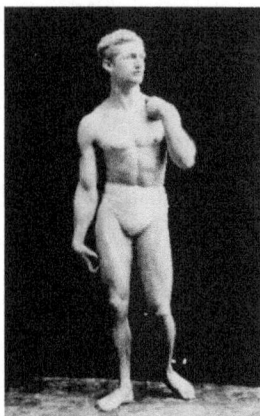

Photos from Wikipedia (Public Domain)

Eugene Sandow – was born as Freidrich Wilhelm Mueller in Germany and later achieved the title of the "Father of Modern Bodybuilding." In a contest held in 1901, Sandow won the title of the "World's Most Perfect Man." Sandow did muscle displays and strongman stunts promoted, by his front man, the famed Flo Ziegfeld. The famous Mr. Olympia Contest awards the annual Mr. Olympia winner the famous Sandow statue taken from an early likeness of this turn of the century bodybuilder and strongman. The first chain of fitness gyms in the world have also been attributed to the great Sandow known as the Sandow Institutes and he also published one of the first physical culture magazines.

Charles Atlas or Angelo Charles Siciliano won the title of the World's Most Perfectly Developed Man in 1921 and again in 1923 in a contest promoted by Bernarr Macfadden. (the first contest was actually called the world's most beautiful man)

Every kid who ever read a comic book knows the famed advertisement about having sand kicked in your face at the beach with your girlfriend by your side. The young reader would get mad; slam his fist on the table in disgust; order the Charles Atlas course; develop a powerful body; return to the beach to kick the crap out of the bully and win the admiration of his girlfriend. Charles Atlas claimed his famous system of "Dynamic Tension" was realized while watching the big cats exercise at the Brooklyn Zoo. Atlas made millions with those simple magazine ads that changed from year to year. Angelo Siciliano was born in 1892 and died in 1972. Many believe he took his famous trademark name from the statue of Atlas that sat atop the Hotel Coney Island, in New York.

Charles Atlas was one of the pillars of the fitness industry and an early inspiration for most of our *panel* members and their friends. We thought it would be interesting to elaborate on the background of Atlas and his fitness programs. We mentioned above that Angelo Siciliano, alias Charles Atlas, developed his concept of "Dynamic Tension," while watching the big cats at the Brooklyn Zoo stretching and appearing to use resistance type, isometric movements, to keep their muscles toned. Atlas developed a 12- week muscle and confidence building course that included a final perpetual lesson. The "Dynamic Tension" course, of the soon to be famous Atlas, appealed to the novice and professionals alike. Legendary heavyweight boxers like Max Baer, Rocky Marciano and Joe Louis subscribed to the course in their early years like many of the so called "friends" of Atlas.

Wikipedia (Public Domain)

Early photo of Angelo Charles
Siciliano (Public Domain)

The Atlas courses were heavily promoted in the 1940s through the comic books and other magazines. Almost every kid read some sort of comic book and had their special super hero. Those Charles Atlas ads were usually contained somewhere in those pages with the same inspirational scenario. The skinny, 97-pound weakling is bullied at a social gathering and eventually exacts revenge, after building a powerful body, with the self-confidence to avenge his prior humiliation. The ads were changed from year to year, but always had the same theme and appeal. Some of the titles were classic and attention getters.

- "Hey skinny, your ribs are showing!"
- How Jack slaughtered the dance floor hog.
- The insult that turned a chump into a champ.
- How Joe's body brought him fame instead of shame.

Perry and Mabel Rader started *Iron Man Magazine* in 1935. This was a fantastic team that promoted weightlifting, powerlifting, bodybuilding, old time strong men and other articles related to health. The advice was sound and appeared politically neutral when compared to others of the time period. Perry is the only known person to be inducted into the Physique, Powerlifting, Old Time Strong Men and Weightlifting Halls of Fame. Perry was born in 1909 and was active in weight lifting and bodybuilding early in life. Perry and his wife, Mabel, built their operation in Nebraska literally from the ground up. They purchased an old army barracks and converted it into their business location by the sweat of their brows. Perry bought an old copy machine and began his newsletter, which evolved into the well- respected *Iron Man Magazine* that eventually had over 40,000 subscribers. The Rader husband and wife duo offered no secrets to results, but believed that a person could transform themselves with hard work that had no price tag. They also believed that a well lived life was a true virtue and just reward for your efforts. Perry died in 1992 and was able to stay out of the fray of the hyped up claims, counter claims and animosity that existed between other rivals and competitors of the fitness industry. The 50th anniversary event of *Iron Man* requested comments from the industry and there were many, but not one negative. Positive comments were sent from many of the editors of rival magazines that included Jeff Everson, Bill Starr, John Grimek, and the well- known Doug Hepburn, Milo Steinborn and

Arthur Jones of Nautilus fame. We believe very strongly that the current owners of Beverly International, Roger and Sandy Riedinger, appear to operate in the same mode.[31]

Bob Hoffman was known as the "Father of World Weightlifting." He authored the publications, *Muscular Development and Strength and Health* (at one time the world's leading health and fitness magazine) which had great information for bodybuilders, weightlifters and power lifters. The Hoffman name was associated with the founding of the York Barbell Company and the York Barbell Hall of Fame. Bob Hoffman was born in 1898 and served his country in WW I. Soon after returning from service Hoffman promoted the first American Weightlifting competition in 1924, at age 26, and by the late 1920s was manufacturing training equipment. Hoffman began his business career by establishing the York Oil Burner Corporation in 1932 and soon after bought the bankrupt Milo Barbell Company, (1935) which evolved into the York Barbell Corporation with the companion publication *Strength and Health Magazine.* [32]

During the mid -1930s his greatest business competition came from Charles Atlas even though Jack LaLanne was also hard at work creating his empire. Hoffman received a challenge from

---

[31] Todd, Terry (Jan 1992) Perry Rader (1909-1992): Our Best Man Gone, Iron game History, Vol 2 (Number 1) Retrieved from http;//www.starkcenter.org/article-archive

[32] Markers, Pennsylvania (9 Nov 1998) Bob Hoffman Highway Marker Dedication, Retrieved from http://www.explorepahistory.com/marker.php?Markehd=1-A-304

rival Joe Weider, in 1951, for a one on one weightlifting and bodybuilding contest. The problem was that Hoffman was 53 and Weider, born in 1919, was twenty years younger at age 32. The January 1952 issue of *Strength and Health Magazine* addressed the absurdity of that challenge and the hype surrounding it. In later years, Bob Hoffman became a member of the President's Council on Physical Fitness and at age 60 still claimed to lift 250 pounds overhead with one hand. His legacy includes him with a distinguished group that spread the gospel of self- improvement to millions around the world and Hoffman and his AAU remained the most dominant force in weight training, bodybuilding and physical culture until the 1970s.

Photos of Bob Hoffman from Wikipedia (Public Domain)

John Grimek became the poster boy for York after winning the Mr. America title twice and was also well known for his weightlifting and feats of strength. John Grimek actually competed in the 1936 Berlin Olympics as a weightlifter and eventually became the associate editor of *Strength and Health* and the editor of *Muscular Development Magazines*. The York

Barbell Company was also the largest supporter of the Amateur Athletic Union (AAU) bodybuilding competitions. [33]

Photo by Geimeier
John Grimek, at the York Hall of Fame, in 1971

Wikipedia.com (Public Domain)   Photo by Geimeier

The great John Grimek is pictured (above, left) in one of his legendary poses, which was obviously taken in his prime. The picture at right has Bob Hoffman, AAU guru and "Father of World Weightlifting" talking with Sergio Olivia, at an early 1970s AAU Mr. America contest, in York, Pennsylvania.

---

[33] Bass, Clarence(1998) John C. Grimek (1910-1998), Ripped Enterprises, Retrieved from http://www.cbass.comGRIMEK.HTM

Jack LaLanne was born Francois Henri "Jack" LaLanne in 1914, the son of French immigrants, and in the 1930s began a 60-year career of fitness and a health philosophy that influenced millions through his mail order business, equipment sales, television programs and later in life the TV infomercials for his line of juicers. Jack brought his fitness concepts to the daily television stations in the 1950s that continued through the 1990s and was known as the "Godfather of Fitness." It is hard to imagine how many lives were motivated and influenced by his TV shows and personal fame from his phenomenal feats of endurance that were well publicized! Jack owned prototype health spas, as early as 1936, that included gyms, juice bars and health food stores later licensed to the Bally Corporation. Jack was an icon of physical culture known for his super human, grueling workouts; that trademark sweat suit that showcased his physique and the basic tools of a broomstick, chair and rubber tubing or tension bands. He made millions selling his training courses through his early mail order and through his other endeavors. In his declining years he was on the infomercials with the juicers of today. Swanson Health Products still offers the Vita-Lanne Instant Meal Replacement Shakes, in a two- page ad, featuring Jack in his famous exercise suit.[34] Jack was a motivational speaker, fitness guru, nutritional expert, but was originally trained as a chiropractor that became a millionaire many times over due to his great business acumen. Like many of the other early role models of physical culture, Jack started out as a meager youth who had many health problems to overcome.

---

[34] Swanson health Products Editors (31 Jul 2013) Jack LaLanne in Vita-Lanne Shake Ad, Swanson Health Products Magazine, 2013 (July) pgs 18-19

At the age of 15, Jack heard an inspiring talk by the noted Paul Bragg that would be the motivational spark he would internalize for his 96 years on this earth.

Jack ate only two meals per day that included an after workout breakfast and an early dinner in a local restaurant. Jack arose each day at 4:00 am and began his day with an intense 90- minute strength training workout to the point of fatigue. That was followed by a 30- minute run or a swim. Breakfast consisted of hardboiled egg whites, a cup of broth, oatmeal with soy milk and fresh fruit. Dinner consisted of a large fresh salad with more egg whites, fish, preferably salmon and a mix of red and white wine. Jack drank no coffee and ate no snacks except for an occasional roast turkey sandwich. One of his famous quotes was, "I can't die, it would ruin my image." Another interesting fact is that Jack advocated that women could exercise in the same gyms, same rooms and same times as men, which was a totally new concept. (1930s)

Since the majority of the *panel* members cited Jack LaLanne and Charles Atlas, as early influences, we decided to elaborate on some of their contributions. Jack LaLanne was known his unbelievable physical endurance accomplishments. Jack swam the length of the Golden Gate Bridge with 140 pounds of weight attached to his body; he swam from Alcatraz to Fisherman's Wharf while in handcuffs; performed 1033 pushups in 23 minutes; towed 70 rowboats with passengers from Queen's Way Bridge to the ship Queen Mary, while shackled and handcuffed, at age 70. He helped to break the stereotype of muscle bound athletes; preached about preventative medical practices; is credited with the invention of several exercise machines (cable pulley, leg extension, Smith Machine, weight stack selection system); promoted the relationship between exercise and nutrition; advocated exercise for women; early pioneer in hydronastics, trimnastics and plyometric training and that athletes should work their muscles to complete failure. [35] There are also claims that Jack was the first to come up with the idea of an *instant breakfast* type food supplement.

Jack posted a $10,000 reward for anyone who could stay with him during a workout and no one ever took him up on the offer. Jack's most unusual philosophy was that he did not believe in warming up or cooling down. **Jack stated, "Lions do not warm up before they kill their prey and after the lions eat they go to sleep."**

Wikipedia photos of Jack LaLanne by Cliff Riddle (Public Domain)

---

[35] Clear, James (22 Nov 2015) Learning from Super Humans: The Incredible Fitness and Success of Jack LaLanne, Huffington Post, Healthy Living, Retrieved from huffingtonpost.com/James-clear/achieving-success_b_3269182.html

Jack in his 90's with permission by Nathan Cremisino [36]

Steve Reeves took his physique of perfect symmetry, balance and proportion to the big screen. Every kid who went to the Saturday matinees saw the great Hercules Unchained and decided they needed to add a little muscle. Steve's approach was different than most. He preferred lighter weights, higher repetitions, natural health foods and pioneered the concept of "power walking." Many physique judges and magazines, from the 1950s until the 1980s, considered Reeves to possess the perfect blend of symmetry, muscularity and muscle mass. His proportions were believed to duplicate those of the statue of David by Michelangelo with his neck, upper arms and calves all measuring the same size.

Joe, born in 1919 and Ben Weider, born in 1925 grew up in Montreal, Canada the sons of Polish immigrants. During their early teens, in the 1930s, they encountered problems with other kids and were looking for a way to improve their bodies and self-esteem. They ordered the famous Charles Atlas course and began

---

[36] Cremisino, Nathan (3 Sept 2007) Lifetime Achievement Award: Jack LaLanne (Muscle Beach, Venice Beach, CA), Creative Commons Arrtibution –Share Alike 2.0 Generic License

his "Dynamic Tension" program. They also read Bob Hoffman's *Strength and Health Magazine* and made their first weight equipment from scrap metal at a local junk yard. As their muscles and strength progressively improved so did their self -esteem, which was key for their eventual success as pioneers and probably the most successful entrepreneurs in the industry. Joe often claimed he became the strongest kid in his Montreal neighborhood. The Weider success was based on a huge promotion of their muscle building, self- defense courses, equipment, health supplements, and contests promoted through their publications.

The original self- copied *Your Physique* publication of 1943 containing twelve pages eventually evolved into *Muscle Builder* and soon spread across Canada with the equipment business a short time later. The lucrative business aspects prompted Joe, on his 30th birthday, to move to Brooklyn, New York while his brother Ben stayed in Canada working on developing the International Bodybuilding Federation. (IFBB) The Weider publication empire that included *Muscle Builder*, with an 80,000 monthly circulation, *Mr. America, Shape, Flex and Men's Fitness* were later sold to American Media for 350 million dollars. The million- dollar business of the Weiders eventually moved to California with Arnold Schwarzenegger as the new face of the IFBB. The standard mail order business for Weider products was basically replaced with a retail sales format. **An**

interesting note is that Charles Atlas once told Joe he was an idiot for selling barbells to build strength. [37]

The IFBB, a professional oriented organization with the Mr. Olympia contest as the top title in bodybuilding, was often in conflict with Bob Hoffman's AAU and the Dan Lurie WBBG (World Bodybuilding Guild) that produced the *Muscle Training Illustrated Magazine.* We remember one incident at the Brooklyn Academy of Music in Brooklyn, New York in the early seventies where that conflict came to a head. Joe Weider introduced Sergio Olivia and stated before the crowd that Sergio was a product of his Crash Weight Formula #7. Dan Lurie was in the orchestra pit and shouted out that Joe lied and tried to leap on stage. We had driven to New York to see the Olympia and by the shows end we were also in the orchestra pit. Lurie said to lift him up, which we did and he rushed Joe saying that Sergio signed an agreement that he exclusively used his Formula #707. We don't remember any other specifics, but that was our limited contact with Joe Weider and Dan Lurie.

There was a heated rivalry between Bob Hoffman, of York Barbell fame, and the Weider brothers (Joe and Ben) about which organization would take control of bodybuilding and reign supreme. The professional International Federation of Bodybuilders ran by the Weider, known as the IFBB, was growing by leaps and bounds, while the long time Amateur Athletic Union (AAU) promoted by Bob Hoffman was in decline. Tom was well aware of that situation, as was Roger

---

[37] Haxha, Tim (Sept 1995) How Joe and Ben Weider Became the Founding Fathers of Bodybuilding, Flex Magazine, 1995 (Sept) Retrieved from http://www.getbig.com/articles/faq.wdr.htm

Riedinger. Both were chairmen of Kentucky's AAU Physique Committee in the late 1980s; promoted numerous bodybuilding events and were official judges for the AAU. Several other members of our *panel* also participated in AAU bodybuilding, power lifting and the martial arts competitions. The National Physique Committee (NPC) was formed in 1981, by Jim Manion, as the amateur arm of the IFBB. The NPC eventually dominated the AAU and by 1999 the AAU voted not to sanction any more competitions. Vince McMahon, wrestling promoter, master showman and billionaire, attempted to form the World Bodybuilding Federation (WBF) in 1990 and add his expertise to make bodybuilding more marketable. That effort lasted a brief two years because there was no profits or demand from pay for view. [38]

Dan Lurie was a notable bodybuilder and strongman. Many will remember Lurie as the Sealtest Ice Crème strongman on that same TV show. Lurie was a bodybuilding promoter, with his own events and had his own magazine, *Muscle Training Illustrated*. Lurie was interviewed, at age 82, in December 2005, by Dave Robson and made some very valid points when he stated, "The golden age of bodybuilding was when they didn't have steroids." Dan also stated, "If I ever competed in the women's division today, in my best shape, I wouldn't even place. They would make me look like a beginner. That is how advanced they are. Like men." Lurie was also an anti-steroid use advocate and warned

---

[30] McFadden, Robert D. "Joe Weider Dies, at 93," New York Times (New York) 25 March 2013: pages A4 print

against their use and side effects. [39] One of his Dan Lurie's often used quotes was, **"Your health is your greatest wealth."**

Photos by Geimeier
(Left) Sergio Olivia visiting an AAU contest in York, Pennsylvania; (right) the great Bill Pearl with fan, Rance Darity.

Arnold Schwarzenegger in York, Pennsylvania shortly after arriving in America.

---

[39] Robson, Dave (Dec 2005) The Dan Lurie Story and Interview, Retrieved from http://www.bodybuilding.com/fun/drobson133html and http://www.davidrobsonelite.com/ Purchasebooks.html

J.I. Rodale was the founder and editor of *Prevention Magazine*. This widely read magazine on nutrition and natural health was devoted to spreading the doctrine that our bodies are not chemical laboratories, but biological organisms. The message was that a simpler, more organic, natural way of life is the best option for health. [40] *Prevention Magazine* eventually reached a one million per month circulation. J.I.'s fame was growing when he was invited to the Dick Cavett nightly show to spread his message. He had a heart attack shortly after his interview session began that resulted in his death and that tape was fortunately never aired.

White House staff photo
White House Staff photo with Dan Lurie joking around
with President Ronald Reagan

---

[40] Rodale, Robert (August 1971) J.I Rodale In Memoriam, Prevention Magazine Vol 23 (Number 6) pgs. 13-17

The *panel's* comments ....

Our p*anel* will discuss their personal all- time favorites, mentors and role models in Chapter 15.

What the research says ....

The information we presented on the evolution of fitness equipment and the early icons can easily be duplicated by surfing the Internet. There will be many, many sources for the evolution and those legendary icons. Bodybuilding, weightlifting and the fitness boom was growing by leaps and bounds in the 1950s and 60s with southern California and that famous Muscle Beach crowd appearing to lead the way. That same basic strategy or template of marketing, used since the 1920s, was now being utilized by the current fitness gurus to make their fortunes. There were a number of competing companies selling equipment, courses, promoting their magazines and nutritional supplements. Numerous bodybuilding titles were contested and there were contests all over the country, which gave more exposure to the athletes and the fitness companies. The movies also had a dramatic impact on strength, muscles and their popularity, especially, the early Hercules and Samson movies featuring two of the all- time legends of the sport, in Steve Reeves and Reg Park.

The bottom line ....

There has always been an interest in staying in shape, as a necessity from the ancient days of the hunter, gatherer mentality, to the modern era of fitness. The information we provided in this chapter has provided a brief overview of the evolution of fitness dating back to the middle of the 19th century. The names which have made outstanding contributions to this evolution are revered in the entire physical culture world. It is also important to point out that many people have pursued their fitness interests, not so much for health reasons, but in order to perform the demanding tasks of their job, military responsibilities, participation in athletics or a unique interest that had physical requirements. The old back alley gyms are relegated to the past and the transition to the modern facilities has occurred over the past 50 years. Today, there is no excuse for abstaining from training, as the links to better health and extended longevity have been well documented. The modern gym chains are easily accessible, convenient, with flexible hours, modern machines and other amenities that make a very attractive package. Every member of our *panel* has spent some time working out in a home style gym, but the modern gyms are usually a better option financially and will save you the expense of setting up your own. Home gyms are obviously a great resource for family oriented fitness activities, but setting up a first class operation is financially out of reach for most people.

The hot tip ….

Unless you live in an extremely rural area, we recommend joining a local fitness center after making a few trial visits. Many fitness centers occasionally advertise special deals that offer a two years for one program and reasonable add on fees for family members. Personally, we do not like the automatic monthly withdrawal programs from one's bank account. Ending your contract under those circumstances and moving to another facility can be very frustrating and possibly time consuming. We both prefer to pay cash for our gym memberships and can often negotiate three years for the typical year and a half rate. If you happen to live in an area, without convenient gym opportunities, then the home gym may be your best and only option. In that case, stay basic and make sure you have a spotter, training partner and some well- made safety equipment!

The great "Sandow" in his prime
Wikipedia (Public Domain)

Chapter 7

Avoiding Injuries

"They have a long term toll on both mind and body"

Our mantra for injuries is to avoid them at all costs by warming up properly and using strict form and technique. **If you believe you have injured a joint, muscle or other body part do not try to tough it out.** Seek medical advice quickly if an injury occurs because that will usually shorten rehab time and lessen the risk of a more extensive injury. We can all think of examples of how a minor injury became more severe by taking the macho approach. **Never ignore pain!** Always get a second opinion regarding your orthopedic surgeon and make certain to check out the expertise of your physical therapist. Remember that many orthopedic surgeons tend to specialize on specific body parts. A doctor who is the best knee expert in town may not be on shoulders. The location of your therapy is also a decision left to you through your insurance provider and does not have to be your orthopedic surgeon's office. Anyone who has experienced surgery and the need for physical therapy can tell you **the success of that surgery is only as good as the therapy you will receive.** Your recovery time will be progressive and in incremental steps to insure a full recovery. Many people have injured the opposite or healthy shoulder, knee or joint by overusing the other during their therapy period. Please follow your therapist's advice and modify your routine, equipment and intensity to be pro-active against further injury and to allow the healing process to be successful.

We also believe that any required joint, tendon or ligament surgery can never replace the original equipment you were born with! Surgeries are intended to repair serious injuries and to provide as much of the original function as possible. You may have a brand new shoulder or knee joint, but the same old ligaments and tendons are probably still in place. We have often talked about professional athletes and their numerous injuries requiring a trip to the table of their orthopedists. How often have notable athletes returned to 100% of their ability after a Tommy John, Achilles tendon, shoulder surgery and lengthy periods of rehab? There are a few examples, but they are the exception rather than the rule. The best advice we can give is to avoid anything at work, in the gym, or your specific sport that can cause you a serious injury. Don't do anything stupid that jeopardizes your original equipment! That may be easy to say, but often hard to do for competitive, alpha type athletes. If you are over extending, straining, or doing activities in awkward positions you are placing yourself at risk.

We classify all injuries into three categories. The first is an **acute** training injury that occurs suddenly, with that dreaded tearing or popping sound, and the immediate accompaniment of a lot of pain. You realize very quickly that you have joint or muscle damage and wish you would have used a lot better judgement. Our guess is that a trip to the orthopedic surgeon will be required. The second type is more of a **chronic**, ongoing injury that never fully heals because you continue to train or attempt to train around. You don't feel comfortable missing workouts so you try to calm down the problem and hope it goes away. The RICE formula with some Advil or Ibuprofen may help to relieve the symptoms, but a period of rest and recuperation is actually needed. It is also advisable to seek professional medical advice if the problem continues to persist. The third category involves **freak accidents** that are out of the gym area. In this case there was no way to anticipate or prepare for the inevitable. There is a fourth category that may require surgery and those are age related problems. Those will be discussed in greater detail in Chapter 9.

Our research indicates that the most common gym and fitness injuries include: shoulders, elbows, knees and the lower back. The surveys from our *panel* will give the reader more insight into the personal problems and injuries they have encountered.

Panel of Experts question #11

What injuries have you experienced, the causes and final outcome?

The *panel's* comments ….

Terry Collis – A few cracked ribs from sparring and a number of stitches in the mouth. Today, customized, protective mouth pieces; protective pads; cups and new regulations for safety to obtain the necessary insurance are required.

Devorah Dometrich- Herbst – My only serious injury was a torn meniscus in my right knee that required surgery. That injury was the result of excessive kicking and doing a lot of those kicks into walls. The knee is fine after surgery and my rehab went well. Always let your pain be your guide.

Dave Guidugli – I've had my nose broken four times and surgery on both shoulders and elbows. Most of those injuries can be attributed to over 20 years of football and boxing. Rehab takes time so take it slow.

Ray Hughes – Prostate surgery at age 60, which is not an injury, but required 18 months to fully recover. I've been very fortunate during my 50 plus years of weightlifting and judo training. I've never had an injury that required surgery because I've had good mentors. That's a blessing!

Lanny Julian – A torn bicep from a non -arm wrestling freak accident; a torn ligament in my elbow; and a torn ligament in my right wrist from a work related accident dealing with a slab of beef weighing 900 pounds. I always resumed training once the doctor gave me the go ahead.

Roger Riedinger – Shoulder injuries from years of very heavy weight training. The final outcome was a radical, total shoulder replacement. After extensive rehab I actually returned to 90% of my former strength and many of my nagging injuries actually healed. Another outcome is that I now perform each exercise in a perfect form.

Jerry Auton –I have experienced rotator cuff damage to both shoulders. I attribute this to the stupidity and brashness of youth that finally caught up with me. Surgery by a highly competent professional is recommended. I researched the best available shoulder specialists in Cincinnati and was able to become a patient of Dr. Kremchek, the orthopedic surgeon for the Cincinnati Reds. Any serious injury can be mentally devastating and depressing because you never know if you can come back to your level of expectations.

Tom Geimeier – The safest statement by me is to claim the fifth regarding ego and stupidity. I experienced a torn tendon in my right shoulder from a baseball injury, which required surgery. The doctor who had previously operated on my left knee performed the surgery, which was a huge mistake. The procedure should have been an arthroscopic procedure, but when I woke up I discovered he had performed a Mumford Procedure. (A Mumford Procedure is making a huge incision completely through your deltoid) **My knee doctor was obviously not the best shoulder man. Remember that!** After my surgery, my upper arm turned a deep red due to a staph infection, which required a lot of antibiotics and a number of trips to the doctor's office. I asked the doctor on one visit, "What is the worst thing that can happen with my arm?" He replied, "I may have to take that arm off for you." I think there is a lesson to be learned, but you can't turn back the clock.

I also had an unfortunate, work related incident that resulted in four and possibly a fifth surgery. While working as a high school science teacher, I was having a conversation with the elementary school secretary, whose daughter was in my class. The elementary, middle and high schools were on the same campus and used the same cafeteria. A mother of a young kindergartener came running into the building screaming and handing me her car keys, "My God, somebody help me. I just ran over my son!" The mother was bringing her young son to the afternoon class session when her son unexpectedly unbuckled his seat belt, stepped out of the car and rolled under the right rear tire. I ran outside, saw the terrible situation and looked around for other men to help. There appeared to be no help so I had to act fast and somehow lifted the right side of the car off the boy, while the school secretary pulled him onto the sidewalk. Ironically and thankfully, the youngster had no significant injuries, since the weight of the car was on his buttocks, but was taken to the hospital for a day or two of observation.

When an adrenalin rush allows you to do something you are normally incapable of and has you hyperventilating and panting like a dog you don't realize immediately that you have injured yourself. My left knee was injured requiring two surgeries; I pulled something in my lower abdomen and a thumb sized object had popped through my left "lat" muscle resulting in two more surgeries. That combination put me out of commission for about two years and after returning, possibly too quickly, I ripped my Achilles tendon in half. All of those injuries came after age 40, when I was just hitting my prime. I would do it again, without question, to save a child, but what makes me very angry is that I found out later that there were other men watching from their cars who could have helped. I also feel that I have never fully recovered from that incident and still have some lingering effects. ***See documentation of that incident from the General Assembly of Kentucky, in Appendix B**

We feel the *panel* answers have covered a wide array of potential injuries that can occur over years of training and can also serve as future "food for thought." **The *panel* believes the main reasons for gym and athletic injuries, which research backs up are: lack of appropriate skill; lack of proper training and condition; doing exercises that are not advisable; injuries from non-sport events; failure to warm up properly or taking unwarranted risks.**

We are very concerned with the injuries that have been credited to the rampant use of drugs, by all ages, whether competing athletes or not. It is important to make the connection with drug use here regarding potential injuries, but **we will discuss the drug specifics, in greater detail, in Chapter 14.**

The widespread use of HGH (human growth hormone) and steroids have given high school, college, and professional athletes muscle mass and strength that will eventually play havoc on their joints, ligaments, tendons and organs. Many college and high school athletes today are lifting weights with amounts that 20 years ago could have only be hoisted by national or world class power lifters and weight lifters. Any savvy fitness or nutritional advisor knows that nutritional supplements alone and the most modern training methods could not produce the size and strength we see in today's athletes.

Yes, we have a drug problem, at all levels, in many sports. We often hear about professional baseball because they have the most intense steroid testing program, but they are obviously not the biggest offender. Think about it! How may baseball players have you seen walking around with 20" arms, handling 500 plus pounds in their workouts, weighing 250 -300 pounds with super low body fat and a very dense muscular look? We discussed the known cases and could count them on one hand! That's because baseball is obviously not the most offensive abuser. You might consider professional wrestling, but remember, that doesn't count as a sport because wrestling bills their events as professional entertainment. We often wonder how the great George Hackenschmidt, Lou Theze, Buddy Rogers, and some of the former great wrestlers would compare to those of today?

Drug use is prevalent, often expected, and has shown up in almost every major sport. Ask the Olympic Committee why they spend so much money on drug testing? It took the IOC almost 30 years to devise a test so sophisticated that it could differentiate between natural and synthetic human growth hormone. (HGH) The costs of trying to perform drug control in the major sports has reached enormous levels.

Think of the sports where size, weight, and strength play the greatest role. Listen to the TV commentators describe to the viewers the physical attributes of a particular player they just saw on the screen and what the viewers are probably thinking. They will often elaborate about the amazing physical prowess of a certain athlete and the unusual gifts genetics have bestowed on them. Common sense should be enough to convince you that lifting weights, taking vitamins, and saying prayers will not achieve the remarkable condition of some athletes, even if they had several lifetimes to accomplish it. There is only one truth and we believe our readers are smart enough to see that fact with great clarity. I would love to hear an interviewer ask one of these athletes how they achieved their remarkable size and strength, at such an early age, and what supplements they would advise their young, impressionable followers to take. Think back just a few years to the natural physical builds of Dave Cowens, Bill Russell, Larry Bird, Pete Rose, Hank Aaron, Mickey Mantle, Jim Brown or Kareem Abdul Jabbar. Enough said!

Train sensibly and don't take unnecessary risks. Trying to prove your manhood by lifting more than you should or doing some super human exercise routine is a prescription for disaster. Train hard, on a regular basis, and continue to challenge yourself with new goals. Avoid reckless challenges that jeopardize all that you have been working for. Avoid extreme motions, especially those that can tear ligaments, rip tendons, and detach muscles. Avoid extreme exercise after periods of illness or rehab and take your time to get back in the groove. Do not make bizarre changes in your diet, supplementation or nutritional program without consulting a doctor or competent nutritionist. Make sure you keep the body hydrated during exercise and at all times. Remember why water has often been called the "elixir of life."

Injuries, especially needless injuries not only take a toll on your body, but also affect your state of mind. Our mind's eye often sees what others do not. We look in the mirror and see ourselves from long ago and then in a weak moment we look again and say, "What the hell happened?" Recuperating from injury after injury can also take a heavy toll mentally and depression can be very difficult to overcome. Depression can also lead to other serious problems. Once you lose a quality skill or ability, it may be difficult or impossible to regain. How very true!

Controversial Exercises: Do's and Don'ts

This timely information about exercise do's and don'ts has been extracted from the ISSA Handbook and asks the trainee to think about three questions before attempting any exercises.[41] 1. What is the purpose? 2. Will the exercise help me to achieve my goals? 3. Can the exercise be performed safely without sacrificing good

---

[41] Knopf, Karl, EdD (2010) Senior Fitness Handbook, "Controversial Exercises: Dos and Don'ts," Carpenteria, CA International Sports Sciences Association, pgs 149-150

biomechanics? All exercises should be performed with a very strict technique, but there are others that have a greater risk of injury when performed haphazardly. A good trainer would ask if there is more risk to the trainee than good and are there safer alternatives? Areas to be concerned with include the neck, lower back, shoulders, knees, ankles and feet. A professional fitness instructor should have their trainee perform exercises in a slow, safe manner; never hyperextend or over flex the lower back or knees; exercise caution on overhead exercises to avoid impingement; insure that the knees and the feet are always pointing in the same direction; and periodically check the trainees gait to make sure there are no ankles, feet or hip problems.

Panel of Experts questions # 8, 9, 10

What are some of the key mistakes you have observed in the gyms or dojos; the leading cause of injury in adults; and what injuries have you personally observed?

Our *panel's* comments ....

Terry Collis – I've observed older adults who try to keep up with younger members of the dojo or gym. No matter how fit you think you are, remember that your body is not what it was 30 years earlier. The majority of injuries seem to be from bad knees. Some injuries come from lower rank students who do not control their kicks & punches. Concerning sparring injuries, there is a speed difference between the younger and older trainees.

Devorah Dometrich – Herbst - Thinking there is such a thing as 'instant fitness." Most injuries are from the lack of patience and failure to stretch properly.

Dave Guidugli – Trying to relive your youth and thinking you can somehow perform like you might have 20-30 years ago. Ego can become your number one enemy. I rank shoulder injuries and elbows as the most frequent injuries that top my list.

Ray Hughes - In judo and karate people try to accelerate the throws and can injure shoulder joints. You can't control disease, but you can and must control technique. Injuries from improper technique can take up to six months or a year to fully recover. The next category of novice mistakes is lack of preparation; no warm ups; no stretching; and trying to lift too much. I've observed a number of shoulder injuries resulting from improper warm-ups, lack of stretching, and possibly over aggressiveness.

Lanny Julian – The biggest problems are over training, not paying attention to your technique and losing focus. **Injuries come easier the older we get.** Make sure you warm up properly, stretch and use the high rep method. I never accepted bar challenges in my arm wrestling career. That was never the place or time to put all my training at risk. I might lock up with a challenger in a handshake to let him feel my grip. That was usually enough. I also trained both arms the same because there are left handed contests and you also want both arms to be symmetrical. I believe many injuries result from overtraining, using too much weight, and being trained by gym staff who don't seem to understand the needs of their clients.

Roger Riedinger – Over work is the biggest cause! Trying to do too much too fast without adequate rest and recovery. The key is progression. Long time heavy lifters will generally develop shoulder problems, at some point during their training, which is usually caused by too much emphasis on bench pressing, at the expense of more balanced training programs.

Jerry Auton - Lack of preparation for the goals you have set. Age does not give you experience in every endeavor or an edge in all things. Do you think you can fly an airplane just because you can fit into the cockpit? Be realistic. Back and knee injuries seem to be the most common and are the result of overworking specific muscle groups or poor technique. Sometimes the result of both!

Tom Geimeier - Failing to warm up and taking unnecessary risks regarding the amount of weight used in your exercise routine. Many injuries also occur outside of the gym in other areas. **Be cautious and think before you act!** You cannot afford any setbacks with your training! Make sure any previous injuries or surgeries have completely healed and then make a gradual transition with your activities.

The Shoulder Ligaments

Ligaments are soft tissue structures that connect bones to bones. Several key ligaments that provide this function are:

Glenohumeral ligaments (GHL): A joint capsule is a watertight sac that surrounds a joint. In the shoulder, the joint capsule is formed by a group of ligaments that connect the humerus bone, of the upper arm, to the glenoid. These ligaments are the main source of stability for the shoulder and are the ligaments that keep the shoulders from dislocating.

Coraco-acromial ligament (CAL): This ligament links the coracoid to the acromion ligament. (CAL). The ligament can thicken, due to age or wear and tear, and cause an **Impingement Syndrome**.

Coraco-clavicular ligaments (CCL): These ligaments (trapezoid and conoid) attach to the clavicle coracoid process of the scapula. These tiny ligaments, along with the acromial-clavicular joint, play a key role in keeping the scapula attached to the clavicle and keeping your shoulders square. They are capable of carrying a massive load and are extremely strong.

Transverse Humeral ligament (THL): This ligament holds the tendon of the long head of the biceps brachii muscle in the grove between the greater and lesser tubercle on the humerus bone.

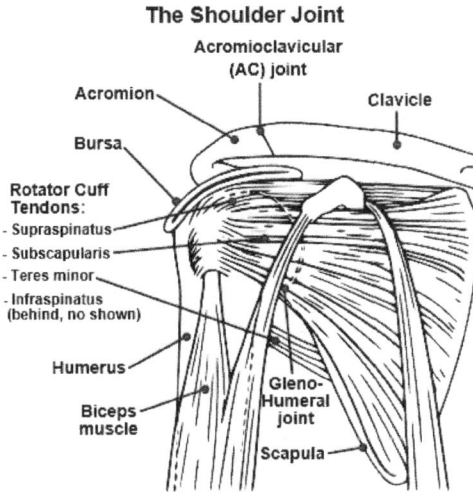

The Shoulder Joint

Public Domain photo
National Institute of Arthritis and Muscular Skeletal -Skin Diseases (NIAMS) by Angelito 7 https://commons .wikipedia.org/w/index: php?curid=29907860

The Knee Ligaments

There are four ligaments that provide stability in the knee, but are prone to injury:

Anterior cruciate ligament (ACL): One of the two major ligaments that connect the thigh (femur) bone to the shin bone. (tibia) ACL injuries have become very common place with over 95,000 reported injuries, in the U.S. each year. *Women are more prone to this specific type of knee injury.

Posterior cruciate ligament (PCL): The second major knee ligament that also connects the femur bone to the tibia or shin bone.

Lateral cruciate ligament (LCL): Connects the femur bone to the smaller lower leg bone or fibula. It is located on the lateral or outside of the knee.

Medial collateral cruciate ligament (MCL): Also connects the femur bone to the fibula and is located on the medial or inside of the knee.

What does a knee injury sound or feel like?

An acute knee injury will have a sudden, acute pain often accompanied by a popping or snapping sound. That is a good indication that one of your ligaments has been torn or ruptured. There may be a feeling of looseness in the joint and the inability to put weight on the knee, without pain. A good point to remember is that your feet should always turn with your body and never allow your upper body or hips to turn with your feet firmly planted. This may happen on an athletic field when the cleats or spikes are caught in the turf. Many knee and shoulder injuries are the result of the aging process or wear and tear.

Treatment of those possible injuries has progressed light years since the 1960s. A significant knee injury 30 years ago may have caused you to buy a cane and use it for the rest of your life, but today qualified orthopedic professionals can repair and replace torn, worn ligaments, tendons, use sophisticated injections and perform knee replacements.

Common knee injuries may include:

Sprained or strained ligaments and/or muscles- caused by a blow to the knee or a sudden twist with the feet planted.

Torn cartilage- Trauma to the protective pads or menisci that act as shock absorbers within the knee structure. Tears can occur with sprains. Surgery often required.

Tendonitis –A condition involving inflammation of the tendons, possibly from overuse. Tendonitis of the patellar tendon is often referred to as "jumper's knee" and is common in basketball, long jumpers and triple jumpers.

Arthritis –Osteoarthritis affects the knee and is a degenerative process where the cartilage in the joint gradually wears away. Repeated stress, injury or being overweight can aggravate this condition.

Torn meniscus – The three bones that meet in the knee (femur, patellar, tibia) are covered with a protective coating of cartilage that acts as a shock absorber and to offset friction. Between those bones we find two discs of connective tissue called menisci that absorb the shock of the upper body on the lower leg.

The Knee Joint

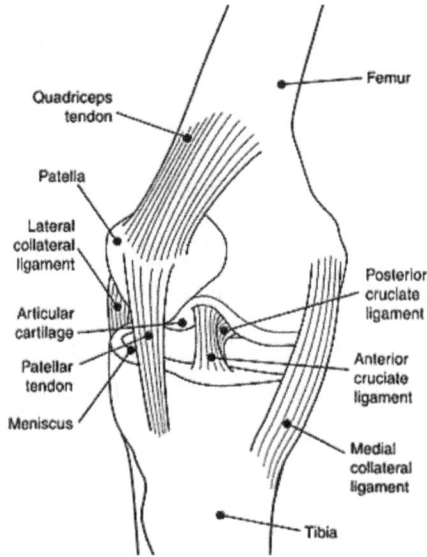

Public Domain photo

What the research says ....

Almost every member of our *panel* has suffered several joint or muscle injuries, which have required surgery, extensive rehabilitation and the needed self- motivation to resume training and possibly accept a few new physical limitations. Many of the injuries in the non –combat types of training could have possibly been avoided with a good mentor and greater personal insight and control. We have listed below a summary of our *panels'* top priorities to avoid injuries:

- Be sure to warm up which includes stretching and your cardio.

- Make sure you have the proper gym clothing, which may vary by season and includes the correct type of shoes for the activity.
- Always use a gradual weight progression on free weights or machines.
- Check the equipment to insure it is in the proper working order. Remember that during the day numerous people use the same equipment and many improperly.
- Never try to work through an injury and never extend the joints to the point of pain or discomfort!
- Use the strictest possible form or technique on every exercise. This greatly reduces the chances of injury and will accelerate your progress.
- When lifting heavy always have a **competent spotter**, especially with free weights.
- Stay within yourself! Nobody really cares what you are doing and we're sure you feel the same about them.
- Stretch during and after your workout. You warmed up and now warm down.
- Breathing is important and should be natural. When exerting you should be exhaling or breathing out. Never hold your breath!

Parting Bits of Advice from Notables in the Fitness Industry on the Importance of Breathing Properly

Vince Gironda, a southern California fitness icon, made the nutritional statement that all units of protein measurement and requirement are taken from the basic egg. Vince also advocated in his July 1966 *Blueprint for the Bodybuilder*[42] that deep breathing caused by vigorous exercise is one of nature's best fat trimming methods. Vince addressed your personal eating habits and food selection by saying that, "What is not in your refrigerator will not be eaten." Vince also advised everyone to drink water between meals to aid digestion, remedy fatigue and cure constipation.

Bill Pearl, winner of numerous bodybuilding titles and one of the strongest bodybuilders in the business, recommended high rep breathing squats followed by stiff or bent arm pullovers to build up the rib box and increase aerobic activity. Bill liked to warm up with dumbbell swings also known as wood choppers. Bill states that when your thoughts accentuate the positive it will give you a happier outlook on life.

Chuck Sipes was one of the pound for pound strongest men in weightlifting, bodybuilding or power lifting. Chuck attempted a bench press of 600 pounds, at one of the Mr. Olympia shows, in Brooklyn, New York in the early 1970s. Chuck stated that oxygen is the life giver to your blood supply and suggested to taking forced breaths during your entire exercise program.

The recommendations of that article were seconded by an article in *titintech.com, menshealth.com, inspiyr.com and fitday.com*. The *titintech.com* site gave a detailed description of how to do a personal assessment of your shoulders, knees and Achilles tendons to determine if they were stable enough to perform heavier lifting. The *titntech.com* site also mentioned that it was a

---

[42] Gironda, Vince (July 1966) Blueprint for the Bodybuilder, North Hollywood, CA91604

good idea to monitor the range of motion required for each exercise; perform a check of the equipment and limit the number of sets and reps in each workout. The *menshealth.com* information, by Michael Easter, offered sound advice on testing your knees for anterior cruciate ligament (ACL) strength; the shoulders for possible impingement injury and the Achilles tendons. The *inspiyr.com* data was written by Dan Cassidy, with a medical review, by Dr. Vonda Wright. (Dr. Wright is the developer of a system of resistance bands called *Strive*) An interesting piece of information was that as we age the cartilage that cushions the joint movement becomes worn, as do the ligaments and tendons. Dan Cassidy categorized injuries as either traumatic, with the accompaniment of the often dreaded popping sound or those from overuse. Dr. Wright interjected that the mirrors in the gym were excellent asset for observing if your technique was being performed correctly. The older person will ultimately lose some of the elasticity in their muscles, joints and tendons so it is **advisable to stretch throughout the entire workout.** The final recommendation was for every individual to take care of themselves outside of the gym. [43] [44] [45]

---

[43] Titin.com Staff (22 Oct 2014) Avoiding Common Weight Lifting Injuries, Retrieved from http;//www.titintech.com/2014/10/122avoid-common-weightlifting-injuries/

[44] Easter, Michael (24 Jan 2013) Injuries and Their Prevention, Retrieved from http://www.menshealth.com/fitnessInjuries-and-prevention

[45] Fit day Staff (Nov 2015) Avoid Injury: 5 Common Strength Training Mistakes, Retrieved from http://www.fitday.com/fitness/exercises/avoid-injury-5-common-strength-training-mistakes/html

The bottom line ….

There was consensus among the *panel* as to the leading causes of injury and mistakes they observed in the gyms and dojos. It was beneficial to learn of the *panels* personal injury history and their final outcomes. The research substantiated what the *panel* stated and that the makes the information very conclusive. The reader is privy to the combined 400 years of *panel* experience and they would be very wise to heed that well intended advice.

The hot tip ….

We believe the *panel* had a unique way of stating their best tips and we have combined them in this section. It might be a good idea to make a few signs, as constant reminders, and tack onto your mirror or refrigerator. Devorah advocated that there was no such thing as instant fitness. Terry, Dave and Lanny were in unison about trying to regain your youth and thinking you could accomplish the same as you did 20-30 years earlier. Lanny also added that injuries come easier with age. Ray was concerned about what we call unbridled enthusiasm. Roger and Jerry mentioned to avoid overwork and Tom concluded with be sure to think before you act.

The *titintech.com* article discusses common injuries that result in torn muscles, damaged joints and broken bones. Cautions against poor technique and limited the amount of sets and reps performed that can lead to over training. One unique piece of advice was to do a self- assessment before doing a new exercise to understand the exercise motions required and constantly monitor your technique. The advice also suggested that a safety check of the machines used was a good idea since dozens or hundreds of people use them every day.

The m*enshealth.com* article by Michael Easter provided insight into doing a self- check of your shoulder, knees and Achilles before doing any exercises on those body areas. An ACL assessment could be performed by doing some free hand or very light weight strict squatting movements. If your knees tended to sway inward while squatting that would indicate your ACL was not up to the challenge. The shoulder impingement assessment was to place your hand on the opposite shoulder and try to raise that elbow as high as possible. Tightness would indicate you had a restricted range of motion and should carefully consider what type of shoulder work would be in your best interest. The Achilles tendon assessment was performed by leaning against a wall while supporting your weight with both hands and taking one step backward trying to keep both feet flat on the ground. Any tightness in the tendon and not the calf was a sign that the tendon was too tight to be stressed.

The *inspiyr.com*[46] article by Dan Cassidy mentioned 9 ways to avoid injury and was reviewed by the noted orthopedic surgeon, Dr. Vonda Wright. He also warned against overuse, traumatic injury, worn cartilage in the joints and any immediate pain. (that would be too late) Looking in the mirror was a new idea, not to be an ego maniac, but to constantly access your form or technique. Other suggestions included: don't be afraid to try something new like a Pilates class; muscles have elastic

---

[16] Cassidy, Dan (reviewed by Wright, Vonda Dr.2014) How to prevent weightlifting injuries, Retrieved from inspiyr.com

properties so a warm up is crucial; avoid the power lifts; have a spotter; stretching should be constant throughout the workout; don't try to do all your exercise on one weekend day (weekend warrior syndrome); rest, eat correctly and stay hydrated. Be sure to take care of yourself outside the gym.

FitDay.com cited many of the same mistakes as: don't train to failure; don't spend excess time on your warm-ups, avoid too many repetitions, get ample rest between sets and use a slow and steady exercise form.

Chapter 8

Rehabilitation and Therapy

"Know your options and avoid crucial mistakes"

We think it is rather obvious that the authors and our *panel of experts* have collectively, experienced most of the common injuries to athletes and non-athletes alike. They are providing you with the wisdom of their personal experiences. Remember that every injury, regardless of whether surgery is required or not, is accompanied with some period of rehabilitation. The perfect scenario is to maintain continuity with your exercise program and avoid injury or at best minimize possible mishaps. Chapter 7 was significant in that it dealt with sound advice on prevention that could also be referred to as preventative maintenance. Unfortunately, in an imperfect world, mishaps will occur, but we certainly have great admiration for the fitness buffs who has never encountered any problems.

A good question to ask your friends is, "How often has the doctor performing a shoulder or knee shoulder told the patient to be very careful not to injure the opposite joint." Experience has taught us that doctors do not elaborate on that fact and we believe it happens more than you think. Doctors are in business to make a living and stay busy. The statistics are quite high for patients having a joint surgery only to injure the opposite joint, within a short time, by over compensating or overusing their good side.

Surgery will cause you lost training time and it may take months or years attempting to regain your previous bench marks. There may be a point in your life, due to age or other ailments, that you will never get back to the condition you were once in. A young, gifted professional athlete could have ligaments replaced in their knees and eventually return to a high performance level, but we firmly believe that once you have surgery, on any major joint, you will never return to your highest level. The doctor told Tom, after his Achilles tendon repair, that completely torn tendons will never reconnect, heal and return to normal. The doctor said, "Your tendon is held together with as much thread as I could put in there. Scar tissue will eventually encase the torn tendon and help in holding it together. You can return to your sports or exercise and basically do what you want, but remember, you will always be more suspect to rupturing it again."

Panel of Experts question # 12

What is your best advice on rehabbing injuries and surgeries?

The *panel's* comments ....

Terry Collis – Rest, recuperate and use Tiger Balm ointment.

Devorah Dometrich – Herbst - Let your pain be your guide. Ice and Ibuprofen has always taken care of my ailments.

Dave Guidugli – Take it slow. Make sure you complete any rehabilitation or physical therapy program.

Ray Hughes - My rehab was incremental starting back with 5 pound weights and eventually getting back to 300 pound plus bench and completing 5 mile jogs at 70 plus.

Lanny Julian – Make sure your rehab work is complete before increasing your training goals.

Roger Riedinger – Follow a progressive rehab period and then use a very strict form.

Jerry Auton - Rehab all injuries slowly and patiently! Keep the positive attitude that you will be back as long as you follow the professional advice of your surgeon.

Tom Geimeier - Be patient and follow the PT's advice if you want to obtain the best possible outcome! You cannot afford any additional set- backs. Trying to push the limits and coming back too soon is not in your best interest. If you feel your physical therapist is doing a poor job and not attentive to your needs do not hesitate to transfer to another location. A lack of proper PT can allow scar tissue to accumulate in the joint, which restricts movement and will often require another surgery to clean out the joint.

A Few Key Terms, Relating to Possible Injuries You May Experience

Sprain - An injury that damages the ligaments, which insure stability of a joint by holding the two bones together. The force that causes the injury may be accompanied by a popping sound and the extent of the injury is rated on a grade of 1, 2 or 3. The injury to the ankle, finger, knee, thumb or shoulder is often indicated by swelling, black and blue bruising and weight bearing pain. The pain and swelling will dictate the extent of treatment, which could be physical therapy and even surgery. A thorough physical exam of the joint, with the results of an x-ray or MRI, will help to form an accurate diagnosis of the injury. A grade 3 sprain is also referred to a tear or complete rupture. Initial treatment would involve the RICE formula of rest, ice, compression and elevation.

Strain – An injury to a muscle or the tendons that attach the muscles to the bones. (ex. Biceps tendon) Utilize the Aspirin, Tylenol or topical pain crèmes to assist with pain relief. The RICE formula should be utilized with rest to protect from further injury until a diagnosis is conducted by a medical professional. Ice should be applied 4-6 times per day for the first 36 hours with a possible compression bandage to reduce swelling. (caution should be used with any compression bandages so they are not too tight and cut off circulation and create numbness) Rehab can begin after a brief recovery period. Strengthening the muscles is a key factor to protect from further injury, as is restoring the full range of motion. Proper technique is imperative to protect against further injury and those who have experienced an injury may be recommended to wear a supporting brace. The extent of the injury could range from an over stretch to a complete tear or rupture. Pain, muscle spasms, muscle weakness, swelling, inflammation and muscle cramping are indicators that would identify the extent of the injury and whether therapy or surgery were the best options.

Tears and Ruptures – Tears and ruptures are very serious grade 3 sprains or strains. The joint ligament or muscle tendon affected can be partially severed to a complete snap or ripping in half by a force to the body. The rehab period for a tear or rupture will be greatly extended and the ability to return to a prior "blue chip" athletic level will be in serious jeopardy. Surgery is a definite treatment and the rehab will take many months with progressive stages. Our belief is that the older person will usually have a slower rehab period than a younger person and your physical condition, before the injury, will also be a major factor in the eventual outcome.

Bursitis – A condition where the small fluid sacs that provide a cushion like, friction reducing function to the joints becomes inflamed. Medical professions can recommend medications to alleviate the inflammation and fluid may have to be drained from the sacs.

Tendonitis - An inflammation and irritation of the soft tissue of a tendon that is of course attached to the muscles. This injury is due to repeated small stresses that were possibly not given enough rest to completely recover. Many athletes try to work through this condition, which is commendable, but not the most intelligent thing to do. Rest, an anti-inflammation drugs, possible steroid injections are probably required with splints and possibly surgery as a more extreme option.

Contusion (bruises) – An injury caused by a direct blow to the connective tissue or muscle. A discoloration, which is evidence of blood pooling, will indicate the extent of the injury. The RICE formula should be followed.

Acute and Chronic – An acute pain or injury comes on suddenly as the result of a broken bone, burn, cut, dental work or following surgery. It begins with a sharp, dull, stabbing, and often described biting pain. Treatment could provide almost immediate relief or the pain could persist for up to six months. Chronic refers to a consistent, ongoing problem even though the injury has been treated and should have healed. Symptoms of a chronic condition may result in tense muscles, limited mobility, lack of energy, anger, anxiety, changes in appetite, constant headaches, low back pain and nerve problems. [47] [48]

What the research says ….

Every member of the *panel* has experienced injuries during their 50 years of participation in their specific discipline. The majority of those injuries come with the territory! Terry Collis mentioned that his cracked ribs and a few stitches were not uncommon in martial arts, especially with sparring and kumite (competition fighting) contests. The same applied to Devorah who has also participated in years of sparring events. Her knee injury was her only significant joint injury and that was probably due to some wear and tear after thousands of kicking movements, over 50 years. Roger, Tom, Lanny and Jerry have experienced joint injuries that can be attributed to years of lifting weights and competitions in their areas. There is a break through treatment currently in the experimental stages referred to as "The Soup." "The Soup" is a mixture of human cells that include stem cells derived from the patient's own fat. The belief is that "The Soup" mixture can help to repair injuries that would typically require surgery. IntelliCell and BioSciences, the manufacturer, think this type of cellular therapy can help to restore injured knees, elbows, hips, shoulders and necks. Several professional athletes have

---

[47] National Institute of Arthritis and Musculoskeletal and Skin Diseases (Nov 2013) Handout on Health: Sports Injuries, Retrieved from http://www.niams.nih.gov/Health_Info/sports_injuries/

[48] American Academy of Orthopaedic Surgeons (July 2015) Sprains, Strains and Other Soft Tissue Injuries, Retrieved from orthoinfo.aaos.org/topic/cfon?topic=A00111

already received the experimental treatment with a price range starting at $15,000. No one is sure if the treatments actually work or are legal under the U.S. Food and Drug Administration (FDA) guidelines. "Baby Boomers" and the athletic patients are anxious for surgery alternatives and the stem cell clinics are expanding rapidly to meet that expectation. **It should be pointed out that the type of stem cells used in this process come from the patient's own fat cells and not another person's bone marrow, embryo or fetus.** The FDA is watching the clinics carefully and have tried to have the process labeled as a new type of drug. [49]

The bottom line ....

Injuries often come with the territory! Regardless of your preparation, high level equipment and expertise, activities often come with various hazards. Terry, Devorah and Dave have all experienced various injuries due to their martial arts involvement. Sparring over a period of time will almost always produce a few nicks and scraps. Hopefully, these can be kept to a minimum. The exception to the rule is Ray Hughes who has been training for over 60 years without any injury that required surgery. Ray's routine has always combined heavy resistance training in conjunction with his judo. That is really amazing when you think that judo is a contact sport and the heavy lifting usually takes a toll on the body. Ray made a key statement when he credited his health and longevity, in fitness, **to the great mentors** he has worked with on that journey!

---

[49] Schrotenboer, Brent "Soup Therapy Promises Healing," USA Today Sports, (New York) 2 Sept 2015: pg 1

The hot tip ....

Every member of the *panel* stated emphatically that any rehab must be incremental and followed to complete recovery. Seniors in rehab will need a longer recovery period than their younger peers and may have difficulty regaining full function. The best advice is to avoid injuries than need surgery and rehab at all costs!

Chapter 9

Age Related Problems to Anticipate

"Aging is a fact of life, life can take a cruel twist, but being proactive is the key"

There have been numerous, recent articles related to how scientific research is finding that exercise has a positive impact on brain health, especially aerobic exercise. Aerobic exercise is any activity that will increase your heart rate or stimulate your heart and lungs by improving the oxygen flow to the vital organs of the body. Some examples of this type of activity would include; a brisk walk, for a senior who has been inactive, to increased activities such as jogging, swimming, cycling and power walking. The basic idea is to increase blood flow, especially to the all- important brain, thus helping to eliminate plaque buildup and increasing the body's ability to carry more oxygen to the vital organs. The facts are that the average person will lose ten percent of their muscle mass each decade over age fifty, but the cardio aspects must take priority in any workout when time is an issue.

Until recently, most people felt they could fit enough cardio work into their exercise routines and busy lives to keep the lungs and heart in decent working shape. Many also relied on some type of strength or resistance training to support the muscular system, which of course supports the skeletal system. The seniors or older trainees obviously need resistance training to maintain mobility, muscle tone, balance and functionality, but if we lose our cognitive ability then the battle will have been lost. What good are all of your positive efforts to maintain your physical condition if you can't find your way to the gym and back home again.

Everyone has experienced firsthand a close friend or loved one suffering the terrible debilitating effects of Alzheimer's disease. This dreaded disease, like a thief in the night, robs the individual of their history, interests and family. It has certainly changed our outlook and priorities when thinking about the quality of the "golden years." As a matter of fact, Jerry lost one sister to that disease the very week we were writing this article and he has another sister recently diagnosed with the early onset. We feel it is important to discuss this dreaded disease in some detail because of the devastating effects on the senior population.

Studies indicate that a gradual hearing loss is a common symptom of aging, but in some people it may also be an early indicator of the onset of Alzheimer's disease or other types of dementia. Older people with mild hearing impairments and those who have difficulty following a conversation in a crowded restaurant are nearly twice as likely, as those with normal hearing, to develop dementia. **Severe hearing loss nearly quintuples the risk of dementia!**

Alzheimer's Disease & Exercise
(Jerry elaborated on this section, due to his research and concern, on behalf of his two sisters, Carol and Cathy)

Jerry has two sisters who have been diagnosed with Alzheimer's disease. Carol began showing signs of this disease in the form of forgetfulness and absent mindedness at the age of 67 and within two years she had progressed to the point that the family had to admit her to a nursing home. Jerry's younger sister, Cathy, developed early-onset Alzheimer's, showing symptoms at the young age of 57. In her case, the progression was very rapid at first, almost what we would refer to as sudden. Cathy had an office position that required a degree of technical computer and typing skills. She had taken a couple of years off for grandmother duties and eventually decided to return to the work force, but the Alzheimer's had affected her to the point she was unable to pass a fairly simple clerical test to return to her previous position. She was even fired from another position, at a local motel /restaurant, because she couldn't remember how to set a table with a plate and eating utensils. Seeing what happens to a loved one when they lose their cognitive abilities was heartbreaking for the family members. Watching his sisters undergo their struggle has motivated Jerry to be an advocate and do everything possible to **warn others of the dangers** and what can be done to fight this terrible disease. (AKA "Old Timers")

Statistics indicate that one in eight older Americans currently has Alzheimer's disease and Alzheimer's disease is currently ranked as the 6th leading cause of death in the United States. Over 15 million Americans require unpaid care for this currently incurable diagnosis or other types of dementias. Payments for the necessary care were estimated to be $200 billion in 2014.[50]

With the "baby boomer" population entering their senior years, we may quite possibly be looking at a problem of epidemic

---

[50] Cole, Diane (2 Nov 2013) New Alzheimer's Research Holds Promise for the Future, Retrieved from nationalgeographic.com/news/2013/11/131101-alzheimers-sleep-brain-proteins-science/

proportions by the year 2050. Today, the number is 5 million people diagnosed, and the forecast is almost 14 million by 2050. Put that into perspective and that roughly equals the population of the entire state of New York. (approx. 19 million) Aging is the strongest known risk factor for Alzheimer's and we advise our readers to pay attention to your body's warning signs. Remember that the brain is the computer center of the body and that is of tremendous significance. Our research on this subject has alerted us to do all we can to fight this disease. There is no current cure for Alzheimer's disease, but scientific research has given us some clues, as to the possible causes, and what preventative measures can be taken to at least slow its progression.

Exercise is vitally important! Think of the arteries throughout your body as highways for blood and nutrient travel. Plaque buildup in these arteries is a main cause of a variety of health issues including high blood pressure, stroke and C.O.P.D. It makes sense that the blood that travels to our brain needs to be rich in oxygen, glucose and many other nutrients to keep that vital organ healthy. Excessive plaque build-up has been found in the brains of Alzheimer's patients. Physical exercise obviously has the effect of increasing blood flow to the brain just as it does to our heart, lungs and all other organs of our body. We well know the damaging effects that a loss of blood flow to the brain or any other organ of the body causes. Think of how that works in reverse with nutrient rich blood flowing to that marvelous organ, which is a key to our future welfare.

If you have been avoiding exercise and staying in shape because you are presently satisfied with your appearance and physical condition, just consider for a moment the possibility of not be able to live independently within the next few years because you have lost mental function. We look at the benefits of an exercise program as a double bonus! Exercise can provide you with a healthy body, feeling better, living longer and with a healthier functioning brain! Quite frankly, Jerry has a bigger fear of mental decline, or cognitive thinking than he does of any other disease! We can have surgeries to correct injuries and medication to fight practically every other disease, but there is no cure for Alzheimer's on the horizon! We can think of nothing worse than the inability to recognize and interact with our loved ones.

Physical exercise, however, is only one facet in the fight against Alzheimer's. Brain games or brain exercises have also proven to help. Staying active mentally by playing board games, cards, crossword puzzles and computer games, which stimulate the thought process, have also been found to be helpful. Staying active socially is also important. Participation in social gatherings with friends and loved ones; going to a dances or movies; and becoming involved in civic work or in book clubs can be to your advantage. Consider taking a class from a local community college or volunteering, as a tutor or mentor, at a local school. There are a number of social activities that will not only be enjoyable, but mentally challenging and helpful, in protecting and exercising this marvelous computer of ours called the brain.

There are certainly a lot of factors that enter into the equation on the causes of Dementia or Alzheimer's disease. Heart disease, cancer and adverse drug related reactions may be the main causes of senior death, but Alzheimer's disease has become so prevalent that is receiving more attention than those other well- known killers. We have seen the devastating affects first hand and the

189

current research has increased our knowledge with data taken on genetics, physical condition and brain injury. We cannot turn back the clock, but we can do everything possible to keep that clock ticking. Visit any gym or fitness center and you will see a tremendous number of seniors involved in a variety of fitness activities making their priority **fighting back against the ravages of time**.

Aging "baby boomers" are fatter and sicker than their predecessors were at the same age, says a new study, by <u>JAMA Internal Medicine</u>, that's raising alarms about future projected costs of health care and disability claims. The study, published online, in February 4, 2014 says "baby boomers" were less likely to report excellent health and to do regular exercise and more likely to suffer from obesity, hypertension, diabetes and other maladies. To pick one sorrowful example, they were twice as likely to use a walking device, such as a cane or walker. "Boomers" who are in poor health will not only require more expensive health care in future years, but they are more likely to retire early depriving employers of their depth of specialized knowledge. [51]

Since the start of the 2006-2007 Recession, there's been a rise in the number of people filing for disability insurance and the U.S. Government's Supplemental Security Insurance Income Program, which undermines the entire Social Security System. The Council for Disability Awareness, in Portland, Maine, which

---

[51] JAMA Internal Medicine Staff (4 Feb 2013) Overall Health of Baby Boomers Appears Lower Than Previous Generation, Retrieved from http://www.media.jamanetwork.com/news-item/overall-health-status-of-baby-boomers-appears-lower-than-previous-generation/

represents insurers, said last year that in its survey, "Most, but not all, companies continue to believe the economic environment is a factor." *The JAMA Internal Medicine* report makes it clear that a genuine deterioration in health is also a factor." The study is by five researchers from West Virginia University School of Medicine and the Medical School of South Carolina, led by Dr. Dana E. King of West Virginia's Department of Family Medicine. It draws on data from the National Health and Nutrition Examination Survey, a project of the Centers for Disease Control. The "boomer" group had an average age of 54, for the study duration, which was between the years 2007-10. It was compared to a group of people who were the same age in 1988-94. The study said that although "boomers" have a longer life expectancy than their elders, their health is another matter and better health habits are necessary. That study clearly demonstrated a need for policies that expand efforts at prevention and healthy lifestyle promotion in the "baby boomer" generation." [52]

When we were in our forties it was rare to see a large group of people older than we were training consistently, in any form. It was the exception rather than the rule. There has been a definite mind shift in older adults working out to live longer and trying to maintain a happier and higher quality of life. It is also rewarding that many insurance companies have offered incentives such as Silver Sneakers®, to adults over 65, so that gym fees are waived

---

[52]Coy, Peter (7 Feb 2013) Scary Health-Care Statistics on the Broken-Down Boomer Generation, Retrieved from http://www.bloomberg.com/bw/articles/2013/02/07/scary-health-care-statistics-on-the-broken-down-boomer-generation

and picked up by these companies. The insurance companies see this pro-active opportunity as a way to offset future expenses typically incurred by this age group because insurance companies report that the sickest 20 percent of seniors allot for 80 percent of the doctor and hospital pay outs. The nursing homes and senior centers have also showed initiative with the inclusion of fitness type programs geared to the ability of their residents. These creative programs have removed the stigma that exercise is a bad thing even though we all know of the 90- year old who still works in their garden every day. In the 1970s bodybuilding, running, cycling, and other athletic contests had senior and master's divisions that started at age 35. Through the last 40 years, that number has moved to 40, 50, 60 and many competitions are considering over 70 categories. Age does not have to be an exercise barrier and adults today are not sitting back waiting to accept their eventual fate!

Yes, our priorities do change with age. The young person in their twenties and thirties wanted to add some muscle mass to their physique; realized in their forties and fifties that cardio was also a necessity and decided somewhere in their sixties that flexibility was also essential. Today, the priority should be to utilize a balanced program that keeps a strong blood flow to the heart, lungs and brain while maintaining as much muscle tone as possible, with flexibility, mobility and injury preventions a priority. Millions of dollars have been spent on researching the aging process in hopes of finding that magic elixir, but so far that quest has been elusive. Longevity is beautiful thing, but a long life with the ability to offset many of the negative effects of the ravages of aging is the key we strive for.

Wellness visits and required screenings

Screenings are proactive tests that look for diseases before you develop the symptoms. Blood pressure checks, rectal exams and mammograms are examples of important health screenings. You can schedule most screenings, with your insurance company's approval, at your doctor's office or a preferred hospital. After a screening test, it's important to ask when you will see the results and who you should talk to about them.[53] When a "red flag" is discovered the doctor may order a biopsy, of the problem area, to discover a more finite evaluation.

Breast Cancer - talk with your healthcare team about how often you will need a mammogram and remember how devastating this type of cancer can be.

Cervical Cancer - have a Pap smear every 1 to 3 years until you are age 65. The frequency depends on your level of sexual activity. If you are older than 65 and recent Pap smears were evaluated, as normal, then future Pap smears may not be necessary. If you have experienced a total hysterectomy, for a reason other than cancer, future Pap smears may not be needed. **This is a decision that should be made after consulting with your urologist!**

Colorectal Cancer - have a screening test for colorectal cancer and a point to remember is this type of cancer has a genetic tie. Several different tests such as a stool blood test and regular scheduled colonoscopies can be early detectors of this cancer.

---

[53] Humana Vitality Staff (Aug/Nov 2014) Required Wellness Visits and Screenings, Humana Vitality Magazine, 2014 (July/Nov) pgs. 2-3

Your health care team can help you decide how often you will need this procedure.

Depression - your emotional health is as important as your physical health. Talk to your health care team about being screened for depression, especially if during the last two weeks you have felt down, sad and hopeless; or if you have little interest or pleasure in life.

Diabetes - get screened for diabetes if your blood pressure is higher than 135/80 or if you take medication for high blood pressure. Diabetes (high blood sugar) can be a serious problem and can cause problems with your heart, brain, eyes, feet, kidneys, nerves, and other body parts.

High Blood Pressure - have your blood pressure checked at least several times per year. This can be accomplished during your annual Wellness Visit and many dentists also take a blood pressure reading for their charts. High blood pressure is considered 140/90 or higher. High blood pressure can cause strokes, heart attacks, kidney and eye problems, and heart failure.

High Cholesterol - high cholesterol increases your chance of heart disease, stroke, and other circulation problems. Have your cholesterol checked regularly if you use tobacco; are obese; have a personal history of heart disease or blocked arteries; or have a male relative in your family who had a heart attack before age 50 or a female relative before age 60.

Osteoporosis (Bone Thinning) - have a screening test at age 65 to make sure your bones are strong and with optimum density. If you are younger than 65 and at high risk for bone fractures, you should also be screened. Talk with your health care team about your risk for bone fractures.

Overweight and Obesity – the best way to learn if you are overweight or obese is to find your body mass index (BMI). You can find your BMI by entering your height and weight into a BMI calculator that can be found on the Internet. A BMI between 18.5 and 25 indicates a normal weight. Persons with a BMI of 30 or higher may be obese. If your rating indicates obesity it will be important to talk to your health care team about seeking intensive counseling and getting help. That advice will usually suggest changing your exercise and dietary habits to lose weight. Obesity and being overweight can lead to diabetes, cardiovascular disease and a shortened life span.

Prostate problems -the prostate gland is an organ that is located at the base or outlet (neck) of the urinary bladder. The gland surrounds the first part of the urethra and is the passage through which urine drains from the bladder to exit from the penis. One function of the prostate gland is to help control urination by pressing directly against the part of the urethra that it surrounds. The main function of the prostate gland is to produce some of the substances that are found in normal semen, such as minerals and sugar. Semen is the fluid that transports the sperm to assist with reproduction. A man can manage quite well, however, without his prostate gland. Current treatments have shown great promise to the patient, regarding prostatectomies, by lessening the side effects of incontinence and sexual function. Current treatment options vary from seeding with radiation, to cryogenics and DaVinci robotic nerve sparring surgery.

In a young man, the normal prostate gland is roughly the size of a walnut or approximately 30 grams, but during normal aging, the gland usually grows larger. This hormone-related enlargement with aging is called **benign prostatic hyperplasia**, but this condition does not necessarily indicate the presence of cancer. An enlarged prostate can cause difficulty with urination and the frequency of night time urination in older men. Patients should seek medical advice from their urologist or primary care physician if these symptoms are present. Your annual prostate exam and the PSA numbers may be indicators of a potential problem, but can be deceptive. There have been men with PSA blood tests of 2.5 or less with prostate cancer and men with numbers as high as 9 and 10 without. Younger patients almost always tend to have more aggressive type cancers while older men tend to have a slower growing cancers and lower Gleason scores. The only true way to know if cancer is present is through a biopsy and analysis by a pathologist. **Several urologists have stated that every man will ultimately have prostate cancer if they live long enough!** The greatest fear with this disease is that it will metastasize and spread to the bladder, bones, lungs and liver. That is usually a death sentence!

Skin Assessment – skin cancer in any form is a definite threat to everyone in the "boomer" generation. A yearly assessment should be performed by your dermatologist and if pre-cancerous growths are discovered they will probably recommend seeing you at least every six months. There were no sun screens in the 1950s or 60s and the damage done to your skin may ultimately reveal itself. Doctors will usually recommend using a quality sun screen, wearing a hat, staying out of the sun during peak hours, and buying a pair of sunglasses that have great UV protection.

Metabolism and Aging

The Webster Dictionary definition of metabolism is the chemical changes in living cells by which energy is provided for vital processes and activities. In simpler terms it is the process that breaks down and builds up substances for the production of energy. Let's take a look at the differences between males or females when compared to those who are sedentary versus those physically active.

Familiar excuses, concerning weight control, from those sedentary are, "My metabolism has slowed down and there is nothing I can do about it." "Fat weighs more than muscle or is it that muscle weighs more than fat?" Realistically, one pound equals one pound whether comparing fat or muscle. We have listed some pertinent facts below:

- Decreased muscle mass may contribute to falls and injuries
- Calorie requirements drop by 2-10% each decade over age 30

There are numerous benefits to staying active and maintaining a healthy lifestyle, which is especially true in the senior years. Research indicates that heredity and genetics play a crucial role in concerning life span and the aging process, as well as gender.

- Men are 88% more likely to die from heart disease than women
- Men are 45% more likely to die from cancer than women
- Men are 18% more likely to die from strokes than women

If you are 65 and over heart disease and strokes are your greatest health risk. The healthy, active lifestyle has some very powerful benefits that will surely interest anyone interested in a longer, happier and healthier life and may help to offset these dreaded diseases. Benefits of an active lifestyle include: increased cardiac output, increased lung capacity, less muscle loss, maintenance of bone density, greater flexibility, balance and coordination, greater muscular strength and heart muscle. Research indicates that physical activity may reduce heart problems by as much as 50% and strokes by 40%.

Exercise and Arthritis

What do Joe Namath, Nolan Ryan and Dorothy Hamill all have in common? They are all great athletes and they cope with osteoarthritis, better known as AO. **More than 36 million people in the United States have arthritis to some degree, making it the number one crippling disease!** Arthritis actually means inflammation of a joint, but a more accurate description would be a problem with a joint. There are different forms of arthritis and the two most common are: osteoarthritis (OA) and rheumatoid (RA), which is categorized as an inflammation joint disease that affects the smaller joints typically found in the hands, elbows and feet. RA has a greater occurrence in women. The non-inflammation OA disease refers to a degenerative joint disease that affects the larger joints such as the hips, knees, ankles and spine. Most adults over age 65 are affected by OA to some degree and this is increased in athletes due to the wear and tear after years of competition.

The obvious question might be if OA is the result of wear and tear on the joints then why is exercise recommended? Certainly caution is advised, as well as, a physician's approval, knowledgeable trainer and proper technique, but there are many potential positive benefits. Proper exercise will increase muscular strength and flexibility, which will ultimately reduce the work load on the joints in everyday living. The increase in bone density will provide blood cell nourishment to the joints and some strength training will increase cardiovascular and upper body strength. That increase in strength is going to help you prevent dangerous falls from routine events like getting out of a chair or from your automobile. If you are having a bad day, with lower body pain, you may be able to do some upper body work. Remember that you will need your triceps to push out of a chair; the grand baby in a stroller; and shoulder strength to carry out the garbage or get out of the tub. You will require all of these to keep from asking someone to help you off the toilet.

Most doctors and experts agree that people with OA should make an effort to exercise at least three times per week; incorporate flexibility training as part of their program; and warm up the body, especially the joints before beginning. Staying active will play a big part in overcoming this obstacle and your efforts to enjoy life in your *Second Fifty*. One final comment: if you need a daily reminder of how much better you would feel if you lost 10 pounds of unwanted body weight then just try walking around the house with a 10 pounds of potatoes strapped to your body. It may be that extra weight that is deteriorating and attacking the joints and not the exercise program. [54]

Fluid intake - it's no surprise that too many drinks, whether water, milk, or other beverages, can be a problem for people with incontinence. However, you can't solve incontinence by severely cutting back on fluids. This can lead to dehydration, constipation, and kidney stones, which can actually irritate your bladder and make symptoms worse. It's important to get the right balance, and many nutritionists recommend about two liters of fluid a day, which is eight 8 ounce glasses. If you're prone to nighttime incontinence, cut back your fluid intake in the evening and drink no fluids after 7:00PM. Remember that alcohol is a diuretic, which causes you to produce more urine and can contribute to more frequent urination. It can irritate the bladder, which is a problem for those with overactive bladder syndrome. Coffee and tea also contain caffeine, which can also act as a diuretic and irritate the bladder. If you love your caffeine, cut back slowly to avoid the withdrawal headaches and other symptoms. Chocolate contains as much caffeine as decaf coffee and excess sugar can also irritate the bladder in addition to carbonated drinks, spicy foods, acidic foods, various medications and artificial sweeteners.

---

[54] Cawood, Frank & Associates (2004) Fitness for Seniors, Frank Cawood & Associates Publishing, Chapter 4, page 83

Panel of Experts question

There was no specific question in this category asked of the *panel* regarding their personal health screenings.

The *panel's* comments ....

The specific information on the topics in this chapter was handled primarily from the research aspect and was not one of the designated questions for the *panel*.

What the research says ....

The Humana Active Outlook Magazine includes a valuable insert that provides a convenient listing of all the prescribed health screenings and shots recommended for seniors. [55]That list for seniors includes the following recommended shots: flu, hepatitis B vaccine, pneumonia and the shingles shot. Cancer screenings include a pap smear, pelvic exam and a thorough skin cancer assessment. The blood work would focus on the HDL, LDL and triglyceride levels. Our bodies must have a specific amount of cholesterol for our hormones, vitamins and other body substances to function properly. Cholesterol builds the outer layer of cells; insulates the nerves; makes sex hormones and converts sunshine to vitamin D. Modifying your diet and incorporating moderate exercise are the best remedies to lower the bad LDL and

---

[55] Humana Staff (Nov 2015) Take Steps to Good Health, Humana Active Outlook Magazine, 2014 (July) Retrieved from http://www.humana.com/medicare-support/benefits/health-resources/

triglycerides. Humana's Health Watch, chief of quality, Dr. George Andrews, targets saturated fat as the instigator in making too much bad cholesterol. (LDL) This sluggish, bad cholesterol, over time, turns into plaque that clogs the arteries and increases your risk for heart disease and stroke. The good cholesterol or HDL picks up excess cholesterol and routes it to the liver where it is broken down. Another substance in the blood, which has a negative effect on the body, is a type of fat called triglycerides.[56] Statins are medicines designed to lower the cholesterol in the body and provide some protection against heart attack and strokes. It is estimated that one in four Americans, over age 45, are taking them. They work to combat the bad cholesterol or LDL in the liver, but they do have potential side effects and regular liver function tests are recommended to monitor their use. The side effects that may accompany the use of statins are: muscle cramps, muscle soreness and eye problems.

Finally, the U.S. Library of Medicine National Institutes of Health stated in Resistance training is medicine: effects of strength training on health, that sedative seniors can expect a 3-8% muscle loss per decade with a decrease in metabolism that promotes an accompanying fat increase. The benefits of regular exercise to seniors were a quicker walking speed, increase in metabolism, fat loss, greater functional independence, improved cognitive abilities and a more positive self- esteem. The article indicated that a short 10- week program could add three pounds

---

[56] Andrews, George Dr. Nov 2015) Humana Inc., Chief of Quality, Retrieved from http://www.linked,com/in/georgeandrews

of muscle, a loss of four pounds of fat and a one to three percent increase in bone density.[57]

The bottom line ....

The natural process of aging will eventually affect every person alive, regardless of their genetic gifts, wealth or personal status. The most important insurance policy you can give yourself is to schedule the recommended health screenings that we have discussed. You may not be able to avoid all of the pitfalls, as you approach the *Second Fifty*, but you can certainly be proactive in your own defense. Regular screenings can detect abnormalities in your body and the onset of illness much earlier, which improves the odds of beating the problem. You have spent a lifetime prioritizing the care of your family, home, career and thinking of others so don't forget to take care of yourself. There are quality years ahead and the best option is to maintain your health at all cost.

We want to clarify that no one on the *panel* is in the medical profession and we are certainly not qualified to give out medical advice. The information we have provided comes from reputable sites that should be of interest and will benefit you in the long run. Do your research and seek the best medical care possible, as you anticipate a problem, or when one arises. You

---

[57] Westcott, WL National Institutes of Health Staff (Jul-Aug 2012) Resistance Training is Medicine: Effects of Strength Training on Health Retrieved from http://www.nchi.nim.nih.gov/pubmed/ 22777332

know your body better than anyone else. Always tell your health care team about any changes in your health, including your *vision* and *hearing*. Ask them about being checked for any condition you are concerned about, not just the ones your visit is for. If you are wondering about diseases such as *glaucoma*, or *skin cancer*, for example, be sure to ask about them.

Other suggestions that will benefit you are: staying physically active, working on a healthy target weight, lowering your Body Mass Index (BMI), creating a healthy eating plan, abstaining from all tobacco products and limiting your alcohol, especially the hard stuff.

Tom remembers observing his great grandfather, who lived with his family, eating lunch with two of his brothers. (great, great uncles) They were all about 90 and drank numerous cups of over boiled black coffee with their heavily buttered rye bread loaded with cheeses and lunch meats. After lunch they listened to the baseball game while drinking lots of beer and limburger cheese. They went to bed early and were also early risers. They had all done their share of physical labor and this was also a typical lifestyle for other seniors back in the 1950s. When health problems were encountered they probably relied on a home remedy or asked the   doctor to make a house call. You only went to the hospital for very serious illnesses, which may have required surgery. For seniors in the 1950s and 60s, life was a survival of the fittest, but in our lifetime we have been witness to some very remarkable progress in the medical field. **Treat yourself as though you have only one life to live, because that is the truth!**

Assessing the Positives and Negatives of the Gene Pool

"The genes are indicators of our possible fortunes and misfortunes"

Statistics from the U.S. Census, Population Reference Bureau, stated in the November 2011 issue of National Geographic that the world population hit the seven billion mark in October of 2011. The article also stated that in 2010 the number of people surpassing the 100 years old mark was approximately 53,364 in the United States, with over 600,000 predicted for 2050. The article stated that a child born today could easily have a fifty- fifty chance of reaching that triple digit milestone. That increase, however, was only estimated for the wealthier, industrialized countries as in the United States, Germany, England, Japan, France and others in that category. Factors mentioned in the article included: early diagnosis of disease, better access to medical care, improved diet and genetics. The ideal candidate for the triple digit club was a female, wealthy, thin, and a non-smoker. [58]

Are you the lucky recipient of a fantastic genetic gift? Unfortunately, none of us were able to screen and select our parents after a genetic assessment. Each year we are expected to

---

[58] US Census Bureau Staff (Nov 2011) World Population Hits 7 Billion, National Georgraphic, 2011 (Nov) Retrieved from http://www.ngm.nationalgeographic.com/2011/11/population-reference-bureau/

have our annual physical and there are a number of key questions asked by the doctor that give him a reasonable indication of the depth of our personal gene pool. Did you parents have cancer …heart disease…diabetes …how old were they when they died? These are some of the common questions. How about your grandparents?

I'm sure we would all like to respond that both of our parents lived to be in their 90s with no known cancer, heart, stroke or other diseases other than old age impairments like some hearing and visual problems. If your parents and grandparents had great mobility into their 90s and were very physically active and mentally alert you may have inherited a genetic edge. We all have pluses and minuses in dealing with our genetic propensities that will figure somewhat into the total picture and future years of our health. It is a fact of life that the older seniors have already outlived many of their friends and family members. Tom had an interesting story on his father and grandfather that emphasizes that point. Tom remembers his father, Harry (70s) having words with his grandfather, John, (97) about frequenting the same hangouts and sharing many of the same friends. Tom's father asked his father, "John, why don't you hang out with your own friends." Tom's grandfather replied, "I would, but the cemetery is a lonely place."

The hot tip ….

Severe hearing loss nearly quintuples the risk of dementia! The loss of hearing can have a devastating effect on family dynamics and the social life of the affected person. There are many new technologies that can help and sometimes provide short term remedies for hearing loss, but we feel that it is important to provide more detail to this dreaded condition that often goes untreated. Our recommendation is to make sure you have a thorough hearing assessment on your next scheduled wellness, physical exam. [59]

Aging is a fact of life, but there is unfortunately, an end date for everyone. We can all share examples of the 90 year olds who still looks pretty good, stays very active, participates in activities that keep them mentally alert, lives independently, drives a car and has no serious illnesses. That is a great picture to keep in your mind as you slowly progress towards those elusive triple digits. There are always going to be pitfalls that threaten to disrupt that positive path you have embarked on, but you must stay focused and true to yourself. Take care of your health by scheduling regular wellness visits and make sure to keep a schedule of all the suggested screenings. Try to surround yourself with others of the same mind set, regardless of their age. Remember that old adage that "birds of a feather flock together." Set quarterly and yearly goals so you are also moving forward with your mind on some special activity. Finally, don't forget to reward yourself when you achieve a goal and be the best example possible for your family.

---

[59] Peeples, Lynne (15 Feb 2011) Hearing Loss May Be an Early Sign of Dementia, Retrieved from http://www.cnn.com/2011/health/02/14 .loss.dementia.health/index.html

Chapter 10

Especially for the Female

Early women icons in physical culture

The earliest known women of the fitness world were known as the "old time strong women," which was not the most complimentary nickname. This timeframe was at the turn of the 19th century (late 1800s) when female school teachers were forbidden to marry, wore black dresses, high top black shoes and had strict rules as to dress and behavior. The old time strong women were truly the first fitness examples for their gender, but they performed in relative obscurity, unless you were a physical culture advocate. They showed that women could be strong, agile, very athletically talented and also very feminine. Because their skills were so unusual, for that era, the women usually performed in side shows, carnivals, circuses, and vaudeville. We have listed several examples of these remarkable athletic prototypes in the fitness or physical culture world. These women lifted heavy barrels, bent a variety of metal objects, lifted thousands of pounds on platforms that consisted of horses or spectators, wrestled, boxed, were capable of trapeze and acrobatics feats, lifted heavy dumbbells overhead, as well as, maintaining outstanding physiques. This was a hundred years ago when women did not have the right to vote until 1920 and very few women worked outside the home. That unrealistic stereotype for women actually existed through the 1950s and most of us can remember the role of our mothers and women in our early neighborhoods. Your authors attended the same inner city high school, in the mid- 60s, and can remember the dress code where girls wore dresses and the boys dress type pants. No jeans! Fortunately, we have all witnessed that equitable transition in our lifetimes. Jack LaLanne is credited as one of the first physical gurus, in the 1960s and 70s, to advocate **that women could train in the same gym and in the same room with men!** Before that time opportunities for women were very limited. After 1980 we saw the women's pentathlon and heptathlon events enter the era of the modern Olympics and high schools, colleges and universities began to offer a wide array of female athletic opportunities. A very limited number of women fitness gurus, athletes and bodybuilders had entered the gym scene in the 1940s and 50s, but by the 1970s they ladies were competing in a variety of national contests which helped change that outdated perception.

The Great Sandwina – born Kate Brumbach, in Austria in the late 1800s, she took her name in honor of the great strongman, Eugene Sandow. She wrestled men, lifted weights, bent iron bars and horseshoes with the Ringling Brothers Circus. She was able to perform many of these feats until she was 64 years old. Sandwina's bio states she was 6'0'' tall and with a pair of 17'' biceps that could lift a 165 pounds overhead with one arm.

Minerva – born Josephine Blatt in Hamburg, Germany she was considered the world's strongest woman, by the Guinness Book of World Records, in 1893. She was capable of breaking chains, catching cannonballs and lifting heavy weights. At the Bijou Theater, in Hoboken, New Jersey Minerva completed a platform lift of 3,564 pounds. She was also known to push horse carts uphill that were stuck in the mud.

Annette Busch – born in Estonia she was employed by the Russian Circus. Annette broke chains, bent coins and iron bars, wrestled a live bull to the ground and traveled to Japan to learn the basics of Sumo Wrestling.

Marie Ford – born in 1900 in New York City she was involved in track and field, acrobatics, running marathons, and "pankration," which was an early form of mixed martial arts, (MMA) that combined wrestling and boxing.

Other strong women of note included: Miss Apollina (Belgium), Marina Lurs (Estonia), Charmion (USA), Luisita Leers Krokel (Germany), Athleta Van Huffelen (Belgium), Vulcana (Wales).

Wikipedia (Public Domain) and Physical Culturist

Pictured above is Luisita Leers Krokel, from Germany. She was an outstanding trapeze artist whose specialty was the *iron cross*. She performed for various German circuses and eventually the Ringling Brothers / Barnum and Bailey Circus until 1936 when Germany was disrupted with the build – up to WW II.

Pictured above is Vulcana from Wales. She was 5'-4" tall and could one hand press a 125- pound dumbbell overhead with one arm. She also did a backbend; had a wooden platform placed on her body; and then had two horses walk onto the platform.

Pictured below are two photos of the Great Sandwina from Austria. She stood 6'-0" tall with a pair of 17" biceps capable of lifting a 165 -pound dumbbell overhead with one hand.

Wikipedia (Public Domain) and Physical Culturist [60]

---

[60] Physical Culturist (13 Aug 2013) Top 10 Old Time Strong Women, Retrieved from http;//www.physicalculturist

Panel of Experts questions # 13 and 14

What special advice or comments can you make regarding the female over 50 and are the priorities for women different than for men?

The *panel's* comments ....

Terry Collis – The sparring is not as aggressive as with the men, although the exercises may be the same, however. Some women may take advantage of this & hit the men harder. Warmups, katas, and techniques must be the same so the only difference is sparring.

Devorah Dometrich – Herbst - Warmups, katas, techniques are the same with the only difference being in sparring.

Dave Guidugli – The woman over 50 will of course go through menopause which will cause some bloating and hormone levels to fluctuate. They may be moody at times and have to fight weight gain. There will also be those difficult areas like the triceps, gluts, and back of thighs.

Ray Hughes - I don't see why women would train any differently than men. There would be some modifications in the throwing and grabbling that is involved in judo.

Lanny Julian – Women have other issues like osteoporosis and bone density issues. These can be addressed through resistance training and proper nutritional supplements. The same advice for men and the younger trainees still applies.

Roger Riedinger - Train on a basic weight training course as noted in #11 above. Forget specialized exercises to tighten up the body part that you are agonizing over. What you should do is a complete course of basic exercises in a systematic manner of progression. And stay with it, 3 days a week, every week. A heavy, light, medium system would be best for women as their energy seems to vary more than men on a day to day basis.

I don't think so. Because women usually have not pursued a regular weight training program, they can experience even greater benefits in promoting bone density and combating age related muscle loss.

Jerry Auton – Osteoporosis has to be taken into account for this age group. Avoid conditions and training that places undue stress on the skeletal system. Ex. Female runners suffer many times the leg stress fractures as men.

Plan your work and work your plan with the help of a professional trainer. Seek a trainer that is certified for Senior Fitness. Many in this age group will qualify for the "Silver Sneakers" ® programs offered by many insurance companies. Those free memberships, to the over 65 crowd, will free up money that can be used to hire a trainer. Make your training routine a good habit because they can be as difficult to break as a bad one. Try to work out three to five times per week and take off enough time to fully recuperate. I recommend 60% cardio and 40% strength /resistance training on the same day.

Tom Geimeier - I've coached women's track and field, soccer and a few bodybuilders and powerlifters. Like anyone else they need motivation and realistic goals. Women over 50 have some common problem areas, but also a few of special concern. Triceps sag, cellulite buildup on the hamstrings, lower back and the buttocks are frequent concerns. The inside of the thighs will lose muscle tone and is problematic for the ladies. During and after the child bearing years the abdomen and lower belly lose their elasticity. Hormonal changes and weight gain accentuate these problem areas.

The benefits of strength and resistance training for women of all ages are many, but for the senior female they are even more important. Strength and weight training can be great allies in the fight against loss of stability and balance. It is no secret that a high percentage of injuries occur from falls in women over the age of 50. Most of these falls are from the lack of balance or stability that could be prevented by utilizing some form of resistance training. Unfortunately, many of these falls are resulting in broken hips and other bones that can result in months of rehab and recovery time. Some can even result in permanent limitations that require the lifelong need for a walker or wheelchair.

Strength training for the senior female is even more important and needed for confidence and physical independence. The life expectancy for females is roughly seven years longer than for males and the need for **living safely alone** will eventually require the best of abilities to move freely about. No one wants excessive limitations in performing everyday activities they enjoy like shopping, babysitting grandchildren, walking, working out, traveling, cooking, gardening and many other enjoyable daily functions. Staying active will also reduce stress levels while improving mood. If you are a female possibly living alone it will be a great asset and confidence builder to stay in good physical condition. **The statistics are very clear that as we age the women will definitely outlive and outnumber the men.**

Maintaining a good dedicated physical training routine will help you continue your independence and not count on the generosity or help of family, professionals and friends to complete your daily activities. In other words, a strength workout performed at least three times a week for a minimum of just 30-45 minutes can provide this for you.

For the female, the menopausal years create more reasons for needing to stay in shape. These years vary by person, but usually occur between the ages of 45-55, and hormonal changes that occur in the body give most women a double whammy. These hormonal changes cause muscle loss combined with weight gain. If you have never exercised before now is the time to start! Consult your physician for clearance to exercise, as we have frequently advised, and don't be afraid to start at this stage of your life. Remember that your age is just a number, but the clock is ticking! Many senior citizens don't start a fitness regime until they are 60, 70, and even older. Add quality to your life by re-energizing and spending more of those "golden years" having a good time. Look at your exercise time as the vehicle that will give you the ability to continue enjoying living. Don't be one of those negative seniors who will be spending much of their time in doctor's offices and bragging about their various medical maladies.

We've given you some important reasons to begin strength training several times per week, but have you read the statistics on osteoporosis? This is another great reason to do everything possible to fend off the natural effects of aging. Osteoporosis is a natural aging effect that results in the loss of calcium than will lessen bone density and weaken the bones. Women are the most susceptible for this disease because of the menstrual cycle and the bone loss that occur after menopause which increases the risk of fractures. Most cases require a doctor's advice that may include improved diet, nutritional supplements, hormone therapy and exercise. Exercise is also very important at this stage to strengthen the ligaments and tendons that are attached to the bones and improve balance, and stability, in addition to the strength component. That combination will work well together to hopefully reduce falls and possible injury.

The female readers will find throughout this book that exercise and a healthy lifestyle go hand in hand. Diet is an essential part of that lifestyle! Managing a proper optimum nutritional diet plan is similar to managing your money. You will need to invest wisely and think in the long term. Many seniors, of both genders, frequently say they are busier after retirement than during the working years, but the truth is you will have the necessary physical training time on your hands. Seniors will need to have more self- discipline than ever before to avoid bad food choices like overeating, mindless snacking and drinking habits. If you have never been willing to start a nutritious, sensible diet you will need to realize that now is the time to start! Don't wait until tomorrow or next week, but now! In reality, you are the only person in charge of your life and with the power to make that decision.

Jerry recently visited several very busy, well known restaurants, at dinner time and made a casual observation of the customers eating habits. Jerry purposely kept his head down and focused his attention at the waist levels of the people passing by. He made his notations on index cards that indicated whether the person appeared average or obese and those casual, non- scientific observations clearly indicated that 75 percent were visibly obese. America is noted as one of the most obese countries on the planet and America is also said to have the most obese, unhealthy poor people on earth. Statistics on life expectancy have the United States listed as 37th overall with a life expectancy of between 77 and 78 years. The top 15 to 20 countries on the list had expectancies of 82 to 83 years. **How is that possible for one of the top three industrialized countries in the world?**

The American public simply eat too much of the wrong foods and appear to have no discipline when it comes to managing a balanced diet. Many families eat their evening or main meal "on the run" or from a fast food restaurant on a daily basis. The overabundance of useless carbohydrates and the most dangerous types of fats have a dramatic and significant effect on their health. Unfortunately, that cycle of self- destruction is often very early imbedded in the minds of the children. Do not be a part of that group! Sure, as a senior female you statistically should out live your spouse and male friends, but make today the time you change that sedentary, lazy lifestyle. Make today the day you begin a new life of routine change in habits (good ones), exercise and diet.

What the research says ....

Realize that a person's skeletal or bone structure cannot be changed. Many females may want to trim their hips, although wide hips tend to be trendy today. **Remember that when reducing any body part or area you cannot reduce any farther than bone!** If you have large arms, thighs or calves it is

217

important to keep them firm with exercise and dropping a few pounds will also aid your efforts. Don't be a slave to the tape measure! Ideal measurements only apply to someone's perception of the perfect body type. On a tall woman they would make her very thin and on a short female too large. Be happy with your uniqueness and work with what you have. You cannot change genetics and the real focus should be on better health, fitness and living an energetic and active life. There are numerous charts available that will provide insight about your type of bone structure. The measurements required for structure identification are taken at the key joint areas. (wrists, elbows, knees, ankles, hips)

An article at *Livestrong.com*, by Jae Allen, was geared for the females and recommended consulting your doctor as a first stop, with a fitness professional as the second. The article was adamant that weight training was **not advised for pregnant women! Weight training was also not advised if the person had a hernia, high blood pressure, a recent surgery or perhaps a hysterectomy.** [61]

Parting and heartfelt advice is to beware of quick fixes and instant results. The condition you are in did not happen overnight, whether good or bad. The ads for the fad diets that bombard the magazines and TV programs may have some benefits, but a basic truth is they have made millions upon millions for their promoters. We actually like the variety and creativity of many of the exercise programs advertised on the TV infomercials. We

---

[61] Allen, Jae (13 march 2013) Is Lifting Weights Bad for Women?) Retrieved from http://www.livestrong.com/article/365618/Is-Lifting-Weights-Bad-for-Women/

believe trainers have become smarter over the years and the programs seem to combine the best attributes fitness seekers are after. The downside is you must have a starting point and that is a slow, progressive, safe and injury free approach. Don't think that when your CDs arrive you will be maxing out with the group promoting the programs on TV. You will need to be in decent shape to begin those aggressive programs and your mentality should be to be satisfied with consistent, progressive results. Keep your goals high and visualize your end point realizing that success will come in steps, not leaps and bounds.

The International Sports Sciences Association (ISSA) article states that the number one killer of women and men is heart disease. Breast cancer is actually ranked as number two. The article mentioned that the National Institute of Health, at Stanford University is spending 628 million dollars on a study of the health habits of women 50-79. One of the components of the study is whether hormone replacement can protect against bone fractures, but at the expense of increasing the likelihood of breast cancer. A large segment of the study will focus on diet, vitamins and calcium on breast, colon and rectal cancer. [62]

The bottom line ....

The good news for females is that every statistical survey indicates that they will outlive their male counter parts by seven to eight years. That also leads to the conclusion that the number

---

[62] Knopf, Karl, EdD (2010) Women's Health, International Sports Sciences Handbook, Senior Fitness Course, Carpenteria, NY: International Sports Sciences Pub. Ch.3, pg. 27

of females in senior citizen centers, assisted living communities and eventually nursing homes will vastly outnumber males. Many females will be living independently and to maintain maximum functionality their decisions regarding exercise and diet are crucial to extend those quality golden years.

The hot tip ….

Find physical activities that you will enjoy, as soon as possible, and make those positive decisions lifelong habits. There are many female, group exercise programs available in every gym and fitness center that will combine balance, flexibility, cardio and some resistance /strength training. Our observations, in many environments, indicate that the group sessions also offer some comradery and socialization benefits.

Distribution of Subcutaneous Fat in Males and Females

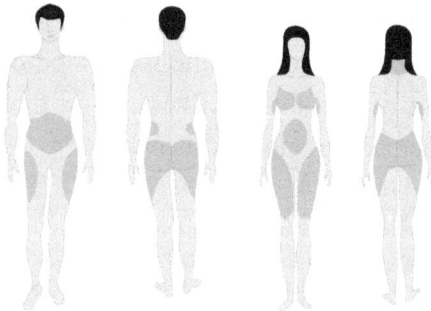

Mean Percentage Body fat by Age Group and Gender [63]

---

[63] US Government Office Site -CDC: Quick Stats "Mean Percentage Body Fat by Age Group and Sex, Retrieved from:
http://www.cdc.gov/mmwr/preview/mmwrhtml/mm 5751a4.htm

Chapter 11

Nutrition and Supplementation

"There is a tremendous correlation regarding health and nutrition which is proven time and time again"

There is no mystical, magical "Fountain of Youth." People have been looking for that elusive location since the days of Ponce de Leon and have found absolutely nothing. Today, people around the world are taking a variety of nutritional supplements; modifying their diets; taking experimental drugs; undergoing plastic surgery; using a variety of beauty products and trying a plethora of physical training systems in their quest to offset the effects of the aging process. The infomercials on TV offer a variety of systems that are guaranteed to get you into fantastic shape within a very short time frame. Health, fitness, beauty, looking better and feeling better are multi- billion dollar businesses. People are willing to spend a small fortune in their quest of retaining their physical appearance, youthfulness, vigor and fighting off the effects of the aging process.

I'm sure most Americans are unaware of how dramatically their life expectancy has increased in the last 50 years. Before 1900 the average life expectancy in America was 46 years old! Anyone making it to 80 or 90 was considered a marvel and probably the possessor of a great genetic gift. Between 1900 and 1950 the life expectancy in the United States went from 46 to 72. Before 1900 75% of the population died before 65. Today, 70% will live past 70. The average height of a Civil War soldier was 5'-5" while the average height today is 5'-10" for men and 5'- 6" for women. An

221

interesting sidebar is that the heights of today are the same as in pre -history, but the effects of protein on attaining full body potential will be discussed in other paragraphs. That is almost unbelievable, but there are reasonable causes for these phenomena. The main reason for this improved longevity is believed to be the conquering of infectious diseases. Other factors that have influence are: reduced infant mortality, improved diets, better access to doctors and hospitals, refrigeration and a balanced day that divides your typical day into equal periods of work, rest and social time. Further research also lends credence that if a person reaches 70 in a reasonable healthy condition they can expect to live at least another 12 years. [64]

The main cause of death in 2015, for men and women, was not the dreaded Cancer, but heart disease. The all- important immune system of the human body is controlled by the diet, which can be a positive or negative and the body's primary defense against disease is a strong functioning immune system. The effectiveness and efficiency of this defense mechanism is controlled by diet, especially the quality and quantity of that diet.

Research will dictate that the best formula for optimal health at any age, but especially after 50, is to avoid dehydration by drinking at least 64 ounces of water daily; taking essential vitamins and minerals; dedicating yourself to daily moderate

---

[64] National Institute on Aging Staff (22 Jan 2015) Global Health and Aging- Living Longer, Retrieved from
http://www.nia.nih.gov/research/publication/global-health-and-aging/

exercise; reducing stress and cutting the empty over loaded carbohydrates from you daily habits. [65]

Free radicals are an important part of cells we should try to understand. Free radicals are molecules that have an unpaired electron and seek out other molecules to bond with. This has to do with the oxygen atoms in the body. They attack other molecules and may affect DNA, proteins and fats. The damage that can be done is similar to the effects of radiation on the human body, whether by a nuclear bomb or the typical radiation used in Cancer treatments. Popular supplements that are helpful in neutralizing the negative effects of free radicals are anti- oxidants like Vitamins C, E, and supplements like CoQ10.

Recommended daily supplements may also include: fish oil capsules, magnesium, a good daily vitamin –mineral supplement with B3, B6, folic acid, beta carotene, calcium, chromium, selenium and zinc. Many people take a variety of herbs (ex. garlic, licorice, ginger, gingko) and there is a word of caution here. Most of our original medicines came from herbs before being synthesized in the laboratories. That is why the destruction of the Rain Forest could have a devastating effect on our planet and other eventual break through medical discoveries. Herbs are basically drugs and consultation is advised before doing a hit and miss or experimental approach with you as the guinea pig.

Remember that one of the keys when selecting quality health food supplements is the quality and the potency of the tablets,

---

[65] Anne, Melodie (26 Sept 2015) How Much Water Should I Drink for Weight Training, Retrieved from http://www.livestrong.com/article/462716-how-much-water-should-i-drink-for-weight-training/

capsules, or soft gels. One bottle might say one capsule equals 100 milligrams and another bottle may offer a 200 milligram dose. Closer inspection of the label often states you will need to take 2 capsules to obtain the 200 mgs. If the dosage isn't doubled then you can be sure the size of the pill, capsule or soft gel certainly is. Make sure you read the labels and make an intelligent comparison considering the dosage, source, price, and potency.

Tom's first association with Roger was in the mid -1970s when they were both teachers and track coaches. Tom worked for a small class A school and Roger worked at a larger inner city class AAA school. Roger was a former Kentucky discus champion and later on won the Masters Mr. USA bodybuilding title. Sandy was a former track star and was working as a dental hygienist with a passion for bodybuilding and nutrition. Tom started the Northern Kentucky Bodybuilding Championships in 1978 and a few years later Tom, Roger, Sandy, and Tom's wife Mary worked together on a number of sanctioned AAU contests. At the 2012 contest, usually held in March, it was announced that the Northern Kentucky had grown to the largest one- day bodybuilding event in America. Tom and Roger were also co-chairs of the Kentucky AAU Physique Committee for several years. After Roger retired as a school administrator he purchased and became the sole owner of Beverly International Health Supplements. The Beverly name is well respected and regarded as one of the highest ranked health food companies, in the world, in terms of quality, variety of product, purity and specific design. Roger and Sandy have several publications that deal with bodybuilding and fitness and they should be recognized for their integrity and as two of the most committed, knowledgeable, and honest people in the business. At the beginning of each annual Northern Kentucky Bodybuilding event Roger and Sandy present a very large check to a representative from Cincinnati Children's Hospital in Cincinnati. (that amount has exceeded well over $100,000 the past four years)

Because of our relationship with Roger and Sandy and their integrity, we asked them to have heavy input into our Chapter on Nutrition and Supplementation. Their response was quick, positive and we are honored to have their professional input. Please heed their advice and take it to heart. It may be the best nutritional advice you will ever receive and has been distributed to thousands of clients through their various publications.

Before going into the specifics of your nutrition program it is important to understand the following basics: (Previously posted in **No- Nonsense Muscle (NNM 18 issue 3 articles)**

- Genetics determine your ultimate potential. Your goal should be to reach your own personal peak potential.
- Proper nutrition is 80% of the battle
- There is no quick fix as often promised in ads by those desiring to make a quick buck in the bodybuilding magazines or through massive "junk mailings" of special offers on a new supplement that is supposed to be the best thing since steroids.
- You do not live off of supplements alone because they are available to bring your nutrition to its optimum level.
- Supplements, however, are the catalysts that make it all go. Proper supplements and timing of intake are important.

- Cycling your supplements is important. Although many supplement companies would like you to think that taking a single miracle optimizer drink or a couple of capsules of one "magic formula" is all you need, don't believe it. Just as your training program is designed to maximize your adaptive response so you must take your supplements at the optimum times to take advantage of your metabolism and regeneration cycles.
- Since you are looking to add quality muscle gains, the food sources you use should also be of the highest quality.
- In order to maximize your nutritional needs, you must first determine how many calories per day it presently takes to maintain your current level of lean muscle, fat, and total bodyweight. This can best be accomplished by purchasing a calorie counter and charting your daily food intake over the course of a seven to ten- day period to determine your average daily caloric intake. Once you have established this figure, increase your calories 300 to 500 per day to gain one pound per week. Conversely, reduce your calories 300 to 500 per day to lose fat. Chart your weight daily to determine your individual calorie requirement. Weigh at the same time daily.

Sample Meal Structure

We recommend that you eat five or more meals daily spaced two and one-half to three hours apart. Your meals should include foods from the categories listed below. The specific ratio of nutrients from each category will depend on your particular training phase and body composition goals.

1. **Protein Foods** - Most of your protein should come from fresh, lean protein sources such as chicken breast, turkey breast, lean beef (flank or round steak, 90% lean ground beef), fish, eggs, (egg whites in particular), and low-fat cottage cheese.

2. **Complex Carbohydrate Foods** - The best sources of foods under this heading are oatmeal, rice, potatoes, sweet potatoes, beans (white, pinto, kidney black or lima) corn and peas.

3. **Fibrous Vegetables** - This category includes green and yellow vegetables. The sources we use most often are asparagus, broccoli, raw carrots, cauliflower, cucumbers, green beans, lettuce, spinach, and zucchini.

4. **Fruit** - Although many bodybuilding nutrition authorities omit fruit from their recommended diets we consider it a valuable source of fiber, vitamins, minerals, and energy. Recommended fruits are apples, bananas, blueberries, cantaloupe, grapefruit, kiwi, oranges, pears, and strawberries.

5. **Dietary Fats** - Make sure you include essential fatty acids (EFAs) in your nutrition plan. They are they essential for health all the way down to the cellular level and EFAs also help in building muscle and fat reduction. Good sources are cold water salmon, walnuts, flax and borage oil.

Nutritional Supplement Basics

Supplementation is a vital part of maximizing physical training and development. Supplements are not even close to steroids no matter what the ads claim. If you're looking for some miracle to happen by taking a particular supplement, you're probably going to be disappointed. Nutritional supplements do play a key role, however, in muscle development. They are the catalysts that can maximize your nutrition. Their benefits include increased growth, decreased body fat, improved endurance, and reduction of destructive cellular processes that hold back your progress. It is virtually impossible to get the nutrients required for optimum muscle growth through food intake alone. But when you eat properly and train intensely, supplements will accelerate muscle growth beyond what dietary food intake alone can provide allowing you to reach new limits in strength and development.

Building muscle at the fastest rate possible requires excellent nutrition and excellent supplementation. The proper combination of supplements taken at the proper time can play a pivotal role in the assimilation and utilization of your food sources. At **Beverly International** we have extensively studied and researched the field of nutritional supplementation. We've found many beneficial supplements and many more that are only beneficial to the pocket book of the manufacturer. The **Beverly** formulas are the result of this research and experimentation.

Nutrition

I recommend a higher protein intake and moderate to low carbs for those over 50 who are trying to build muscle and strength while losing fat.

30 grams of protein per meal is the minimum you should shoot for and 4–6 meals per day. Some current research shows that the older person may need more protein than the younger one, so don't be afraid to go up to 50 grams of protein in a meal.

Unfortunately, as we grow older, our metabolism does slow down a little. It becomes more important that we watch our caloric intake. I'd estimate 12–13 calories per pound of bodyweight is about right if your goal is to add muscle and strength while tightening up. Keep your total carbs under 150 grams per day on most days.

Supplements

Many of **Beverly International's** best clients are in the 40, 50 and 60 age brackets. I think one of the reasons for this is these guys have been around, tried it all, and settled on what works.

Editors' note –the products mentioned above are formulated by Beverly International and have the highest level of quality and purity. There are other brands available on the market, but we recommend checking the labels to see if they actually meet the same standards.

Final Thoughts from Roger

We hope that this article has given you some new thoughts and insight regarding strength training and muscle building for those over 50. [66]

Things you should know about fats

Energy is stored in the body in fat from excess food. Fats are solid at room temperature. Fats are needed by the body as insulators and to absorb shock. Fats may store unabsorbed drugs from years ago. Most saturated fats are from animal fats and should be very limited in your diet. Unsaturated fats are from mostly plant oils, with the exception of coconut and palm oil. Fatty acids in the body can suffer oxidation that damages cells and could possibly lead to cancer. The medical community refers to fats as triglycerides. Polyunsaturated fatty acids include omega -3, oleic, linoleic and linolenic acids. These are considered beneficial and may decrease heart disease and some cancers. Cholesterol is increased in the bloodstream by animal fats, trans fats, and other animal products. The recommended daily intake of cholesterol is 200 mg per day and your daily intake of fats should be no more than 25% of your food intake. Recommended levels from your Wellness Visit blood test should be: Total cholesterol 200 mg, LDL 100 mg, HDL 50 mg and Triglycerides 150 mg.

---

[66] Riedinger, Roger (Vol 8) A Basic Course in Nutrition, Body Muscle Journal, 2014 (8) Retrieved from http://www.bodymusclejournal.com/volo8/

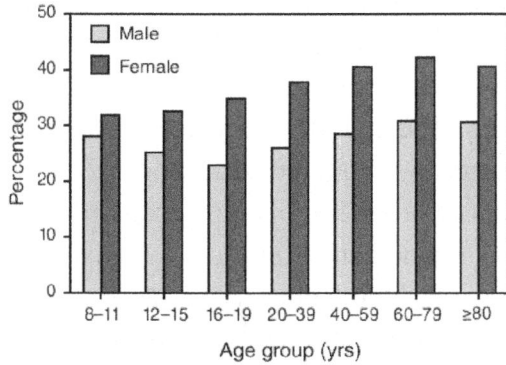

(Above) Body Fat Comparison Chart

Things you should know about protein

The basic building blocks of protein are the amino acids divided into the sub classes of essential and nonessential. There are nine essential amino acids that are not made by the body and are dependent on food intake and supplementation. There are 11 non-essential that can be produced in the body from protein rich foods. **The egg is the standard** by which all other protein measurements are compared. Proteins are subdivided into complete and plant proteins. A complete protein contains all essential amino acids and if the source is easily digestible it is referred to as a high-quality. Plant proteins are of a lower quality, but it is recommended to add or compliment the complete proteins. The recommended daily intake for females and males, over 50, is 0.8 g/kg of bodyweight.

Things you should know about carbohydrates

Carbohydrates usually make up the largest daily food group. They also supply the body with a steady supply of energy. Excess carbohydrates are stored in the body as fat. Carbohydrates are classified as sugars or starches and are further subdivided into three classes: monosaccharides, disaccharides and polysaccharides. The complex polysaccharides must be broken down into disaccharides or monosaccharides to be utilized by the body. The Glycemic Index (GI) ranks carbohydrates according to their effect on blood sugar levels. Low Glycemic carbs have little effect on the blood glucose or sugar level, while high Glycemic carbs can have severe effects, especially if someone's weight has spiraled out of control. The ideal diet should have a majority of low Glycemic carbs and a good source is fibrous fruits and vegetables.

Reading the Food Labels

Remember that the ingredients on a food label are listed in order according to the volume or percent of each. (ex. If sugar is the main ingredient by volume then it must be listed first) There are many government loopholes companies take advantage of regarding the accuracy of their labeling. A .5 or less gram of a specific ingredient may be regarded as a zero. The wise consumer should take a minute or two to look over the labels and beware of products that promote: fat free, sugar free, zero trans- fat, free range, immunity booster, all natural, no sugar added or multi grain. The benefits you actually seek from a particular product may actually have other contained items that neutralize the advertised advantages and may have negative health consequences.

The most important ingredients for a consumer to scrutinize are: size, fats, calories, sodium content, fiber, sugars, vitamins and minerals.

- Size – the data listed on food packages is for specific portions, often smaller than the average person consumes.
- Fats – look for the healthier unsaturated fats. Saturated or trans-fat can elevate bad cholesterol (LDL) and decrease your good cholesterol. (HDL)
- Calories – high calorie content alone can often be deceiving. Be sure to look at the total number of nutrients included, which should take precedence over calories.
- Sodium – an excess of this ingredient can elevate blood pressure, which increases the risk of stroke and heart disease. The recommended daily value (DV) may be 2300 mg, but 800 is preferred.
- Sugars – labels usually do not differentiate between natural sugars like fructose (fruit) and lactose (milk) from the negative added sugars like corn syrup. Strive for the natural and avoid products that have multiple sources of sugar added.
- Fiber – The key word here is whole grain and not multi grain or enriched.
- Vitamins and minerals – A worthwhile nutritional product should contain at least 10-20 percent of the daily value for those specific vitamins and minerals.

Body Mass Index (BMI)

This is a common assessment tool to determine if your body weight, muscle mass and amount of body fat are in the proper, recommended proportions. A determination of your BMI can be made by multiplying your weight, in kilograms, by your height in meters. The normal BMI categories for those over 50 are:

Females (age 40-59) = 23-33.9   Females (age 60-79) = 24-35.9

Males (age 40-59) = 11-21.9   Males (age 60-79) = 13-24.9

A lower BMI would indicate an underweight condition that may not be in your best interest, while a higher BMI would indicate being overweight. A very high of over 40 for females and over 30 for males would indicate an obese condition.

CoQ10 (coenzyme Q10)

A research report, on CoQ10, by *Life Extension Magazine* regarding the Longevity Factor, states the user could potentially add nine years to your life expectancy. CoQ10 is one of the most popular supplements in Japan and one that has been very popular in the U.S. for about 10 years. The main basis for taking CoQ10 is for heart and vascular health, but the research indicates that CoQ10 is an important antioxidant that can reduce the oxidation rate in the cellular mitochondria believed responsible for aging. **Antioxidants** are responsible for reducing harmful free radicals that damage the cells and open the body up to a variety of diseases and of course aging. One of the functions of the mitochondria, which are components of the body's cells, is to transfer energy. One of the side effects of this process is oxidation, which creates harmful free or rogue oxygen radicals. Rust is an example of oxidation pertaining to metals and that process, left unchecked is totally destructive. The Japanese also believe CoQ10 can alleviate the onset of Alzheimer's disease, lower blood pressure and alleviate the effects of Parkinson's disease. [67]

CoQ10 can be easily taken as a nutritional supplement, in pill form, in a variety of strengths. (50, 100, 200, mg) CoQ10 is found in a variety of foods (oily fish, organ meats and whole grains), but the aging process has a natural tendency to deplete the body of optimal levels. One of the side effects of taking this supplement is symptoms which mirror a low blood sugar problem, diarrhea, heartburn, rash, and headaches can also appear. Beta blockers and **statins** will decrease the body's ability to absorb and produce CoQ10. Make sure you consult a physician if any of these problems surfaces.

Flaxseed Oil and Fish Oils

Flaxseed oil is an excellent source of omega -3 essential fatty acids needed for optimal functioning of the cardiovascular system, brain, skin, bones, and other vital organs. (linoleic, linolenic, oleic) There are also a variety of fish oils that also provide the same benefits such as Krill Oil, Salmon Oil, Cod Liver Oil etc.

Multi Vitamin /Mineral Tabs

Many nutritionists state that a human being should be able to obtain all the daily required of vitamins and minerals from a well-balanced diet. Unfortunately, times have changed. Many families or groups of people living together do not have regular sit down

---

[67] Life Extension Staff (20 Aug 2015) CoQ10 –The Longevity Factor, Retrieved from http://www. Lifeextension.commagazine/2013/1/CoQ10-The Longevity Factor

type meals, as in prior years. Americans have done an outstanding job of butchering the well- balanced diet. We have also heard doctors state that taking nutritional supplements will only give you expensive urine and they are a waste of money.

Tom was a teacher and school administrator for almost 40 years. The best meal of the day for most of his students was the well balanced lunch with lots of choices including; a full hot lunch, salad bars, fruits, yogurts, and a fast food line with good nutritional choices. He remembers casually surveying students how many ate at least one meal a day with a knife and a fork. Less than half the class raised their hands. Most of the students grabbed their carbohydrate filling grub on the go and grazed on whatever was in the fridge or the cupboards. Most public schools also offered a breakfast programs and at times after school program with snacks. The free and reduced meals in any public school can range from 15-100%. For many students the school programs are the best and possibly the only, full sit down meal of the day.

We agree that a well- planned diet and nutritional plan with plenty of all the food groups on the food pyramid would be ideal, but that is not always the case. We feel strongly that taking daily vitamins and minerals is a great back up insurance plan. Imagine a competitive athlete or anyone training for optimum health and benefits leaving their nutrition to chance.

Chondroitin / Glucosamine/MSM and Hyaluronic Acid

The combination of chondroitin, glucosamine and MSM have been used for years by active people trying to relieve joint pain. The last few years have seen the addition of hyaluronic acid to the mix with increased benefits. Hyaluronic Acid is one of the main ingredients in the synovial fluid, which provides the lubrication for the joints and reduces friction as the joints wear with aging and injury.

Vitamin C

Vitamin C increases antioxidant protection required every day in cells and assists to strengthen capillary membranes. Rose hips are often added because they contain bioflavonoids which help fight free radical damage. Free radicals basically are chemical changes in the cells that promote aging.

Protein Powders

Protein is the most important of all the nutrients. Muscles are 90% protein and this fact alone should show all athletes the value of having ample protein in their diets. Old school athletes believed you needed one gram of protein for every two pounds of bodyweight. Amino acids (22) make up protein and the past 20 years and seen unbelievable refinement in the benefits of taking the individual amino acids. A protein shake also has far less calories than a protein rich meal.

Creatine Powder

Creatine is usually taken in a powder from with a pleasant taste additive. Adding creatine monohydrate to your pre or post workout nutritional plan is advertised to increase strength, muscle performance and endurance, while building lean muscle. Creatine provides energy to the muscle cells which improves workout recovery between sets of exercises; allows greater intensity to be utilized and also the upside of aiding your post workout recovery period. Supplement directions advise the user to mix their creatine with water, fruit juice or their favorite workout drink.

Human Growth Hormone (HGH) Natural Releasers

There have been all sorts of miraculous claims for Human Growth Hormone (HGH), but most appear to be just promotional claims. We recently read an unbelievable advertisement in the *American Legion Magazine* that their miracle HGH would restore hair loss, virility, youthful appearance, lean body mass and more. Obviously a lot of hype and such claims are to be taken with much suspicion, but there are actual benefits and some solid research behind some of the claims. Most health food companies sell a product called a natural HGH releaser, which is supposed to increase the body's HGH hormone levels to what they were years earlier. The theory is if those hormone levels increase then you might regain some of the vitality that you normally lose past age 30. HGH is vital to the healthy aging process and research data verifies that the human body decreases the secretion of HGH after age 30 and two percent per year after that.

Most health food and supplement companies offer these natural HGH releasers as an alternative to the illegal "performance enhancing drugs" (PEDs) that can result in fines, jail time and embarrassment at the end of many stellar athletic careers. The natural HGH releasers report less belly fat, improved skin tone, offsetting the loss of muscle mass and greater all around vitality.

Most companies have formulas that are very similar and with a combination of vitamins, minerals, herbs and amino acids. Other recommendations include: adding 2 grams of the amino acid Arginine two to three times per day; drinking Fenugreek tea several times per day; using a sleep mask to enhance sleep since HGH is produced during deep sleep periods; utilizing weight training as a natural HGH stimulant; intense physical training of various types; weight loss; periodic 12-14 hour fasting and laughter. To insure a good night's sleep, it is advised that you consume no food three hours before bed and drink no caffeine after your last afternoon cup.

Arginine and Ornithine

This combination is believed to stimulate muscle growth. The suggested dosage is two parts L Arginine and one- part L Ornithine. One rare side effect that can occur is the lowering of your blood sugar, which can cause light headedness and dizziness that mirrors a hypoglycemic type of reaction. The Ornithine is needed to maximize the efficiency of the Arginine.

Several years ago Tom was taking a supplement of L Arginine and L Ornithine and had the same hypoglycemic reaction. His morning blood sugar was between 60 and 90 for a period of several weeks (normal 100-125) and there was numbness in his hands and forearms. There was also light headedness and the feeling he was walking on a cloud. The school nurse where he worked thought the symptoms were stroke like and sent him to the hospital. His family doctor ordered an MRA, MRI, ultrasound of my carotid arteries, and a complete physical. The good news was he did not suffer a stroke. He researched the possible side effects for all the supplements he was taking and the culprit seemed to be the Arginine and Ornithine, which he had taken numerous times before. Tom stopped taking that supplement; kept a close eye on his blood sugar and in a few weeks everything was back to normal.

239

Vitamin E

Considered one of the key anti-oxidants associated with heart health. The natural sources through food are high in fat content so the supplement alternatives may be the best option.

Carnitine

Derived from an amino acid and has a primary role in energy production within the mitochondria. It also removes toxins from the cells. There is a decline in the natural mitochondrial function and production, which affects aging. Advocates of this supplement cite improvements in mental function and cognitive related diseases.

Carnisine (a combination of two amino acids)

An anti-oxidant composed of two amino acids (histidine and beta-alanine) that is found naturally in the human body, but whose production is known to decrease with age. The research indicates that this amino acid has the ability to enhance exercise performance, protect against stroke and offers protection to the heart muscles and blood vessels. Dr. Oz has promoted carnisine as the miracle anti-aging pill! Other benefits that have been credited include reducing wrinkles, preventing cataracts and improving brain function. [68]

Anti -Oxidants

A special group of vitamins, minerals and foods that combat the dreaded "free radicals" that are generated by cells as by-products of turning food into energy A specific group of vitamins,

---

[68] Life Extension Staff (20 Aug 2015) Carnosine: A Proven Longevity Factor, Retrieved from lifeextension.com/magazine/2012/6/Carnosine-Proven-Longevity-Factor

minerals and foods that combat "free radicals" that are generated by cells as byproducts of turning food into energy. The "free radicals" can damage cells and genetic material, while other "free radicals" can be the result of exposure to sunlight, the air we breathe or certain foods. The most notable anti -oxidants are: vitamins C, E, beta –carotene, selenium, manganese, coenzyme Q10, lipoic acids, flavonoids and phenols. They work to give extra electrons to the "free radicals," to inhibit oxidation, without turning them into cell scavengers and destroyers. [69]

Urinary / Prostate

An assortment including; cranberry, lycopene, Saw Palmetto, and Stinging Nettles Root.

Women's Health

Supplements recommended strictly for the females would include: calcium to offset bone loss; vitamin D, which is required for calcium to be absorbed; (believed beneficial against breast and colon cancers) omega -3 fatty acids to ward off internal inflammation; and probiotics for gastrointestinal problems.

Men's Health

Recommendations for men include: a multi- vitamin, without iron; a high quality protein powder; creatine for energy, recovery and lean muscle mass; green tea, which is known as a fat fighter; and fish oil for the heart. The higher quality fish oil is more expensive, but does not contain that fishy taste. [70]

---

[69] WebMD Staff (4 June 2014) Antioxidants-Topic Overview, http://www.webmd.com/food-recipes/antioxidants-topic-overview

[70] National Institute on Aging Staff (8 Oct 2015) Healthy Aging, Retrieved from http://www.nia.nih.gov/healthy/publication/dietary-supplements

Cardio vascular

Ribose supplements have been a hot item on the market. The heart needs a supply of ribose to function properly. Ribose aids in the production of cellular compounds needed to create cellular energy.

Beta –carotene

A precursor to vitamin A in the body. Benefits affect the mucus membranes, immune system, eyes, vision, cancers and heart disease.

Lutein and Lycopene

Related to beta-carotene and vitamin A. Often referred to as the eye vitamin and advocates believe serves as an eye filter and can target macular degeneration, cataract formation and retinitis pigmentosa. Research is currently being conducted regarding the benefits against types of cancers, type 2 diabetes and heart disease.

Selenium

Plays a key role in metabolism and believed to be beneficial for prostate cancer, HIV and Crohn's disease. Early research states it may also increase the risk of non- melanoma skin cancers.

Herbs and Spices of Value

One of the most popular we would like to mention is the use of curry. Some companies are currently selling products that offer turmeric and black pepper in a combination as an anti-inflammatory. Curry is a great choice because it offers turmeric, black pepper, nutmeg, cumin, fenugreek, ginger, coriander and clove in one source. Initial reports state that adding this powerful anti- inflammatory to your diet may lower the risk of heart disease, diabetes, sooth the stomach and improve cognitive function. The use of curry, turmeric and other Indian spices has been linked to dietary practices in India called Ayurvedic that attempts to balance the body and the mind. This practice can be documented as far back as 5000 years We suggest adding a little to your snacks, side dishes and doing some personal research.

Anti-Aging Food Factors

A lot of factors come into play when we give in to seriously thinking about living a longer, fuller and healthier life. In recent years there have been a lot of discussions taking place with many who are suddenly realizing that this thing called EXERCISE has a real impact on living longer. Suddenly more *Second Fifty* adults are paying attention and many of these senior citizens are showing up at fitness facilities in numbers greater than ever before. The media and the business community certainly realize the benefits of this new phenomena and are helping to promote this healthy lifestyle for the 'boomer" generation.

We mentioned before that many insurance companies offer the *Silver Sneakers®* program because they understand that motivated "boomers" who exercise regularly and follow a sound nutritional plan will statistically require a lot less outlay of money than a gym membership. Many of these same companies also offer cash incentives for yearly Wellness Visits and home assessments by a visiting nurse program. We're sure you are aware of the discounts that many restaurants and retail businesses have recently began offering on purchases from this age group. They understand that this age group holds a lot of money and are in pretty good financial shape. They need us to support their business interests and are trying to get us to live longer to get a share of our spending. Believe us when we say that you will never see a *teen* discount in your lifetime!

The counter part of exercise in living longer and aging healthier is of course nutrition. The grocery stores have taken due notice and are making more foods available that are healthier choices. Remember the days when you went to the health food store to try to maximize your daily vitamin and mineral intake? Today the buzz words are fresh, natural and organic with every large store presenting an array of these choices. The research on the foods we eat has also reached a new level. Chemists, scientists and the medical professionals have published numerous articles that document the best, as well as, the worst possible foods we consume. The bottom line for those of us who wish to live longer and age healthier is to prioritize nutrition and healthy eating habits alongside of exercise.

In prior days we had the food pyramid that gave us a visual representation of the number of servings of fruits, vegetables, grains, dairy and meat recommended daily for an individual. Today we are hearing about the anti-aging super foods that may not be our favorites and have the best flavor, but are reported to have special benefits. The bio-chemists and scientists now have the ability to analyze many of those common foods and tell us the exact nutrients that may have anti-aging properties. Below are some of the most touted:

- Kale, sardines, berries of all types, spinach, sweet potatoes, quinoa, peppers, curry, turmeric, eggplant and many more.

Panel of Experts questions # 15 and 16

Give us some insight about your beliefs on nutrition? Do the same on the use of dietary supplements.

* **Roger and Sandy Riedinger, from Beverly International, gave us some valuable information on nutritional supplementation. The survey answers below will give us some insight as to the *panels* beliefs. Remember that our *panel* members are not professional nutritionists and many of their recommended supplements are from trial and error or what has worked best for them. Our *panel* members have been unbelievably successful in their athletic pursuits, but we couldn't help wondering if their overall health could have been improved by having a more thorough knowledge of nutrition.**

The *panel's* Comments ....

Terry Collis – I take a One a Day vitamin and a calcium tablet. The doctor advised me to take Fish Oil capsules. I have no special nutrition program. I do tell people to eat a lot of Sushi. No limitations.

Devorah Dometrich - Herbst - I raise beef cattle, but eat very little beef. I eat mostly chicken and fish and avoid "plastic food" like burgers and pizza. I take a daily vitamin and mineral supplement and also a 400 IU Vitamin E.

Dave Guidugli – Your nutrition becomes more important the older you get. Add a lot of fruits and vegetables, no fast food, which may contribute to the increase in Diabetes, due to carbohydrate excess. The problem is a healthy diet is expensive and eating starches is less expensive. Many older people are dehydrated because they limit their fluid intake. Drink more water. I take a One a Day vitamin, fish oil and a mineral tablet with extra calcium.

Ray Hughes - I drink two good beers a day and take in at least 40 oz. of cool water. I drink no sodas and eat no fried food. I may eat fast food once every two years. I also try to eat as much fruit and vegetables as possible. I take no meds or supplements. **Maybe I should be taking something?**

Lanny Julian – My wife and I take a daily vitamin / mineral supplement; fish oil; supplements for bone density; and a glucosamine – MSM- chondroitin supplement for the joints. We also like to have blood work done twice a year to check on our baselines. I eat whatever my wife fixes. Some supplements are necessary, but I adhere to the basics. No type of protein, creatine etc.

Roger Riedinger - Protein is of first importance. Our body is made of protein and in fact, the term protein means "of first importance." Fats, in general, are not as bad for you as the popular thinking purports. Too much of anything is, but many fats are beneficial and in fact, some are essential to life. Learn about healthy fats. Finally, carbohydrates need to be limited to some extent if you wish to lose body fat, especially as you age. Good carbs are those found in their natural state like fruits and vegetable. Processed carbs like sweets and grains are not so good.

(Disclaimer: My wife, Sandy, and I own a nutritional supplement company, Beverly International.) Supplements do not take the place of food that is found in its natural state – eggs, meat, vegetables, and fruit. However, they are very helpful in providing nutrients that we may not get in our normal diet. We have a supplement recommendation chart for various categories of athletes including those over age 50. For over 50 we recommend in this priority: (1) protein (preferably Milk Protein Isolate – a natural milk protein with carbs, sugar, and saturated fat removed), (2) creatine (anti-aging and muscle cell integrity) there have been thousands of studies on the benefits of creatine, and despite the press, the overwhelming majority show benefits for not only muscle and strength, but also neurological and anti-aging benefits, (3) glutamine for recovery and immune system enhancement, (4) HMB, which prevents age related muscle wasting or sarcopenia.

Jerry Auton – Nutrition is vital to good health. Why put forth the sweat and effort of your workouts if you are not going to replenish your system with healthy eating habits. I recommend: drinking 64 oz. of water per day; avoiding junk foods; and consuming plenty of fresh fruits and vegetables. I also take fish oil, Vitamin C and a high quality protein drink several times a day.

Tom Geimeier – Many people say you don't need supplements if you eat right, but that is probably a foolish statement for those over 50. Eating correctly is crucial, but I take a few supplements as an insurance policy and some my family physician thinks are a good idea. I eat a lot of fruits and vegetables and quality grains. I like my egg whites, low fat milk, chicken, fish and some pork. I cut out all beef about four to five years ago. I need to consume more water, which is difficult because I am never thirsty. A friend of mine, Dr. Larry Leslie, told me that some older adults lose their ability to detect thirst and I must force myself. I started adding some lemon and lime juice for a little flavor. Jerry and I have also become big fans of the *Nutri Bullet* for juicing. I currently take a 60 mg low dose Aspirin, several capsules of flaxseed oil, a multi-vitamin tablet, CoQ10, a little creatine in my workout water and an occasional protein shake.

What the research says ....

Roger and Sandy Riedinger are some of the foremost authorities in the country and their Beverly line of nutritional supplements is an international business. The success of that business is very dependent on keeping current on the latest developments in the industry. On a recent visit to the Beverly International headquarters, Roger discussed the extensive research and testing that was done on all new products and to improve those already offered to the public. We will add a few research sites, but are very confident that the information provided by the owners of Beverly is beyond dispute.

The bottom line ....

It is virtually impossible to get the nutrients required for optimum muscle growth through food intake alone. But when you eat properly and train intensely, supplements will accelerate muscle growth beyond what dietary food intake alone can provide allowing you to reach new limits in strength and development. After reading our *panels'* views on nutritional supplementation, our over 50 crowd may want to think hard about adding a few supplements to maximize their exercise efforts. The research has leaped light years since the 1960s. Many will remember your old high school coaches giving athletes wheat germ capsules before a big event and salt tablets during. That was years before the electrolyte drinks that are now used. State, regional and national level seminars and workshops have certainly improved the physical training knowledge of the youth, college and professional coaches. There has also been an improvement in their knowledge of nutrition.

The hot tip ....

Our motto is to eat a balanced diet and take a few key supplements as a low cost health insurance plan. Supplements can vary widely in price so we recommend doing some comparison shopping to check labels for potency, daily doses, source and the expiration date. Even if you decide to take a number of supplements they would still total less per month than a smoker or moderate alcohol drinker would spend.

Chapter 12

Eliminating the Negative Baggage

"There is power in positive thinking or your PMA."

It really doesn't matter if your goals are addressing responsibilities at home; being a better parent; better father; better co-worker or starting a fitness and wellness regime. Start your journey by letting your mind tell you, **"I can do this!"** Remember to begin slowly, with one step at a time, keeping that picture of success within your focus. Week by week you will see the life changing benefits appear before your eyes. You will feel a whole lot better, especially when your spouse, friends, and family, start asking questions about your new enthusiasm. You will start reaping the rewards that are due all because of that positive mental attitude or PMA. Congratulate yourself on taking that first step and not procrastinating. That first step may be difficult, but it could never compare or be as frightening, as Neil Armstrong taking his first step on the moon.

Jack LaLanne often gave the TV audience and book readers his views on staying motivated. Jack often said, **"Get mad and do something about it!"** He also advised his fans to read as many articles and books on fitness so they would be better educated and informed. It was essential to make an effort to break bad habits, eat well, organize your day, set specific goals and to **visualize the image of what you would like to become**. [71]

---

[71] LaLanne, Jack (20150) Jack LaLanne Website http://www.jacklalanne.com

Panel of Experts questions # 17 and 18

What has motivated you to continue training and maintaining your PMA or positive mental attitude for over 50 years? List any personal mentors who helped you develop your fitness concepts and training philosophy?

The *panel's* Comments ....

Terry Collis – What started out as an interest in self-defense and sports became a life- long habit. I believe that any type of martial arts training is the best way to exercise. I firmly believe there are excellent benefits that improve flexibility, stamina and the training will add quality living with longevity to my life. My Tai Chi Chuan instructor, Mok Lau, was a fitness expert and emphasized that a person must remain active. Tai Chi is an excellent form of martial arts to enhance good health and fitness and also compliments other styles. Most of my Japanese instructors have been an inspiration. Dr. Tsuyoshi Chitose did a demonstration in Canada, at age 70 plus, where he threw students around like they were nothing. He was able to roll around the floor like a young kid. I told myself, **"That's my goal!"**

Devorah Dometrich – Herbst - My father William Dometrich set me on the right path and taught me my personal values. I have utilized those values throughout my entire life to great success. My Okinawan and Japanese sensei's: Akamine, who taught me Kobudo or weapons; Onaga, who taught me the secrets of karate; and Inomoto, who was like an older brother to me.

251

Dave Guidugli – My positive mental attitude is all about looking for a better way of getting and keeping the edge! Trying to find that edge physically, mentally and psychologically, through various types of exercise, becomes a life-long habit. Have you ever noticed that the best trainers are usually older because they have learned, through the years, how to find that special advantage or edge? I've found a lot of good training advice from Kim Wood, Strength Coach for the Cincinnati Bengals; Dick Harbors, Billy Joiner, and Roy Dale in boxing; Mike McGraw, Baltimore Colts, and my semi pro coach, Bob Bradford, in football.

Ray Hughes - Various Japanese instructors and some of the early members of the U.S. Air Force Judo Team.

Lanny Julian – PMA is always something I have included in my training. I have always used self- talk to maintain a positive mindset for my competitions and workouts that affect my body. When I began in arm wrestling there were no mentors or role models. I think I was in the first generation of the sport's popularity. The TV always showcased the Petaluma, California Championships.

Roger Riedinger – My PMA or positive mental attitude has been a priority in my life during the 53 years since I started training. I believe progressive weight training is one of the best activities to promote longevity and the quality of life. Peary Rader, Stuart McRobert, Bob Hoffman, and Brooks Kubik were excellent resources on basic, progressive resistance training.

Jerry Auton – My desire for success has always been greater than my fear of failure. I believe firmly that my fitness program will increase my longevity and overall health. I have always been able to compare notes and progress with Tom Geimeier my lifelong friend and frequent training partner. It is good to have that inner circle of friends who will give you honest and sincere input.

Tom Geimeier – Working out energizes me physically and relaxes me mentally, which tells me that perfect balance must be good for you. Working out eventually becomes a need, but there is no doubt that it has a positive effect on longevity, aging and the quality of life everyone would like to have. When my PMA waivers, due to an injury, I think back to those early mentors and keep that image in my "mind's eye." I belong to several organizations that contribute to WW II, Korean and Vietnam veterans. I have observed the very good health some of those 90 year olds are still in and think to myself, "Maybe I can do that." My mentors include a neighbor who had a basic gym in his garage, along with a stack of muscle magazines; Gil Benson and Dick Zimmerman who gave me some training advice at the local Turner's Club when I was in my late teens. A lot of thanks goes to my training partners over the years.

You're not happy with your present condition because don't have the strength or measurements, from earlier years, if you were foolish enough to be a slave to the tape measure. You look in the mirror and you don't seem to recognize the face and body before you. What happened to that shoulder to waist taper and that smaller waistline? Hopefully, you haven't let yourself go to the extreme, but in some cases that will be the vision in the mirror. Remember that there must be a starting point, but it is the end game that counts.

Going to the gym or fitness center for a workout can indeed be the "magic elixir" for the mind. Even as young kids working out in an old basement or a neighbor's garage we felt a certain energy and decided to continue with regular workouts. You became addicted to your workouts because of all the positive benefits and the people around you radiated that same positive culture. Regardless of the problems you have upon entering the gym there is a certain calming effect on the mind. Your thinking becomes a little sharper and more focused; the workout relaxes you mentally; problems seem trivial; confidence rises; and you feel healthier, with the need to take better care of your body. We remember our early days at the local YMCA and their motto inscribed on the triangular logo of mind, body and spirit. Regular, lifelong exercise habits can have that same effect on us.

O.K. you have read this far so you must have a genuine interest in fitness and your health. Those interests possibly being a combination of living longer, being healthy, stronger, avoiding prescription drugs, avoiding or delaying dementia, being able to play and interact with your grandchildren and the list goes on. You may periodically question if you have the commitment to follow a routine of healthy living as we have discussed in the previous chapters. **Are you ready to change your lifestyle to attain the desired and needed benefits?**

The most important positive aspect is that you have made it through the first 50 years, regardless of your personal habits, and have outlived many of your friends and relatives the same age or younger. The older you become the more apt you are to read the daily obituaries which can be quite shocking. The variety of ages, especially those a bit younger, and the occasional person you know can be a large dose of reality. The *Second Fifty* encompasses a long life ahead with five additional decades of living. One of our *panel* members, Ray Hughes, has been an escort for the remaining famous Doolittle Raiders (five years); is compiling an oral history project on WW II combat veterans that will be archived in the Library of Congress; and conducts a monthly meeting with a U.S.S. Hornet Reunion Group. The majority of these men are over 90 and still quite active despite some of the horrific experiences they suffered in battle. Their will has never been broken and their zest for life is still strong. Ray recently returned from Texas where he attended the 100th birthday party for Col. Dick Coles, General Jimmy Doolittle's co-pilot on the famous Tokyo Raid. [72]

Change of almost any kind is always going to be a bit scary, especially the life altering kind that affects longevity and increasing your chances of making it to those elusive triple digits. You may be able to gain a better perspective by thinking of your previous significant decisions that involved; get married or not; your first child; a great new job opportunity; or losing one job and moving on to a new position and career. There have been

hundreds of books and articles written regarding the importance of a positive attitude toward achieving personal goals and a person's ultimate success. Jerry spent over forty years in the sales field working strictly on commission and was able to win numerous American, North American and world sales titles and

---

[72] Raiders, Doolittle (2015) Col. Dick Coles, http://www. Doolittleraiders.com

competitions. Jerry utilized dozens of motivational books, tapes, CDs, conferences and seminars on attaining a good "positive mental attitude" or PMA for the rookies. Jerry was always looking for that secret sales pitch that would make him rich and famous so he studied all the great motivational speakers, like Zig Ziegler and Dale Carnegie. He posted all sorts of quotes in his daily journal. At home Jerry also had a bulletin board full of quotes and reminders hoping for the sales dollars to flow his way. He anticipated that the dollars would soon be coming in fast and furious if he followed the advice of the experts. Jerry mastered those concepts well and shared that PMA message as a motivational speaker and outstanding member of the American Toastmasters.

When reality settled in Jerry had actually learned a valuable life lesson. **If you procrastinate on any venture, or that moment in time, that window of opportunity may well fall from your grasp**. If your mind is not on board, or in synch with the rest of your body, negative thoughts may begin to enter the picture and offset your initial positive first steps. How many times will a door of opportunity open for you? How many chances will you have to commit to a specific and life altering decision? The day Jerry realized the all importance of a "positive mental attitude," or PMA, a proverbial light bulb went off in his brain. **Get your PMA into the game; commit to your goals; and then achieve them!**

What the research says....

Hundreds of research projects will substantiate the connection between the mind and the body. Think of the millions of people, from all walks of life, who have taken and benefited from the

Dale Carnegie Success Courses? The Carnegie Website states that over eight million people have actually completed the course, which is offered in 90 countries and 25 languages.

Carnegie's *How to Win Friends and Influence People* and *How to Stop Worrying and Start Living* have sold millions.[73] The success of the Carnegie course and book sales is a strong indicator that self- improvement is a powerful driving force within us. We know of several high school dropouts who had a lot of untapped potential, but could never seem to find their niche. After one friend was convinced to take the Dale Carnegie Course, at the expense of his employer, his life turned around in dramatic fashion. Ironically, he found a rewarding career in another profession by rising to the top of the food chain and eventually bought the company. Being highly motivated, he then did the same in a second career. There are dozens of other similar courses, sold in the millions, to people who want to improve their positive mental attitude. Many companies, schools and organizations hire occasional motivational speakers to inspire their employees; keep them in a positive mindset and allow them to reach their full potential. The most successful motivational speakers are in high demand and this is exemplified by one of the best, Zig Zigler. Zigler is considered one of the top ten speakers in the United States and his bio states he traveled over five million miles giving motivational speeches around the world.

---

[73] Carnegie, Dale (1936,1948)) How to Win Friends and Influence People and How to Stop Worrying and Start Living, Retrieved from http://www.wikipedis.org/wiki/dale_carnegie

One of his favorite quotes was, **"What you get by achieving your goals is not as important as what you will become by achieving those goals."** Another Ziglar quote that rings very true, **"You were designed for accomplishment, engineered for success and endowed with the seeds of greatness."**[74]

The bottom line ....

Our *panel* was in agreement about the power of a positive attitude. Lanny talked about "self- talk" in preparation for his daily workouts and world class arm wrestling competitions. Dave mentioned about getting and keeping that all important edge while Jerry stated his desire for success was stronger than his fear of failure. Every member of the *panel* stated emphatically that maintaining a life style, with fitness as a priority, would add to their longevity and quality of life. Several members also commented that the positive benefits from training had a significant impact on other major areas of their lives. You have nothing to lose and potentially years to gain from maintaining a habit of regular exercise, which will also improve your mind and spirit. We also like Jack LaLanne's to the point quotes on positive mental attitude: **"Get mad and do something about it!"** and **"Visualize the image of what you would like to become."**

---

[74] Ziglar, Zig (15 Feb 2014) Top 10 Motivational Speakers in the World, Retrieved from http://www.motivationalgrid.com/top_motivational_ _speakers/

The hot tip ....

Arnold Schwarzenegger came to the United States, as a young man from Austria, and immediately decided to take advantage of the "American dream." It only took a few years for the "Austrian Oak" to reach the heights of the bodybuilding world, go on to become a movie star, marry the niece of JFK and enter the political arena with great success. Arnold is also considered one of the top 10 motivational speakers on many of the lists you will find on Google. Arnold was asked to reflect on his formula for his immense personal success and his answer was **that he always believed in himself and he used his immense work ethic, strong self- discipline and determination to accomplish his goals. Arnold further stated, "For me life is continuously about being hungry. The meaning of life is not to merely exist, to survive, but to achieve and to conquer."** [75]

---

[75] Schwarzenegger, Arnold (Nov 2015) The Arnold Schwarzenegger Official Website, Retrieved from http://www.schwarzenegger.com/

Chapter 13
Stress Management

*"The 24- hour day should have three distinct parts
...work, personal time and rest"*

When we ideally break the 24- hour day into three equal parts we find that we have eight hours for our career or vocation; eight hours for personal or family time; and eight hours for rest and relaxation. In today's world most people are lucky to get their eight hours of rest and how many people work only an eight- hour day? The rest and personal, family time are seriously eroded as we strive to get ahead in our careers or assume more responsibility as our career paths takes shape. The personal life suffers, as does the quality of family time, which is especially true in today's world where mom and dad are in the work force. The *panel* members in this book were born in an age where the majority of mothers were at home and the fathers were the sole bread winners. How times have changed and at what price? That change has created additional stress, which is one of the biggest causes of those related ailments, illnesses, and diseases on the planet. Read the statistics and they are very convincing about the relationship of stress to major diseases like heart, cardiovascular and even cancer. **Stress is the number one killer and believed to be the main cause of disease!**

Stress Management & Fitness

There are all kinds of theories on aging and what causes it. Jerry has to smile when he reads an article on aging or watches a documentary by a so called expert who appears to be about thirty years old. What do they know about aging? Let us say this, and say it with authority: **You have to live it to really know it!** We hopefully, will still be 68 years old when this book is finished and we have tried to live every day of those 68 years. Our theories, like those of the other *panel* members include: 100s of books and articles read; dozens of seminars, workshops, personal experience, training others, countless interviews and time spent acquiring various certifications, degrees and leadership positions. That combination is a treasure trove of practical and educational expertise. That depth of experience, much like yours, is very valuable if you have lived life fully. As the saying goes, **"Been there and done that!"**

The *panel's* comments ....

There was no specific question in the *panel* interviews that was specifically related to reducing stress. We felt that due to the impact of stress on health and the body's performance that it should be included in our book. The *panel,* after being consulted, agreed that it was an important issue for each member and recommended that it be addressed.

We have seen what stress does to the human body and how excess stress adds years and ages the human body. Jerry will always remember that his parents looked older than what they really were, especially his dad. Even today, as he reflects back at old photos, he was struck by the wrinkles, grey hair and general elderly appearance of his dad, starting with photos of him at about age 45. Jerry has even gone so far as to look at his old photos, at these same ages and made comparisons. After making the comparisons, he found out that it is not just his imagination, but it was real and in front of his eyes. Jerry's dad seemed to age quickly and starting at about age 40 always appeared to be 15-20 years older than he actually was. His father, Dan, only lived to age 76, which was the average life expectancy at that time.

Reflecting back, Jerry connected the dots and developed a logical and sensible conclusion. Jerry's dad was a house painter by trade and was able to keep steady work and income only during the warm weather months. When winter came each year he was virtually unemployed and add to that inactivity the stress of a house with eight children to feed, clothe and maintain; five daughters to worry about keeping out of trouble; and being able to pay the family bills on time. There was a lot of responsibility! Is it possible that stress really could have given him the appearance of being 20 years older than he really was? Jerry mentioned that his mom also looked older than she was too, but not by that many years. Jerry thinks the biggest difference was that she had a great relationship with God and he truly believes her stress reliever was those daily trips to morning Mass.

Here is the answer: Stress is mental and psychological in nature, but depending on how we react to it, it may cause us to have a chain reaction train wreck concerning the delicate balance in our health and welfare. When Jerry's dad was stressed, what did he do about it? He smoked a cigarette or two or three and had a few more cups of coffee. At night, feeling the effects of all the nicotine and caffeine, he didn't sleep very well. The combination gave him heartburn so he didn't have the desire to eat well and thank goodness he wasn't a drinker! What do we do if we are under stress? We have found that physical exercise relieves stress and allows the mind to relax and put the problems in a better perspective. As a bonus, this same exercise does all the physical things that not only make you feel better mentally, but works to keep you looking and feeling better physically. Kind of like a "magic elixir!"

Ulcers, high blood pressure, migraine headaches, chest pain, sleep problems and IBS (irritable bowel syndrome) are just a few of the side effects of stress. We all feel stress at different times in our lives, but how you deal with it is what is going to keep you from aging prematurely and shortening your lifespan. A regular exercise program is the best prescription for stress management. Remember the old rubber stress ball that was the tool of the physicians for so many years? That was based on the same concept of engaging in a physical activity to relieve mental and emotional anxiety and stress.

Jerry had a very insightful perspective regarding people trying to guess his age. Jerry says he feels very good when he hears someone comment that he doesn't look his age, but he feels he actually does. He also gets a frequent comment that, "You certainly don't act your age." If Jerry had a choice in life, he would rather be able to act and perform like a person much younger than his years, than to look younger and not be able to perform as well. This is a pretty easy formula. If you want to minimize the negative effects of stress, simply manage it by participating in a regular program of exercise. When the stress starts to creep in, chase it away with your own favorite method of exercise. This can be a brisk walk, some strength workouts, or even dancing with your wife. (That will alleviate her stress too!) **Do not allow stress to rob you of your vitality, zest for life and your golden years.**

If you have a pulse rate and are breathing you have experienced various degrees of stress throughout your life. If you are a senior citizen you have encountered and accumulated years of stressful situations. Stress has the ability to destroy the body, as well as the mind, but the key to longevity is your techniques in dealing effectively with it. Something as simple as watching the local and national news can create stress. If you have never experienced stress you are probably not human. Stress causes people who are otherwise very normal to lose or quit their jobs; get divorced; make enemies of people who were once friends; and even do the bizarre that may result in their incarceration. There is no age barrier to stress, but we must make every attempt to reduce this horrific health offender to the very minimum.

Many times throughout this book there have been references to the least expensive, non-pharmaceutical and possibly best option to alleviate the problem. Exercise! Look at the index of almost any book on solutions to health problems and you will see that exercise is a key to helping people heal, from Alzheimer's, varicose veins, constipation to osteoporosis and many others in between, including stress. The message is very clear that stress is your enemy and you must have the skills to neutralize this threat and protect your future.

As a side note, there are different aspects of stress, when comparing the problems of men to those of women. Judith Sachs, in her book, *Break the Stress Cycle, 10 Steps for Reducing Stress for Women"* [76] found one big difference between the way stress is handled in women as compared to men. Her references were to

---

[76] Sachs, Judith (Sept 1997) 10 Steps for Reducing Stress in Women, Mass: Adams Media Corp., Retrieved from http://www.mtd4u.com /resour04.htm

a study by Dr. William Malarkey, an endocrinologist at the Ohio State University. The study found, for example, that women can't stand to fight with the one they love and that distress colors everything else in their lives. Their stress hormones rise after an argument and remain that way for, as much as, twenty- four hours. Men in the study were more likely to immediately vent their frustration and get their hormone levels within the normal range in a few minutes.

What the research says ....

An article from the Mayo Clinic, Healthy Lifestyle in July, 2013 focused on Stress Management.[77] The article stated that stress may be the underlying culprit in a variety of illnesses that affect not only your body, but your mood and behavior. Recognizing these common symptoms can give you a jump start on managing them. The article categorized the symptoms into three classes: body, mood and behavior. Effects on the body may be indicated by: headaches, muscle tension, chest pain, fatigue, change in sex drive, upset stomach and sleep problems. Effects on mood include: anxiety, restlessness, lack of motivation, anger and sadness or depression. Likewise, those affecting behavior were: overeating, under eating, drug or alcohol use, tobacco use and a general social withdrawal. The recommended stress management techniques from the Mayo Clinic article focused on finding a physical activity, utilizing relaxation techniques, meditation,

---

[77] Humana Outlook Staff (July 2013) Stress Symptoms: Effects on your body and behavior, retrieved fromhttp://www.mayoclinic.org/healthy-lifestyle/stress-management/in-depth/stress-symptoms/july2013

yoga or Tai Chi classes. *The Humana Active Outlook Magazine,* spring 2013, printed an article titled, <u>Tai Chi' A Gentle Way to Fight Stress.</u>[78] The article was adapted from one from the Mayo Clinic Foundation for Medical Education and research. (MFMER) Tai Chi, as an exercise form, was referred to as a martial arts form that appeared to be meditation in motion that increased balance, flexibility, self- defense skills, while reducing joint pain and stress.

The Website aarp.org/healthy-living presented an article titled <u>Stress and Disease –Conditions that May Be Caused by Chronic Stress.</u>[79] A study by the Harvard University –Robert Wood Johnson Foundation conducted a poll that indicated that 37% of adults, over 50, experienced a major stressful life event in the past year, such as the death of a family member, chronic illness or a job loss. Many people affected by stress combat the problem by eating, drinking, smoking more, with less sleep and exercise. All of those tendencies have an obvious negative impact on your health. The human body reacts to stress by pumping adrenaline and then cortisol into the bloodstream to signal the mind that immediate action is required. This natural fight or flight reaction has ensured the survival of man since creation. Continued stress, with that adrenalin and cortisol rush into the bloodstream, poses

---

[78] Mayo Clinic Staff (Spring 2013) Tai Chi, A Gentle Way to Fight Stress, http;//www.humanaactive outlook.com, Tai Chi, A Gentle Way to Fight Stress/

[79] Agnvall, Elizabeth (14 Nov 2014) Stress and Disease Conditions That May Be by Chronic Stress, Retrieved from http://www.aarp.org/health-healthyliving/info-2014/stress-and-disease.html

significant health risks. The normal function of cortisol is to shut off inflammation in the body, but chronic or persistent stress can cause the cells to become desensitized and inflammation goes wild damaging blood vessels, brain cells, causing insulin resistance and promoting painful joint diseases.

Another article that reinforces the Mayo Clinic and AARP articles is from webmed.com titled *10 Health problems Related to Stress That You Can Fix,* by R. Morgan Griffin and reviewed by Joseph Goldberg, MD. The 10 health problems discussed in order included: heart disease, asthma, obesity, diabetes, headaches, depression / anxiety, gastrointestinal problems, Alzheimer's disease, accelerated aging and premature death. The physiologic response involves the release of adrenalin and cortisol, as previously discussed, accompanied by increases in blood pressure, breathing, and restriction of blood vessels.[80]

The bottom line ….

A fact in stone is that everyone will have stress during various times in their lives! Every doctor, family member and friend will tell you that stress is bad for your health and may eventually be the cause of a disability or even your death. There is only one option and that is to fight back. If you have any doubts about the advice we have presented, please visit your library or get on the Internet and do some research. Experts on stress relief suggest focusing on the present and not something in the distant past or

---

[80] Griffin, Morgan (14 Sept 2015) 10 Problems Related to Stress That You Can Fix, Retrieved from http://www.webmd.com/balance/stress-management/features/10-fixable-stress-related-health-problems/

the uncertain future. Your best bet is to live in and control the present. Other suggestions include: performing deep breathing exercises, finding quality time for yourself, and reflecting on all the positives in your life.

The hot tip ….

The recommended stress management techniques from the Mayo Clinic article focused on finding a physical activity, utilizing relaxation techniques, meditation, yoga or Tai Chi classes. Many insurance companies offer mental health classes, as one of their benefits, and we suggest taking advantage of those. There are numerous gyms and fitness centers in every area that you can select from. An exercise program can be quite successful within your home, but sometimes a change in atmosphere is an extra boost. The larger gyms also offer a variety of those extra classes that can help with stress reduction. Maybe your best option, at present, is to start with a nice relaxing walk every day. Possibly a morning and an evening walk with your spouse. Your basic goal may be to add minutes to you walk or increasing the distance. You will begin to feel a reduction in your stress levels, sleep better, and feel better knowing your health is back on the right track.

Chapter 14

The Drug Solution Affects All Ages

Drugs cannot be your answer! The pharmaceutical companies and their products comprise a significant billion- dollar industry worldwide. They would like to see every man, woman and child on some type of medication. Boxing promoter, Don King, once said, **"It's not about black or white, but about the green."** The human body was not designed to work with drugs at the cellular level! The Lobbyists representing this interest are some of the heavy hitters greasing the palms of our Washington Congressman. Dave, Roger and Tom were school administrators with a combined 100 plus years of experience and can attest to the number of students who are on a menagerie of prescriptions so they can supposedly function. The American public educational system is in trouble and common sense dictates that creating a climate of learning should be the main priority, without undue distractions. All students should have the opportunity to learn. The public schools have become the dumping grounds, however, a cure all for all for our social ills and there are many daily duties for teachers that were formally under the expertise of the medical professionals. One of the first daily duties of some Special Education teachers is to determine which students have missed their meds and make adjustments so the school day can proceed as normal. The problem is not just in the schools or in the daily rations that millions of Americans find in their medicine cabinets, purses, pill boxes or desk drawers.

There is an epidemic among the athletes in many sports and is spread across all continents. The class of drugs we are referring to is called anabolic or performance enhancing drugs. (PEDs) Some may be prescribed by legitimate professionals, but the majority of these drugs are the product of the **"black market."** Everyone is looking for the edge and many athletes have sold their souls to find that elusive "silver bullet" that will put them on the top of the podium. The idea that a blue chip, premier athlete would risk their health, career, reputation, longevity and family relationships to possibly set the bar a little higher defies all logic to the common reader. The athlete who has pursued a lifetime of training to reach the pinnacle of their sport and the admiration of followers may believe that they cannot live without the super high of fame and are willing to risk everything. Unfortunately, the problem is not something that has reared its ugly head in our lifetimes. **The first international anti-doping rule was initiated in Amsterdam and approved in 1928! The IOC, IAAF and the World Anti-Doping Agency (WADA) have currently** been working together to try and find ways to remedy the situation and dish out punishment to the offenders. [81]

Anabolic steroids are technically called anabolic-androgenic steroids referred to on the streets and back alleys as "roids, gym candy, pumpers, stackers or juice." They are basically synthetic forms of the male hormone testosterone. Common steroids include, but are not limited to: Androl, Anavar, Deca Durabolin,

---

[81] WADA Staff (Nov 2015) WADA Prohibited List, World Anti-Doping Agency, Retrieved from http://www.olympic.org/ioc-governance-affiliate-organizations?=wada

Dianabol, Equipoise, Oxandrin, Promobolin, and Winstrol. he anabolic refers to muscle building qualities, while the androgenic refers to increased male characteristics. The user can take the "roids" through tablet, crème, gel or injection form. Many users will combine or "stack" an oral and an injectable form combining two different types in an attempt to enhance the muscle building effects. The steroid or "roid" use can also be cycled for 6-12 week periods to improve the sought after benefits while reducing the negative aspects. Cycling means to increase the doses and then back off before the negative effects are evident. [82] [83]

We became aware of the problem when watching the Olympics of the 1960s, 70s and 80s to current times. The USSR and the East Germans dominated the Olympic Games, especially track and field and the weight lifting events with some of their records still standing today. A lot of people cried foul and said the members of the USSR and the East Germans were on some sort of performance enhancing drugs. (PEDs) That premise turned out to be true, but in truth there were many top athletes from other countries, including the U.S., experimenting with the same drugs. Any person, with the most basic knowledge of physical training, can look at the extreme muscularity of athletes in almost every sport and come to the obvious conclusion that it cannot be and is absolutely not natural development.

---

[82] WADA Staff Nov 2014) Steroid Use and Abuse: Most Popular Steroids Abused by Athletes, http://www.steroid.com/steriod-use-abuse.php

[83] National Institute on Drug Abuse (NIH) Staff (Aug 2006) The Science of Drug Abuse and Addiction, Retrieved from http://www.drugabuse.gov/publications/drugfacts/anabolic-steroids/

We're sure you have seen the super extreme muscularity of some of the professional wrestlers, football, basketball, track and field athletes and others. There have been several key baseball players caught for cheating by using PEDs when baseball doesn't require the same muscular mass or strength of some of the other sports. Think for a minute that Hank Aaron was about 5'-10" tall and 180 pounds. The equally great Willie Mays was 5'-11" and about 185. Maybe those examples say something about real talent, natural ability and the high level performance capable of the body.

The people who developed and made profits from illegal drugs were certainly not going to categorize anyone who had the money to spend. It is also hard to keep a secret from other competing athletes when there are so many contacts through international competitions. Drugs are expensive, regardless of the user's intent. They are vastly over -priced and the only reasonable prices for legal prescription drugs we know of are contracted independently by the Veterans Administration. An example would be medications for men with Erectile Dysfunction (ED) Viagra which sells 10 blue pills for about $150.00 while Cialis sells 10 for about $240.00 The VA will provide their veterans with the same prescriptions for $10.00 and mail it right to their front doors, but the pharmacies mark them up 15-20 times that cost! **Imagine the mark up on the black market!**

The hormones of the body have a delicate balance and to upset that balance can have devastating effects. Men who use these "black market" drugs will risk: increased acne, shrunken testicles, a low sperm count, gynecomastia (breasts), and their hair falling out. The females who use these same drugs will risk:

cessation of their menstrual cycle, decrease in breast size, a deeper voice, and increased facial hair, especially a beard. Both genders would risk: liver tumors, "roid rages," strokes, heart disease, depression and a shorter life span. Research and data indicates that teens may see a stunted growth effect, due to the closing of the growth plates. Taking the synthetic hormones would signal the body that a certain hormone level was achieved and it was time to stop puberty resulting in stopping the teen's natural genetic growth potential. [84] [85]

The "black market" business has also been busy producing **"designer drugs"** that have the anabolic effect, but contain masking agents in an effort to make them very difficult to detect. Some athletes have tried to beat the drug tests given to top athletes by using a class of drugs called **"diuretics." "Diuretics"** are used as a masking agent by trying to balance body fluids and the salts or electrolytes. This practice can lead to exhaustion, dizziness, stomach and muscle cramps, fainting, drops in blood pressure, heat stroke and possibly death.

Creatine or creatine – monohydrate is another frequently used supplement that helps the muscles release energy. It makes the muscles produce more adenosine triphosphate (ATP) which stores and transports energy in the cells. The use is not

---

[84] Mayo Clinic Staff (June 2015) Performance Enhancing Drugs: Know the Risk, Retrieved from http://www.mayoclinic.org/healthy-lifestyle/fitness/in-depth/performance-enhancing-drugs/art-20046134

[85] Men's Health Staff (14 Nov 2014) Abuse of Anabolic Steroids, Retrieved from http://www.web_md.com/men/guide/anabolic-steroid-abuse-

recommended because the body produces a natural form and any detected excess is removed by the kidneys. **The use of creatine can alter the negative test results for performance enhancing drugs by causing a positive reading!** Creatine can have the effects of weight gain, diarrhea, nausea and muscle or stomach cramps.[86]

Human growth hormone or HGH known as somatotropin has been widely used by athletes since at least 1982 and was impossible to detect using the standard urine tests. The substance was banned by the IOC and other organizations, but was not enforceable until the early 2000s when sophisticated blood tests could detect between artificial and the body's natural production of the hormone. HGH is a natural amino acid secreted by the pituitary gland that stimulates growth, cell reproduction and regeneration in humans. HGH is typically prescribed for children with severe growth deficiencies and the current research has attributed numerous benefits to older adults. There has been an ongoing controversy about the use of HGH in livestock production and possible transference to the meat we eat. Side effects may include high blood pressure, diabetes, high cholesterol and joint pain. Long term users may show several physical changes including the thickening of the lower jaw and the enlargement of the fingers and toes.

Another frequently used banned substance is **erythropoietin** commonly known as **Epoetin. Epoetin** is actually a protein produced in the kidneys that promotes the formation of red blood

---

[86] Jerczak, Dave Website (2 Aug 2013) Urine Tests and Creatine, Retrieved http://drugteststips.com/urine-drug-tests-and -creatine/

cells and hemoglobin. The synthetic version was designed to treat anemia, but has been used and referred to as blood doping or oxygen loading by endurance athletes. This conversation has been ongoing especially regarding distance runners and the cyclists in the Tour de France. The theory is to improve the muscles ability to take in more oxygen thus delaying fatigue. This topic has also been discussed at high altitude athletic events where oxygen deprivation can be a key performance factor. Side effects can be very serious such as stroke, heart attack and pulmonary edema. [87]

Stimulants such as energy drinks are high in caffeine and will cause: tremors, high blood pressure, nervousness, psychiatric conditions, heart palpitations, stroke and heart attack. Visit any gym you desire and you will see a few coolers with numerous energy drinks that have caffeine as one of the key ingredients. Other ingredients may include various types of amino acids, herbs and sugar. Many middle school, high school and college students actually prefer these to the common colas for the mental and physical lift they provide. Think about the automobile or truck driver who needs a caffeine jolt and buys the shots available at every store's checkout line. There is definitely an abuse problem across all age groups. Soft drinks and colas are not considered energy drinks, however.

---

[87] Karriem-Norwood, Varnada, MD (28 Aug 2014 Blood Doping, Retrieved from http://www. webmd.com/fitness-exercise/blood-doping

The *panel's* comments ....

Very few of the *panel* members had a working knowledge of performance enhancing drugs, but reached consensus that the drug issue has crept into almost every competitive sport from the intermediate to the professional levels. The reader must remember that our *panel* members are old school and have never looked for pharmaceutical assistance to gain notoriety in their specific area. Hard work, sweat and seeking out great mentors went into the work ethic of that generation. There was concern about the limitations of how drugs could affect performance and the eventual health risks for those who are willing to take a chance.

What the research says ....

The Mayo Clinic recommends no more than four cups of coffee per day, two energy shots or a maximum of 400 milligrams of caffeine per day. [88]

The bottom line ....

If you over 50 and reading this book, what would be the ideal risk factor be for your age group? We are suggesting zero as a risk factor pertaining to using any type of performance enhancing drugs. (PEDs) Why would any sane person invest their hard earned dollars when some of the dividends could mean eventual disaster for your health and future enjoyment? There are, unfortunately, people in your age group who took a variety of

---

[88] Mayo Clinic Staff (2014) Caffeine: How much is too much? Retrieved from http://www.mayo clinic.org/healthy-lifestyle/nutrition-and-healthy-eating/in-depth/caffeine/art-20045678

drugs and wish they could turn back the clock to re-think that grievous misstep. Many are paying the unexpected price of trying to gain an edge or unfair advantage in their specific athletic pursuit. We are issuing a strict warning because we have seen, first hand, competing seniors who are taking a variety of testosterone related drugs. You have enough on your plate beginning the fight against age related illnesses incremental muscle loss. **We implore you to think before you act!** The U.S. Department of Justice Website contains a section of the use and sale of illegal steroids. Possession of non- prescribed steroids carries a penalty of one year in prison and a $1000.00 fine. Trafficking in illegal steroids carries a potential five- year prison sentence and a $250,000. 00 fine, which is doubled for a second offense. The DEA has obviously seen the rampant use and distribution as an epidemic problem, which unfortunately, many of the youth role models have continued to use to maintain that all important edge in professional sports. [89]

The hot tip ....

Be smart, treat your body with the utmost respect and depend on healthy living habits. You've made it through the first fifty or the half century and there is still a life time ahead. We're sure everyone has some sort of a "bucket list" and now is the time to address that fun filled list.

---

[89] U.S. Dept. of Justice Staff (Sept 2015) Trafficking in Illegal Steroids, Retrieved from http://www.Deadiversion.usdoj.gov/publications/brochures/steroids/public/

Chapter 15

Parting Advice and All Time Greatest Examples

"A quick reading of these keys can move you ahead or send you in reverse"

Panel of Experts question # 20

Add any other information that may have value to the reader?

The *panels'* comments ....

Terry Collis – Find an activity that you have an interest in and commit to it. Read up on the history to create more interest & knowledge.

Devorah Dometrich – Herbst - I am Akamine's only foreign student in the world. I also have my own Kobudo Federation.

Dave Guidugli – Be in harmony with yourself. Use a realistic program. Dave Cowens might be the best all- around athlete of any that I have met or trained. He was exceptional at all aspects of fitness.

Ray Hughes - I work with several military groups and the majority of the veterans are over 90 years old. I conduct a monthly meeting of the U.S.S. Hornet Group and have escorted the remaining Doolittle Raiders, on their United States tours, for over five years. I have been able to observe these remarkable veterans and that unbelievable drive that still has them very functional.

Lanny Julian – Keep working out! You should never work out alone and have a reliable training partner with similar abilities. Be careful to avoid injury at all costs.

Roger Riedinger – I've said it over and over again in the above questions – progressive resistance. Take it slow and steady like the tortoise. You will beat the hare in the end and be much stronger, healthier, and injury free. Get a basic program. Set realistic goals. Stick with your program, progress slowly and you will eventually accomplish your goals – then you'll have to set new ones, adding years to your life and a better life to your years.

Jerry Auton - To be successful in any and all ventures of life it takes a combination of three components: hard work, knowledge and enthusiasm. 1. Educate yourself to be knowledgeable in the facts regarding proper training and nutrition; 2. Go into your daily workouts with proper enthusiasm that you are helping you; 3. Work hard on your commitment to continue your workout and nutrition plans from now until the casket. It may take you longer than you think, hopefully, a full *Second Fifty.*

Tom Geimeier - Hopefully, with any luck, you should get smarter with age. You cannot afford to make poor decisions during your *Second Fifty*. Take the time to think ahead, analyze your decisions beforehand and have a good friend or family member you can bounce ideas off of.

What the research says ....

The *panel* members have given you the benefit of their years of experience and that should expedite your progress. Once your training becomes a lifestyle the rewards will start coming in. There is no doubt that you will feel better, look better and have a more positive outlook on life. You will have the satisfaction of knowing that you did your very best to offset the effects of aging and have made a wise decision to extend your lifeline.

The bottom line ....

What motivates you? As a youth you were influenced by the ads of the Charles Atlas Dynamic Tension System or the Saturday afternoon movie matinees with Steve Reeves and Reg Park emulating the great Hercules. The limited TV shows of the 1950s had the amazing Superman, Tarzan and the 1960s Bruce Lee, alias Kung Fu Kato, of the Green Hornet. These early idols were instrumental in planting those early seeds that muscle, strength, fitness and martial arts skill were highly desirable. No one wanted to be the proverbial 97pound weakling; have sand kicked in their face and watch the neighborhood goon walk away with their girl.

The cartoons of the era also had their influence with Popeye and the super muscular Little Abner from the funny pages. Even today a person with a large set of forearms may well be admired and nicknamed Popeye. These early influences set the generations of the 50s and afterward on a path to fitness. Those early images were ingrained into our minds and have left a lasting legacy of those early pioneers.

To further prove our point, no one in their right mind ever made Laurel and Hardy, Abbot and Costello, W.C. Fields, Don Knotts of Mayberry or the three Stooges their role models unless they pursued a career in comedy. There is something to be admired about being fit, strong, well- toned, powerful and athletic. These qualities depict health and virility. These are positive attributes admired by most people.

The females of the early days were left well behind, although there were some very accomplished ladies plying their skills, in virtual obscurity. Women did not gain their role models and icons until the 1980s when the female Olympic athletes took center stage. There were earlier remarkable achievements by women, but they gained little in comparison to the men. Outstanding women athletes at the turn of the century were likely to find employment and notoriety in vaudeville or as a circus act. Several names that comes to mind were Annie Oakley, of side show fame, and in the 1940s Esther Williams and other great female swimmers. Participation in female fitness events, athletics and martial arts involvement was not popular and a difficult stereotype to break. Our *panel* member, Devorah, certainly deserves credit for her contribution and for being a true pioneer for female equality.

Today is a different story. All of those early images and motivations are years behind us in life's ancient history. Realize that the best motivation for a life of fitness and drive for longevity must be intrinsic. It must come from within, after understanding that a person can fight against aging, while striving for greater longevity. Ask any person, of average health, how long they want to live and the answer will always be, "As long as possible." No one wants to check out early unless they are in total chronic pain, misery or have an incurable disease. The encouragement from your spouse, children and friends is certainly a wonderful asset, but your fate is ultimately in your own hands.

A training partner can also be a great benefit and can give you that extra push toward achieving your personal fitness objectives. Whether working out in a home gym or in a high end fitness center, a regular time, convenient access, and avoiding distractions will help you stay focused. Don't forget the power of the mind in your training. There are a number of systems that employ the use of aroma therapy, mood music, special lighting, special chants and dedicated spaces to meditate, relax and seek harmony with the mind, spirit and body. Remember the early mottos of your association with the YMCAs, Turner Societies and Boys Clubs of America. The answers may have been right in front of you!

The hot tip ....

You may not make it to triple digits, but you will have certainly opted to add quality to the years that lie ahead. The **glossary** in this book has an ample supply of fitness terminology and all that you will really need. Many of the articles you will read in magazines or during your individual research will add a variety of others, but we don't advise you to worry about them. Too many terms have been invented and some of them are simply re-creating the wheel. Keep it simple! Don't worry about terms like: squat specialization, tonnage system, peak contraction, quality interval training, single rep training, extended sets, cheating /forced reps, instinctive training, muscle priority, density workouts, giant sets, isolation, reverse action, staggered sets, super sets, tri sets, multi poundage sets, split and double split routines. Use the KISS formula and keep it simple! Trying to memorize a lot of the technical jargon will only add to your confusion.

Panel of Experts question # 19

List any fitness role models you think are worthy to mention?

The *panel's* comments ….

Terry Collis – Mr. Mok Lau (Tai Chi Chuan Assoc.), Dr. Tsuyoshi Chitose, Teruyuki Okazaki (Chair – Shotokan Assoc.) Yutaka Yaguchi (ISKF), Shojiro Koyama (Japan Karate Federation), Bill Dometrich (Instructor – Chito Ryu), Shigeru Takashina (JKF)

Devorah Dometrich – Herbst - William Dometrich, my father, who at one time was the highest ranking non-oriental in the U.S., in his style of karate. You also have to remember that there were no females in martial arts in the 1960s.

Dave Guidugli – People in the business that have given me additional insight: Red Auerbach, Joe B. Hall, Denny Crum, Mohammad Ali, Ernie Schafer, Larry Bird, Dave Cowens, and Oscar Robertson. That knowledge and inspiration helped me coach my four sons to Division 1 scholarships in athletics.

Ray Hughes - Jack Lalanne had some Revolutionary ideas in training, fitness and design of machines.

Lanny Julian – I also had a high regard for the symmetry and training philosophy of Frank Zane.

Roger Riedinger – John Grimek, Jeff and Cory Everson.

Jerry Auton – Bill Pearl, Jack Lalanne, Dave Draper and Larry Scott.

Tom Geimeier – People you see, read about and meet certainly have an impact on you. Many of the gurus have already mentioned Jack LaLanne. Think about the Hercules movies and Steve Reeves and Reg Park. Do you remember the old Superman TV shows and the super heroes in the comics? I've attended a number of AAU and IFBB shows in York, PA and NYC where I was inspired by some of the great physiques and fitness gurus. I've been fortunate to have met some of the legends: John Grimek, Bob Hoffman, Dan Lurie, Chuck Sipes, Frank Zane, Sergio Olivia, Chris Dickerson, and Casey Viator. I was also one of the original students of martial arts expert Sin The. (Shaolin do)

What the research says ....

Selecting a good role model in your youth can serve as an early inspiration and a blueprint for how we conduct ourselves as adults. Devorah Dometrich-Herbst mentioned that her values were instilled very early by her father and martial arts master, William Dometrich. Every member of the "panel" named one or more mentors who were inspirational even if the contact was not hands on. In psychology there is a pyramid of basic human needs and self-actualization or self- satisfaction that sits at the top. Numerous articles reinforce the concept that an ideal role model can guide you in life decisions, provide support when needed and exemplify how to live a happy, fulfilling life. [90] [91]

The bottom line ....

As youngsters, our parents became our first role models teaching us rules of behavior, morals and many of life's important values. Horizons were expanded and we found other role models that exhibited non- destructive behavior, specific success, appeared to operate on a higher moral plain and could motivate one to pursue their passions. These models were not the fictional characters of TV or the comics, but realistic people that you could pattern your life after.

The hot tip ....

A survey of people who are driven to improve themselves find a common thread in that they credit excellent role models as the main reason for their self- improvement and success. [92]

---

[90] Thomas, Mark (23 May 2012) The Importance of Role Models in Your Life, Retrieved from http://www.healthguidance.org/entry/13288

[91] Ask.com Staff (2014) Why are role models important? Retrieved from http://www.ask.com/world-view/role/models-important-bc10ble441c757

[92] Life Style Updated Staff (2014) The Importance of Having Role Models in Your Life, Retrieved from http://www.lifestyleupdated.com/2012/05/23/Role-Models-important/

Appendix A
The *Panel of Experts* Interviews
Terry Collis

Why is your form of exercise / fitness the best?

I'm interested in a total exercise program. I became interested after reading a True Magazine article. They had articles on karate in 1955-56 and the Charles Atlas articles in Popular Science about having sand kicked in your face. I try to combine both.

How long have you been active in your special area of fitness?

I wrote a thesis in English class in 1957 on Judo. I took some lessons in Hamilton, Ohio.

What benefits have you gained from your fitness program?

Each type of self -defense and fitness have a different flavor. Shotokan Karate is more fighting oriented style of Japanese origin with block –kick- & punch movements. Chito Ryu is an Okinawin style with more emphasis on self- defense. With some Ju Jitsu techniques. One old Karate Master described Aikido as just Karate.

List your priorities in training

Trying to keep in shape and continue my training.

What do you look for when selecting a gym?

I look for all white gis or uniforms, with no black or red, because I think that reflects the old system of humility and the Buddhist philosophy. I consider the charges, dues, & type of credit card system used. I like to see a disciplined approach, especially with the younger kids.

What advice would you give to a young person starting out? Expect gradual progress, take it easy. The body and the mind need time to adjust. Practice, learn the basics, build a proper foundation, stick with it thru the initial stages …give it a fair chance.

What advice would you give to the over 50 age person? Basically the same as in any sport. Realize your physical limitations. Stretch, warmup, and the instructor probably determines intensity. Stay within yourself. You can't come back to the same level of fitness or competition after years of layoff. The over 50s try to do things the same as when they were teenagers. They get discouraged after one or two training sessions. Stay within themselves. Work the special katas 4-5 times per day & do a lot of routine stretches. The shoulders and hips especially need to be stretched & assoc. muscles.

What are some of the key mistakes you have observed in a gyms and dojos?
Some advanced members push the new students to do exercises their body is not accustomed to. Ex. The Makawara Board where the young guys injure fingers & knuckles …they think they have to have big calloused knuckles. Same with feet and these injuries can become arthritic in later years. Same with the heavy bag.

What are the leading causes of injury in older adults trying to maintain their fitness levels?

Older adults try to keep up with younger members of the dojo /gym. No matter how fit you think you are, your body is not what it was 30 years ago.

What injuries have you personally observed and the causes in the over 50 age crowd?

The majority are bad knees. Some injuries come from lower rank students who do not control their kicks & punches. Sparring injuries …young vs. old with a speed difference.

What injuries have you experienced, the causes, and final outcomes?

Cracked ribs, stitches in the mouth and a few other minor injuries. Today, mouth pieces, cups and pads are required. There are a lot of new regulations due to insurance policy demands.

Your best advice on rehabbing injuries appreciated

Rest and Tiger Balm.

What special advice or comments can you make regarding the female over 50 age group?

The sparring is not as aggressive as with the men. The exercises may be the same, however. Some women may take advantage of this & hit the men harder.

Are the priorities for women different than for men?

Warmups, katas, and the techniques are basically the same. The only difference is regarding sparring.

Give us some insight about your beliefs on nutrition?

I have no special nutrition program. I do tell people to eat a lot of Sushi. No limitations.

Comment on the use of nutritional supplements.

I take a One a Day vitamin and a calcium tablet. The doctor also advised me to take fish oil capsules.

What has motivated you to continue training and maintaining your PMA or positive mental attitude for over 50 years?

My motivation for staying with martial arts training for over 50 years is as follows: what started out as an interest in self- defense and sport has become a daily habit, routine and occupation based on exercise and personal health. I have found that the Karate and Tai Chi Chaun forms are one of the best ways to exercise. They can be practiced in private or with a group of friends. The body benefits from the forms as the practice provides flexibility and stamina. As we get older these are both crucial for quality living. Another benefit that benefits my overall health is I am continually learning about various martial arts applications that improve basic body movements. Besides visiting Dojo's, I use YouTube as a learning tool. You Tube is easily accessible and there are top instructors sharing information about their life experiences and ideas that enable me to constantly improve.

List some of your personal mentors who helped you develop your fitness concepts & training philosophy?

My Tai Chi Chaun instructor, Mok Lau, was a fitness expert and emphasized that a person must remain active. Tai Chi was a perfect form to develop good health and fitness. Most of my Japanese instructors have been an inspiration. Dr. Tsuyoshi Chitose did a demonstration in Canada, at age 70 + where he threw students around like they were nothing. He was able to roll around the floor like a young kid. I told myself, "That's my goal."

List any role models that you think are worthy of mention?

289

Mr. Mok Lau (Tai Chi Chaun Assoc.), Dr. Tsuyoshi Chitose, Teruyuki Okazaki (Chair – Shotokan Assoc.) Yutaka Yaguchi (ISKF), Shojiro Koyama (Japan Karate Federation), Bill Dometrich (Instructor – Chito Ryu), Shigeru Takashina (JKF)

Any other information that may be of value.

Find an activity that you have an interest in and commit to it. Read up on the history to create more interest & knowledge.

Devorah Dometrich Herbst

Why is your form of exercise / fitness the best?

Martial Arts has as much internal value, as well as, the physical benefits. I have learned more in a dojo that in church. There is a confidence built within that is more important than an empty shell. I have also been involved in police work for over 35 years and know my limitations to both.

How long have you been active in your area?

I started at 12 years old and at 64 that gives me over 50 years of training in kata, kumite, and Kobuto.

What benefits have you gained from your fitness program?

My gym or dojo is wherever I am. I don't need expensive equipment or a special place to work out. My bodyweight and inner motivation are all I need to be successful. Recent physical exams and tests indicate I still have the bone density of a person 30 years old.

What do you look for when selecting a gym?

The knowledge of the martial artists there, but I will state again that I don't need a specific gym or facility. My gym or dojo is anywhere I chose.

What advice would you give to a young person starting out?

Find your passion and pursue it. That gives the person a solid foundation from which to set realistic personal goals.

What advice would you give to the over 50 age person?

Regardless of what you want to do listen to your body. Start with realistic goals; build a strong base; evaluate yourself and build from there. Find a trainer your own age that has the experience and knowledge to guide you to your goals without injuring you. Be patient with yourself or forget it. Set realistic goals. Moderation is the key and nothing extreme.

What are some of the key mistakes you have observed in the gyms and dojos?

Exceeding moderation in training. Don't spend two hours doing kicks or punches. Diversify your training and work different areas of the body and different techniques. Many people torture their bodies and don't know how it will affect them until later years. Martial Arts is about your opponent getting hurt ...not you!

What is the biggest mistake those over 50 make in their training regimen?

The biggest mistakes are: not stretching or warming up properly; forgetting about moderation; not enough time to invest for best results and thinking a pill can heal all.

What is the leading cause of injury in older adults trying to maintain their fitness levels?

Thinking there is such a thing as "instant fitness."

What injuries have you personally observed and the causes in the over 50 age crowd?

The lack of patience and the failure to stretch properly can often result in an injury.

What injuries have you experienced, the causes and final outcomes?

My only serious injury was my right knee that required surgery. That was the result of excessive kicking and kicking into walls. The knee is fine after surgery and my rehab.

Your best advice on rehabbing injuries and surgeries

Let your pain be your guide. Ice and Ibuprofen has always taken care of my ailments.

What special advice or comments can you make regarding the female over 50 age crowd?

Warmups, katas, techniques are the same with the only difference being in sparring.

Are the priorities for women different than for men?

There are probably no necessary differences in training, but possibly modifications for sparring. A female should also be able to train as hard as a man, do the same katas, techniques and weapons.

Give us some insight about your beliefs on nutrition

I raise beef cattle, but eat very little beef. I eat mostly chicken and fish and avoid "plastic food" like burgers and pizza.

Comment on the use of nutritional supplements.

I take a daily vitamin and mineral supplement and also a 400 IU vitamin E.

What has motivated you to continue training and maintaining your PMA or positive mental attitude for over 50 years?

My father, William Dometrich, and other role models I have met along my martial arts path.

List any of your personal mentors who helped you develop your fitness concepts & training methods

My father William Dometrich set me on the right path and taught me my personal values. My Okinawan and Japanese senseis: Akamine, who taught me Kobudo or weapons; Onaga, who taught me the secrets of karate; and Inomoto who was like an older brother to me.

List any role models that you think are worthy to mention

William Dometrich, who was the highest ranking non-oriental in the U.S., in his style of karate. You also have to remember that there were no females in martial arts in the 1960s.

Add any other information that you think may be of value.

I am Akamine's only foreign student in the world. I also have my own Kobudo Federation.

Dave Guidugli

Why is your form of exercise or fitness the best?

My system is all encompassing. I work on developing speed, flexibility, strength, conditioning (endurance), performance, mental toughness, cardio with specific skills and the proper motivation. My system is normally geared to the blue- chip college and pro athletes, but can be adapted to any individual.

How long have you been involved in athletics or training?
I developed my program in 1979 while living in Boston and working with Dave Cowens and some of the Boston Celtics.

What benefits have you gained from your fitness training?

I have met and worked with a huge network of athletes from the Special Olympics to the pros. I have made contacts from the East Coast to the West Coast and was nicknamed the "Guru of Fitness" by several sports writers. My system develops athleticism in competitive athletes and a better conditioned, more confident regular trainee.

List your priorities in training
My priorities are always the same ...cardio, core work, increase energy, staying mentally sharp, staying flexible with a full range of motion. My personal concern is monitoring my blood pressure.

What do you look for when selecting a gym?
I look for a training environment that allows me the flexibility, space and resources to implement my program. I need an area open for speed and quickness drills; a variety of machines for resistance / strength training; boxing equipment and hopefully, a ring.

What advice would you give to a young person starting out?
"Rome wasn't built in a day." Expect gradual improvement as you work on stretching, toning, core, and especially cardio.

What advice would you give to the over 50 age person?
Perform a total evaluation of yourself to establish a starting baseline. This would include: speed, strength, flexibility, explosion, and mental toughness. Your weak areas become your priorities and no matter what has happened the night before you never miss your workouts. Fitness must become your lifestyle and an extension of yourself. Also, try not to get bored by keeping variety in your training sessions. Joining a gym that does not meet your needs is a big mistake. Select a location that offers you the opportunity to work on your total health. Think about your heart, blood pressure, and hormone levels. It's too bad you can't find a gym with everyone your same age.

What are some of the key mistakes you have observed in the gyms and dojos?
Lifting more than you are capable to impress someone. Improper warm ups and not stretching the tendons and ligaments to stabilize them before beginning.

What are the leading causes of injury in adults trying to maintain their fitness levels?

Trying to relive your youth and thinking you can somehow perform like you might have 20-30 years ago. Ego can become your number one enemy.

What injuries have you personally observed in the over 50 crowd?
Shoulder injuries and elbows top my list.

What injuries have you experienced, the causes, final outcomes?

I've had my nose broken four times and surgery on both shoulders and elbows. Most of those injuries are from 20 years of football and boxing.

Your best advice on rehabbing injuries?

Take it slow. Make sure you complete any rehabilitation or physical therapy program.

What special advice or comments can you make about the female trainee over 50?

The woman over 50 will of course go through menopause which will cause some bloating and hormone levels to fluctuate. They may be moody at times and have to fight weight gain. There will also be those difficult areas like the triceps, gluts, and back of thighs.

Are the priorities for women different than for men?

Give us some insight about your beliefs on nutrition?

Important the older you get. Add a lot of fruits and vegetables, no fast food, which may contribute to the increase in Diabetes, due to carbohydrate excess. The problem is a healthy diet is expensive and eating starches is less expensive. Many older people are dehydrated because they limit their fluid intake. Drink more water.

Comment on the use of nutritional supplements.

One a day vitamin, fish oil and a mineral tablet with extra calcium.

What has motivated you to continue training and maintaining your PMA or positive mental attitude for over 50 years?

It is all about looking for a better way of getting and keeping your edge. Trying to keep an edge physically and psychologically becomes a habit. Most of us started out in our athletic activities with ego as the prime motivator and personal pride enabled us to stay on that course. An active life is always the best option, especially if you continue looking for the best way and sometimes the least way to keep that physical, mental and psychological edge. Have you noticed that the best trainers are usually the oldest because they have found the best ways of finding that all important edge?

List some of your personal mentors who helped you develop your fitness concepts and training philosophy?

Kim Wood, Strength Coach for the Cincinnati Bengals; Dick Harbors, Billy Joiner, Roy Dale in boxing; and Mike McGraw, Baltimore Colts, and my semi pro coach, Bob Bradford, in football.

List any role models worthy of mention?

People in the business that have given me additional insight: Red Auerbach, Joe B. hall, Denny Crum, Mohammad Ali, Ernie Schafer, Larry Bird, Dave Cowens, and Oscar Robertson. That knowledge and inspiration helped me coach my four sons to Division 1 scholarships in athletics.

Add any other information that may be of value?

Be in harmony with yourself. Use a realistic program. Dave Cowens might be the best all- around athlete of any that I have met or trained. He was exceptional at all aspects of fitness.

Ray Hughes

Why is your form of exercise the best?

The mental aspects of self- confidence and defensive skill were the best fit for me.

How long have you been active in your area?

Since age 10 (1949) at the Cincinnati, Downtown YMCA. I began Judo at 17 and have practiced for over 57 years.

What benefits to you has your fitness training provided?

Judo and grappling builds a lot of self- confidence, which is a great mental aspect. The US Air Force SAC Judo Team practiced 3 x per day, with morning, afternoon and evening workouts. Our fitness cycle consisted of walking a minute; jogging a minute; and then running a minute. These were the toughest workouts I ever had. I like the use of free weights because of their versatility and I also use a few machines, but my priority has always been to train for endurance and durability.

List your priorities in training

My current training schedule focuses on stretching, core / abdominal work, cardio in several forms and very light resistance training. I enjoy being in the outdoors, hiking, walking and will do nothing that places limitations on what I enjoy.

What do you look for when selecting a gym?

Cleanliness is first on my list and then the variety of the equipment that is available. I like to train every day in my old neighborhood, even though that means a longer commute. I like to mix my workout with free weights, machines and add in some cardio with the treadmill. I like to finish off with a sauna, steam or a dip in the pool.

What advice would you give to a young person starting out?

Find a good mentor and don't pay any attention to what others are doing in the gym or dojo. Stay within yourself. Progress is incremental. Come into the gym and begin your workout with proper preparation and warming up. Don't just come into the gym and load up the bars.

What advice would you give to the over 50 age person?

Never try to prove anything. Warmup, stretch, and stay within yourself. You can't come back to where you were after years of layoff. Continue cardio, but if you have been inactive, start slowly and try to maintain a healthy lifestyle with workouts at least three to four days per week.

What are some of the key mistakes you have observed in the gyms and dojos?

With age I have spent more time on grappling techniques than throws, although I can still bench 265 at 74. I include walking and jogging in my daily work and also enjoy hiking in the outdoors.

What are the leading causes of injury in older adults trying to maintain their fitness levels?

In judo and karate people try to accelerate the throws and can injure shoulder joints. You can't control disease, but you can and must control technique. Injuries from improper technique can take up to six months or a year to fully recover. The next category of novice mistakes is no preparation; no warm ups; no stretching; and trying to lift too much.

What injuries have you personally observed and the causes in the over 50 age crowd?

A number of shoulder injuries resulting from improper warm-ups, stretching, and possibly over aggressiveness.

What injuries have you personally observed and the causes in the over 50 crowd?

A number of shoulder injuries resulting from improper warm-ups, stretching, and possibly over aggressiveness.

What injuries have you experienced, the causes, final outcomes?

Prostate surgery at age 60, which was not an injury, but required a year to 18 months to fully recover. I've been very fortunate and have never had an injury that required surgery because I've had good mentors. That's a blessing!

Any advice on rehabbing injuries appreciated?

Rehab was incremental starting back with minimal 5 pound weights and eventually working up to 300 pound plus bench pressing and completing regular 5 mile jogs.

What special advice and comments can you make regarding the female over 50 crowd?

I don't see why they would train any differently than a man.

Are the priorities for women different than for men?

There are no differences needed for women, with the exception of the grabbling and intensity of the throws.

Give us some insight about your beliefs on nutrition?

I drink 2 good beers a day and take in at least 40 oz. of cool water. I drink no sodas and eat no fried food. I may eat fast food once every two years I also try to eat as much fruit and vegetables as possible.

Comment on the use of nutritional supplements.
I take no meds or supplements. Maybe I should be taking something?

What has motivated you to continue training and maintaining your PMA or positive mental attitude for over 50 years?
10 years from now I plan to be doing the things I enjoy that include: walking and hiking anywhere in the outdoors with very few physical restrictions. I plan to continue my training, with modifications, that allow me maximum functionality and with my weight under control. I don't want my pride to cause me to over train and place future physical limitations on myself.

List any of your personal mentors who helped you develop your fitness concepts and training methods?

Various Japanese instructors and some of the early members of the U.S. Air Force Judo Team

List any role models that you think are worthy to mention?

Jack LaLanne – had some Revolutionary ideas in training, fitness and design of machines.

Add any other information you think may be of value.

Lanny Julian

Why is your form of exercise or fitness the best?
I believe in training the whole body with a system that incorporates light weight, very little maxing out, and high

repetitions. I think this is the best system for me and for any individual who wants to avoid injuries. My form also concentrates on additional exercises that focus on hand and grip strength; wrists and forearms; tendon and ligament strength; and bicep strength. That specialized training is essential if you want to compete and have goals on the national and world levels.

How long have you been active in your special area of fitness?

I started training with my homemade dumbbells in the late 1950s and early 60s. I entered the U.S. Army in 1963 and resumed my weight training after my enlistment was up. I started entering local Cincinnati contests in 1969 and competed until 1981. I still advise many arm wrestlers and my son, Dom, (age 46) is also an active participant.

What benefits to you have your fitness training provided?

I have been able to maintain a healthy lifestyle and good physical condition, with very few injures, for over 50 years. I have also learned the importance of good training partners and the power of "self- talk" or focusing my mind for world class competition.

List your priorities in training

Training is a gradual and success comes with time. Light weight with high reps is the key. Be consistent, but also train to avoid injury.

What do you look for when selecting a gym / dojo?

My wife and I have trained in many gyms including all of the popular fitness chains. The modern fitness centers have every possible type of equipment, but the key is still cleanliness. There is no excuse for not wiping down the machines and maintaining high sanitary standards. I would advise anyone using a fitness club or center to take their own bottle of spray to wipe down the machines before and after.

What advice would you give to a young person starting out?
The advice is the same regardless of age. See your doctor first. I like to have a physical twice a year with blood work included to monitor my body's key functions.

What advice would you give to the over 50 age person?
Use your head, start slow, and use common sense! "You cannot do what you did years ago or when you were younger." Start light and work your way up. Your personal goals may take years of commitment and dedication. Also, be sure to see your doctor first to make sure you have their approval. Don't forget to enjoy your training

What are some of the key mistakes you have observed in the gyms and dojos?
I was in a particular tournament and had five or six long pulls that left me tired. (a quick match might be four seconds and a long pull 20 seconds to a minute) My last match went a minute and there was a loud "pop" as I tore a ligament in my forearm. Proper rest and recuperation is also a key to progress without injury. I also have a problem with many of the trainers I see in the gyms. They seem to have everyone on the same program regardless of sex, age or ability.

What are the leading causes of injury in adults trying to maintain their fitness levels?

The biggest problems are over training, not paying attention to your technique and losing focus. Injuries come easier the older we get. Make sure you warm up properly, stretch and use the high rep method. I never accepted bar challenges in my arm wrestling career. That was never the place or time to put all my training at risk. I might lock up with a challenger in a handshake to let him feel my grip. That was usually enough. I also trained both arms the same because there are left handed contests and you want both arms to be symmetrical.

What is the biggest mistake those over 50 make in their training regimen?

Make sure you have a knowledgeable training partner. Expect progress to be gradual. Make sure any hired trainers on site know what they are doing. They may not know your limitations or health status, but you do.

What injuries have you personally observed in the over 50 crowd?

Overtraining, using too much weight and being trained by gym staff who don't seem to understand the needs of their clients.

What injuries have you experienced, the causes and the final outcomes?

Torn biceps from a non- arm wrestling, freak accident; torn ligament in the elbow; and a torn ligament in my right wrist from a work related injury dealing with a slab of slaughterhouse beef weighing 900 pounds. I rehabbed all of my injuries successfully using very light high repetition exercises.

Your best advice on rehabbing injuries and surgeries?

Make sure your rehab work is complete before increasing your training goals.

What special advice or comments can you make regarding the female trainee over 50?

Women have other issues like osteoporosis and bone density issues. These can be addressed through resistance training and proper nutritional supplements. The same advice for men and the younger trainees still applies.

Are the priorities for women different than for men?
The same as the above.

Give us some insight about your beliefs on nutrition
My wife and I take a daily vitamin / mineral supplement; fish oil; supplements for bone density; and a glucosamine – MSM-chondroitin supplement for the joints. We also like to have blood work done twice a year to check on our baselines. I eat whatever my wife fixes.

Comment on the use of nutritional supplements.
Some supplements are necessary, but I adhere to the basics. No type of protein, creatine etc.

What has motivated you to continue training and maintaining your PMA or positive mental attitude for over 50 years?
Positive mental attitude is always something I have included in my personal training. My strategy was to look into a mirror and talk to myself until I knew I was ready for my next arm wrestling match. I've continued to use that same mental attitude and approach since retiring from competition. I use it when working out and preparing myself for anything I need to do.

List any personal mentors who helped you develop your fitness concepts and training philosophy?
When I began in arm wrestling there were no mentors or role models. I think I was in the first generation of the sport's

popularity. The TV always showcased the Petaluma, California Championships.

List any other fitness role models you think are worthy to mention?

I also had a high regard for the symmetry and training philosophy of Frank Zane.

Add any other information that may have value to the reader?

Keep working out! You should never work out alone and have a reliable training partner with similar abilities. Be careful to avoid injury at all costs.

Roger Riedinger

Why is your form of exercise or fitness the best?

My preferred form of exercise is basic progressive resistance weight training. You can experience near maximum benefits from 30-60 minutes three times per week. For the over 50 crowd, the main benefit is maintenance of muscle tissue and prevention of osteoporosis. It also lends itself to goal setting and self - discipline which are key to a successful and prosperous life.

How long have you been active in your special area of fitness?

I started weight training regularly at age 14; I'm now in my 51st year of weight training.

What benefits to you have your fitness training provided?

The self -discipline and principle of systemized progress has been a big part in creating a very successful business. Health, strength, vitality, skin tone, and appearance are all benefits of progressive weight training properly applied.

List your priorities in training
Full range of movement, maintain strength and flexibility, maintain muscle tissue.

What do you look for when selecting a gym?
I'd look for a gym that includes a mixture of free weights and machines. More importantly, I'd look for one run or managed by an experienced weight trainer who can identify the good in each new fitness fad, but who also has a solid grounding in the fundamentals of progressive weight training.

What advice would you give to a young person starting out?
Not that they would listen, but start well within your current ability and gradually increase each week. Start with a classic weight training program, not with one that you read in a muscle mag, or where you do bench and arms every workout day.

What advice would you give to the over 50 age person?
It's not too late. Start with very basic goals. If you are inactive, start with a walk of 50 steps there and back, three days a week. Increase the next week to 60, etc. Soon you'll be walking a mile, then two. Act like you're 16, start lifting weights with just the bar. Add a small amount each week. Don't make your goals too hard to achieve. Set realistic lifetime goals. Break them down into yearly, quarterly, monthly, and even weekly sub goals. For example: Lifetime goal is a clean and jerk with bodyweight. Starting point is 65 pounds and bodyweight is 165. Your first 1-week goal would be 67.5lbs. Year 1 goal might be 115 lbs. (just 1 lb per week increase). 1st 3- month goal is 2.5 lbs. per week, 2nd

3- month goal is 2.5 lbs. every other week – that gets you to your 1st year goal with 6 months to spare. It's usually better at this point to drop back about 10% and start again with the same progression. Another round of the above progression will take you to 135 at the end of year one. And you still have a lifetime to go to add just 30 more pounds. Do not try to increase strength or endurance too quickly.

Balance. However, I tend to lean to resistance (weight) training. It would be a great time for an over 50 to start with one of the basic weight training courses (York*, Weider, etc.) and actually go through the courses starting with the basic course and staying with it until progress stalls, then going to the next course. I have not seen anyone in years follow this advice, they always want more and think more training will get them where they want to be faster – it actually results in burnout or injury.

What are some of the key mistakes you have observed in the gyms and dojos?

The mindset that more is better. Trying to train too much and with too much intensity. Doing five exercises for each body part.

What are the leading causes of injury in adults trying to maintain their fitness levels?

Over work! Trying to do too much too fast without adequate rest and recovery. The key is progression.

What injuries have you personally observed in the over 50 crowd?

Long time lifters generally have shoulder problems – mainly caused by bench pressing at the expense of a more rounded program.

What injuries have you experienced, the causes and final outcomes?

Shoulder injuries (see #12 above). The final outcome was a shoulder replacement, but by following the type of progression system illustrated in #13 above, I was able to regain 90% of my former strength and many nagging injuries healed during the recovery period. Another outcome was that now I perform each exercise in perfect form and continue to progress in many at 65 years of age.

Your best advice on rehabbing injuries and surgeries?

Shoulder injuries (see #12 above). The final outcome was a shoulder replacement, but by following the type of progression system illustrated in #13 above, I was able to regain 90% of my former strength and many nagging injuries healed during the recovery period. Another outcome was that now I perform each exercise in perfect form and continue to progress in many at 65 years of age.

What special advice or comments can you make regarding the female trainee over 50?

Train on a basic weight training course as noted in #11 above. Forget specialized exercises to tighten up the body part that you are agonizing over. What you should do is a complete course of basic exercises in a systematic manner of progression. And stay with it, 3 days a week, every week. A heavy, light, medium system would be best for women as their energy seems to vary more than men on a day to day basis.

Are the priorities for women different than for men?

I don't think so. Because women usually have not pursued a regular weight training program, they can experience even greater benefits in promoting bone density and combating age related muscle loss.

Give us some insight about your beliefs on nutrition

Protein is of first importance. Our body is made of protein and in fact, the term protein means "of first importance". Fats, in general, are not as bad for you as the popular thinking purports. Too much of anything is, but many fats are beneficial and in fact, some are essential to life. Learn about healthy fats. Finally, carbohydrates need to be limited to some extent if you wish to lose body fat, especially as you age. Good carbs are those found in their natural state like fruits and vegetable. Processed carbs like sweets and grains are not so good.

(Disclaimer: My wife, Sandy, and I own a nutritional supplement company, Beverly International.) Supplements do not take the place of food that is found in its natural state – eggs, meat, vegetables, and fruit. However, they are very helpful in providing nutrients that we may not get in our normal diet. We have a supplement recommendation chart for various categories of athletes including those over age 50. For over 50 we recommend in this priority: (1) protein (preferably Milk Protein Isolate – a natural milk protein with carbs, sugar, and saturated fat removed), (2) creatine (anti-aging and muscle cell integrity) there have been thousands of studies on the benefits of creatine, and despite the press, the overwhelming majority show benefits for not only muscle and strength, but also neurological and anti-aging benefits, (3) glutamine for recovery and immune system enhancement, (4) HMB – prevents age related muscle wasting (sarcopenia).

Comment on the use of nutritional supplements. (see above)

What has motivated you to continue training and maintaining your PMA or positive mental attitude for over 50 years?

Progressive weight training is still a priority in my life 53 years after I started. I believe that systematic, progressive weight training is one of the best activities anyone can do to promote longevity and quality of life. As the years begin to creep up, continuing to set and achieve new goals keeps me motivated in all areas of my life. Progressive weight training lends itself easily to setting SMART (specific, measurable, achievable, realistic, timely) goals. Here's how I set my training goals: I establish goals for each exercise in six-12 week intervals; then systematically work backwards from my six -12 week goals to set weekly and daily workout goals; and each workout is planned in advance. Each workout day I look forward to putting my plan into action. For example, one of the exercises I regularly do is the one arm dumbbell press. I set a 12- week goal to add five pounds to my best poundage for my current age. This year my goals are based on my best performances while 67 years old. I perform this regular exercise one session per week. My plan is to add one repetition per week over six weeks. (Editors' note – Roger mentioned previously that he had a complete shoulder replacement and continues to train hard) See progression chart below:

Week 1   Warm-up, perform 5 sets of 2 reps (with previous 2 rep maximum)

Week 2   1 set of 3 reps and 4 sets of 2 reps

Week 3   2 sets of 3 reps and 3 sets of 2 reps

Week 4   3 sets of 3 reps and 2 sets of 2 reps

Week 5 4 sets of 3 reps and 1 set of 2 reps

Week 6 5 sets of 3 reps

Week 7 - I would then add 2.5 pounds and start back at 5 sets of 2 reps. If I continue this same progression through the 12th week, I'll add another 2.5 pounds and on week 13 I will have achieved my goal of adding five pounds to my best effort!

Relating this back to my SMART formula goals, you can see each workout is a goal in itself and is specific, measurable, achievable, realistic, and timely. You can find small incremental improvements in every part of your life. Whether you are starting a fitness program or some other discipline, take it one small step at a time and build slowly on each success. Remember inch by inch, it's a cinch; yard by yard it' hard.

List any personal mentors who helped you develop your fitness concepts and training philosophy?
Peary Rader, Stuart McRobert, Bob Hoffman, Brooks Kubik – excellent resources on basic, progressive resistance training.

List any fitness role models you think are worthy to mention

John Grimek, Jeff and Cory Everson.

Add any other information that may be of value.

Gosh, I've said it over and over again in the above questions – progressive resistance. Take it slow and steady like the tortoise. You will beat the hare in the end and be much stronger, healthier, and injury free. Get a basic program. Set realistic goals. Stick with your program, progress slowly and you will eventually accomplish your goals – then you'll have to set new ones, adding years to your life and a better life to your years.

*York Barbell Course No. 1

Jerry Auton

Why is your form of exercise the best?
Thousands of hours spent on research, sets and workouts at various times during my lifetime.

How long have you been active in your special area of fitness?
I have been active for fifty- two years. I started lifting weights after my dad purchased my first 110 pound set of Billard barbells. I've competed as a powerlifter, bodybuilder, arm wrestler, physical fitness major, and at one time was the Lexington, Kentucky fencing champion.

What benefits to you has your fitness training provided?

Endless benefits! I have been able to be free of any prescription drugs and other medications that most men my age are required to take. I can still compete in the 60 and over class of men's bodybuilding; run solid times in 5 km road races; and have the resting heart rate of a person 40 years old. I feel that I project an aura of personal fitness and take proud in my conditioning. My health care professionals seem very complimentary of my fitness level after taking and reviewing my vitals.

List your priorities in training
Always plan your workouts ahead on a weekly schedule. It is imperative for maximum results to workout with an experienced

partner or spend the money and hire a qualified and certified personal trainer

What do you look for when selecting a gym?
My highest priority is cleanliness. I go the gym and dedicate myself to maintaining my health and condition. I don't expect to pick up and infectious germs or staph. The second priority is to find a gym with a variety of strength and cardio machines.

What advice would you give to a young person starting out?
The two most common mistakes are actually direct opposites. Train too hard; too fast; too often and you become discouraged by soreness and possible injury. The opposite fault is training too light, being afraid to challenge yourself by increasing the weight; and training infrequently. That also results in discouragement due to little improvement. The key is to find the happy medium.

What advice would you give the over 50 age trainee?
A certified trainer is a must in this situation, especially if it has been years since you last regular sessions. Take the time to think about what you actually want to accomplish on a particular workout day. Again, plan, warm-up, stretch and seek professional, experienced assistance. All ages are prone to poor technique and trying to lift more weight than can be properly handled. Poor technique alone can result in injury, but combined with too much weight is a recipe for disaster. Muscles, tendons, and ligaments that are torn can have an adverse effect on your training for a lifetime.

What are some of the mistakes you have observed in the gyms and dojos?

The improper use of the equipment and very poor technique ranks at the top of the list.

What are the leading causes of injury in adults trying to maintain their fitness levels?

Lack of preparation for the goals you have set. Age does not give you experience in every endeavor or an edge in all things. Do you think you can fly an airplane just because you can fit into the cockpit? Be realistic.

What injuries have you personally observed in the over 50 crowd?

Back and knee injuries seem to be the most common and are the result of overworking specific muscle groups or poor technique. Sometimes the result of both!

What injuries have you experienced, the causes and final outcomes?

I have experienced rotator cuff damage to both shoulders. I attribute this to the stupidity and brashness of youth that finally caught up with me. Surgery by a highly competent professional, proper recuperation and rehab finally got me back into the gym and regular training.

What is the best advice on rehabbing injuries and surgeries?

Rehab all injuries slowly and patiently! Keep the positive attitude that you will be back as long as you follow the professional advice of your physician /surgeon.

What special advice or comments can you make regarding the female over 50?

Osteoporosis has to be taken into account for this age group. Avoid conditions and training that places undue stress on the skeletal system. Ex. Female runners suffer many times the leg stress fractures as men.

Are the priorities for women different than for men?

Plan your work and work your plan with the help of a professional trainer. Seek a trainer that is certified for Senior Fitness. Many in this age group will qualify for the Silver Sneakers® programs offered by many insurance companies. Those free memberships, to the over 65 crowd, free up money that can be used to hire a trainer. Make your training routine a good habit because they can be as difficult to break as a bad one. Try to work out 3-5 times per week and take Sundays off. Even our Heavenly Father wants you to rest on His day. I typically do 60% cardio to 40% strength /resistance training on the same day.

Give us some insight about your beliefs on nutrition

Nutrition is vital to good health. Why put forth the sweat and effort of your workouts if you are not going to replenish your system with healthy eating habits. I recommend: drinking 64 oz. of water per day; avoiding junk foods; and consuming plenty of fresh fruits and vegetables.

Comment on the use of nutritional supplements.
I take fish oil, Vitamin C and a high quality protein drink several times a day.

What has motivated you to continue training and maintaining your PMA or positive mental attitude for over 50 years?

I always felt that the desire for success must be stronger than the fear of failure. That mindset has been my motivation from my high school days until today. I have never outgrown my competitive nature. Whatever the activity, I put 100% effort into it. I also knew from research and association that I was more likely to increase my chances of living a longer and healthier life as a result of that attitude. After I started my family I wanted to be a good example as a father and that was an added incentive to live a longer, healthier life. You may have all the possessions that wealth may bring, but if you cannot maintain your health what good are they?

List any personal mentors who helped you develop your fitness concepts and training philosophy?

Tom Geimeier, my lifelong friend and frequent training partner. (co-author)

List any fitness role models you think are worthy of mention?

Bill Pearl, Jack Lalanne, Dave Draper and Larry Scott.

Add any other information that may have value?

To be successful in any and all ventures of life it takes a combination of three components: hard work, knowledge and enthusiasm. 1. Educate yourself to be knowledgeable in the facts regarding proper training and nutrition; 2. Go into your daily workouts with proper enthusiasm that you are helping you; 3. Work hard on your commitment to continue your workout and nutrition plans from now until the casket. It may take you longer than you think, hopefully, a full *Second Fifty*.

Tom Geimeier

Why is your form of exercise or fitness the best?

I think the best form of exercise is what contributes best to maximum health. I spent years powerlifting, bodybuilding and playing other sports part time, which was not in my best interest. Total fitness should be the key and that form will change with time and age.

How long have you been active in your special area of fitness?

My father bought me a YMCA membership when I was 8 and dropped me off every Saturday to swim and learn the basics of other sports. Like many other early teens of that time I bought a Joe Weider course when I was about 14 and also watched Jack LaLanne on TV. At 17 I joined a local Turner's Club and did some gymnastics and tumbling. I started baseball at 12 and kept playing until about 30. I picked up martial arts in college and continued in the military. I coached track for 15 years and practiced every event but hurdles. I'm not a purebred athlete, but some sort of a hybrid.

What benefits to you has your fitness training provided?

The type of training I focused on added to my self- confidence and the ability to relax physically and re-charge mentally. I had a lot of strength and specific sports skills that allowed me to play a variety of sports.

List your priorities in training

I've always been proud of my flexibility and have tried to maintain that edge. I have concentrated on gaining strength and utilized power type workouts. Today my priorities are: do nothing to aggravate old injuries; be moderate and sensible; do cardio first followed by resistance exercise; be consistent in training and try to maintain a sound mind and a positive mental outlook.

What do you look for when selecting a gym?

I've belonged to a number of gyms since age 12 from the back alleys to the deluxe. I like a variety of machines and I always select machines that do not give me pain while exercising. Cleanliness is a key in the exercise room and locker room. Finally, a gym where people know how to use the machines properly and the staff keeps everything in working order.

What advice would you give to a young person starting out?

A good mentor can set you on the right path, motivate you and save you years of mistakes and lack of improvement. Too many people I know have learned through trial and error. A good mentor can also serve as a life- long role model. Build a good foundation because a house built on sand cannot stand.

What advice would you give the over 50 age trainee?

Find a type of fitness that you can use with regularity and gives you cardio, flexibility, and resistance training for muscle tone. The training must have a low risk of injury and be convenient. Have a thorough physical before you begin and set sensible goals. Know thyself and your personal limitations. Do more than mere exercise. Work on your nutrition, relaxation, and set realistic goals. Make sure you pass all aspects of your physical exam; find an ideal place to train; set sensible goals; and concentrate on the life habits that will take you to triple digits. (100)

What are some of the key mistakes you have observed in the gyms and dojos?

The improper use of the equipment and very poor technique used by all ages is difficult to watch. It is too bad the gyms don't have a roving instructor to correct the flaws. Many people training are ignorant of gym etiquette and the biggest mistake is using a weight that is too much too soon.

What are the leading causes of injury in adults trying to maintain their fitness levels?

Failing to warm up and taking unnecessary risks regarding the amount of weight used in your exercise routine. Many injuries also occur outside of the gym in other areas. Be cautious and think before you act.

What injuries have you personally observed in the over 50 crowd?

I have observed almost every type of injury over the past 52 years that include: shoulders, knees, elbows, head injuries, Achilles Tendons, back, foot and hand problems.

What injuries have you experienced, the causes and final outcomes?

I had two knee surgeries from an incident where I lifted a car from off of a trapped kindergartener. I did not realize the severity of the injury and fell several weeks later doing squats. I had shoulder surgeries: one from a baseball injury along with some facial reconstruction; and the second from a faulty piece of equipment in another school setting. I ruptured my Achilles tendon playing basketball.

Your best advice on rehabbing injuries and surgeries?

Be patient and follow the PT's advice if you want to regain full motion or most of it. You cannot afford any set- backs. Trying to push the limits or coming back too soon may cause re-injury or there is a tendency to reinjure the opposite side.

What special advice or comments can you make regarding the female over 50?

I've coached women's track and field, soccer and a few bodybuilders and powerlifters. Like anyone else they need motivation and realistic goals.

Are the priorities for women different than for men?

Women over 50 have some common problem areas, but also a few of special concern. Triceps sag, cellulite buildup on the hamstrings, and the buttocks are some of concern. During and after the child bearing years the abdomen and lower belly lose

their elasticity. Hormonal changes and weight gain accentuate these problem areas. The weight gain can also be visible near the face, which we call turkey neck. That also affects men.

Give us some insight about your beliefs on nutrition

Many people say you don't need supplements if you eat right. I believe that eating correctly is crucial, but I take a few supplements for insurance and some on doctor's orders. I eat a lot of fruits and vegetables and quality grains. I like my egg whites, low fat milk, chicken, fish and some pork. I cut out all beef. I also need to consume more water.

Comment on the use of nutritional supplements.

I take a low dose Aspirin each day and a flaxseed oil or fish oil on doctor's orders. I mix a little creatine with my water when I go to the gym and take a protein shake after working out or sometimes in place of a meal. I also take a multi vitamin /mineral tablet. My daughter has been a vegetarian since age two and I encourage her to take a high quality protein, multi vitamin, calcium and B-12.

What has motivated you to continue training and maintaining your PMA or positive mental attitude for over 50 years?

Every young person finds a role model in the activities they have interest in or would like to excel in. They initially try to emulate that person and found out how to develop the same skills and physical attributes. That initial interest combined with some success drives you to raise the bar a little higher. Your regular exercise program gives you a great mental high and re-charges you physically. Those feelings become addictive. As we get older we see how inactivity and a poor lifestyle can affect aging and longevity of the people around us. What other option would an intelligent person take?

List any personal mentors who helped you develop your fitness concepts and training philosophy?

I had a neighbor who was a bodybuilder when I started and another mentor at a Turner's Club when I was in my late teens. Many of the guys with the same interests pooled our equipment and followed some of the routines in the muscle mags.

List any fitness role models you think are worthy of mention?

People you see, read about and meet certainly have an inpact on you. Many of the gurus have already mentioned Jack LaLanne. Think about the Hercules movies and Steve Reeves and Reg Park. Do you remember the old Superman TV shows and the super heroes in the comics? I've attended a number of AAU and IFBB shows in York, PA and NYC where I was inspired by some of the great physiques and fitness gurus. I've been fortunate to have met: John Grimek, Bob Hoffman, Dan Lurie, Chuck Sipes, Frank Zane, Sergio Olivia, Chris Dickerson, and Casey Viator. I was also one of the original students of martial arts expert Sin The' (Shaolin do).

Add any other information that may have value?

With any luck you should get smarter with age.

Appendix B

✓ Copy of the Senate Resolution No. 9, from the KY
Senate & House for Heroism

MRS. MARJORIE WAGONER

CHIEF CLERK

STATE SENATE

ROOM 319 STATE CAPITOL

FRANKFORT, KENTUCKY

40601

COMMONWEALTH OF KENTUCKY
STATE SENATE
FRANKFORT, KENTUCKY

October
Twenty-seventh
1 9 8 7

Mr. Thomas Geimeier
5936 Vice Lane
Burlington, Kentucky 41005

Dear Mr. Geimeier:

We are enclosing a copy of Senate Resolution No. 9,
which was introduced and adopted by the Senate on October 21,
1987.

This resolution honors you for your heroic behavior of
Benjamin Overbay. As directed a copy of this resolution is being
mailed to you.

Sincerely,

(Mrs.) Marjorie Wagoner
(Mrs.) Marjorie Wagoner
Chief Clerk of the Senate

MW:PQ

Enclosure

87 SS BR 36

A RESOLUTION honoring Thomas Geimeier and Medrith Jo Hager of Ludlow, Kentucky for their heroism.

WHEREAS, in November of 1986 Benjamin Overbay, five years old, was tragically struck by an automobile which came to rest upon this small child; and

WHEREAS, Benjamin Overbay was heroically rescued from imminent death by the swift and selfless actions of Thomas Geimeier and Medrith Jo Hager; and

WHEREAS, Thomas Geimeier, a teacher at Ludlow High School, single-handedly lifted the automobile off of Benjamin while Medrith Jo Hager, a secretary at Ludlow Elementary School, pulled Benjamin free of the incredible mass of steel, rubber, and glass which rested upon him; and

WHEREAS, Benjamin Overbay is alive today due to the quick response and gentle care administered by Thomas Geimeier and Medrith Jo Hager;

NOW, THEREFORE,

Be it resolved by the Senate of the General Assembly of the Commonwealth of Kentucky:

1   Section 1. That the members of this august body do
2 hereby honor and praise the heroism and heroic behavior of
3 Thomas Geimeier and Medrith Jo Hager in their rescue of
4 Benjamin Overbay.

5   Section 2. That the Senate of the General Assembly
1 of the Commonwealth of Kentucky does hereby proclaim
2 Thomas Geimeier and Medrith Jo Hager of Ludlow to be
3 outstanding citizens and exemplary representatives of the
4 Commonwealth.

5   Section 3. That the Clerk of the Senate is hereby
6 directed to transmit a copy of this resolution to Thomas
7 Geimeier, 5936 Vice Lane, Burlington, Kentucky 41005, and
8 to Medrith Jo Hager, 1605 Park Road, Ft. Wright, Kentucky
9 41011.

ATTESTED: _Marjorie Wagone_
Clerk of the Senate

Appendix C

Recommended resources that may have value

Age Related Problems, Ch. 7, Fitness for Seniors, 2004, Frank K. Wood &
Associates

Aerobics and Fitness Association of America
15250 Ventura Blvd., Ste.200
Sherman Oaks, CA 91403-3297
www.afaa.com

Alliance for Aging Research
2021 K Street, NW, Ste.305
Washington, DC 20006
www.agingresearch.org

American Association of Retired Persons
601 E St., NW
Washington, DC 20049
www.aarp.org

American Heart Association
7272 Greenville Ave.
Dallas, TX 75231
www.americanheart.org

American Senior Fitness Association (SFA)
P.O. Box 2575
New Smyrna Beach, FL 32170
www.seniorfitness.net

Become a Certified Personal Trainer by Robert Wolf, PhD, McGraw Hill 2010, New York, NY

Beverly International Nutrition
www.beverlyinternational.com
1157 Industrial Road
Cold Spring, KY 41076
1 800-781-3475

Encyclopedia of Self-Hypnosis, by Melvin Powers, 1975, Improvement Books Company, Opa Locka, FL

Faster, Better, Stronger by Eric Heiden, MD, and Massimo Testa, MD with Deanne Musolf, 2008 HarperCollins Publishing, New York, NY

Fitness Educators of Older Adults Association
759 Chopin Drive, Ste. 1
Sunnyvale, CA 94087
www.fitness educators.com

Fitness Illustrated by Brian Sharkley, 2011, Human Kinetics, Champaign, IL

High Intensity Training by John Philbin, 2004, Human Kinetics, Champaign, IL

High Performance Health by James M. Rippe MD, 2007, Thomas Nelson, Inc., Nashville, TN

International Society for Aging and Physical Activity (ISAPA)
Wojtek Chodzko-Zajko, PhD
University of Illinois Department of Kinesiology
Louis Freer Hall, 906 S. Goodwin Ave.

Urbana, IL 61801
www.isapa.org

International Sports Sciences Association (ISSA), Senior Fitness Course Handbook
(Second edition), Copyright 2010, by ISSA, Carpenteria, CA 93013

Jack LaLanne .com

Kenpo Karate for Self Defense, by Jay T. Will, Ohara Publications Inc., 1977, Burbank, CA, pgs. 14-15, "Relationship of Martial Arts Systems

Medical Facts and Myths Everyone Should Know, by Drs. Sanjiv Chopra and Alan Lotvin with David Fisher, 1st edition, 2010, St. Martin's Press, New York

National Alzheimer's Association
919 N. Michigan Ave., Ste. 1100
Chicago, IL 60611-1676
www.alz.org

Pilates 2004 by Matthew Aldrich, Hodder Headline Ltd., London

Super Joints – Russian Longevity Secrets, by Pauel Tsatsouline, Dragon Door Publishing, Inc., St. Paul, MN

The Fit Senior, Customized Fitness Training
"In home option"
Jerry Auton @ jerryauton@gmail.com

The Insiders Tell All handbook on Weight Training Technique, 3rd edition, by Stuart McRobert, 2009, CS Publishing Ltd., Connell, WA

The New Aerobics, by Dr. Kenneth Cooper, #1, Bantam Books, New York 1982

Interviews with the *Panel of Experts*
Jerry Auton
Terry Collis
Tom Geimeier
Dave Guidugli
Debbie Dometrich - Herbst
Ray Hughes
Lanny Julian
Roger Riedinger

Total Tai Chi by Andrew Popovica, Annes Publishing Ltd. 2004, London by Lorenz Books Publisher in US

Walking for Fitness and Health by Dr. Klaus Bos, 1995, Sterling Publishing Co., Inc., New York, NY

Weight Training for Dummies, A reference for the rest of us, by Liz Neporent, Suzanne Schlosberg, and Shirley Archer, 3rd Edition, Wiley Publishing Company, Inc., 2006 Indianapolis, IN

Women's Strength Training Anatomy, by Frederic Delavier, 2003, Vigot Publishing, Paris, France …U.S. Human Kinetics, Champaign, IL

Which Comes First, Cardio or Weights? By Sifu Philip Bonifonte, The Career Press, Inc., 2004, Franklin Lakes, NJ

Yoga RX, A step-by-step program to promote wellness and healing for common ailments by Larry Payne, PhD and Richard Usatine, MD, 2002 Broadway Books, Random House, New York, NY

Glossary

The terms listed in this Glossary are for reference only. There are probably more than needed, but there may be times a quick look up will answer questions you have from reading an article, overhearing a comment, or something you observed at a gym. Our purpose is to provide the reader with an informative book that will be easy to use, practical, and covers all the basic information necessary to initiate and maintain their personal fitness program.

Abduction - Any movement or motion of the extremities toward the center or mid line of the body.

Abdominals - Commonly referred to as the "abs." The large group of muscles in front of the abdomen that assist in breathing, supporting the trunk, spine, and protect the internal organs.

Acute - A pain that begins suddenly due to an injury such as: broken bone, cut, burn or surgery. The pain may persist up to six months after the cause is treated.

Adduction - Any movement or motion of the extremities away from the center or mid line of the body.

Aerobic - Exercise that is sustained for a period of time that taxes the cardio system, by increasing the flow of blood and oxygen, which temporarily increases the heart rate and eventually improving endurance.

Amino acids - The building blocks of the all- important protein food group.

Anabolic - Any substance, natural or synthetic, which causes tissue buildup and increases muscular growth.

Anaerobic - Strength or resistance training. Sprinting versus jogging and power type movements taking a priority over cardio benefits.

Antioxidants - A substance or nutritional supplement that reduces damage to the cells due to oxygen damage facilitated by "free radicals."

BMI - Commonly referred to as Body Mass Index. An index used to evaluate the ratio of lean muscle mass to body fat. Height, weight and body type are taken into account. The ideal index is between 18-25, with over 30 having a tendency toward obesity and under 18 very lean and not recommended.

Breathing - The proper breath control used to maximize results during training.

Carbohydrates - A food group commonly known as sugars and starches. They provide quick energy and yield 4 calories per gram. Excess carbohydrates will be stored as fat in the body. They typically provide the main source of caloric intake in the normal diet.

Cardio -   Aerobic training focusing on the cardio vascular system
Chronic – Consistent, ongoing pain even though a past injury has healed.
Circuit training – Performing a series of 8-10 exercises, for the total body, without rest. Used for definition and adding endurance.
Core - Refers to exercises for the abdominals, oblique muscles, and serratus muscles.

Concentration – Clearing your mind and focusing on the exercise, the technique, and the muscle being worked.

Cross training – Incorporating running, swimming, martial arts, and other activities in your training regime.

Definition - The refined appearance of the muscle which many people refer to as "cuts."

Ectomorph - One of the three basic body types which features a more elongated and skinny appearance, with a lighter bone structure.

Endomorph - One of the three basic body types that features a heavier, thicker boned appearance.

Endurance - The aerobic capacity or ability to continue training without fatigue.

Fats - Fats serve as an energy source in the body second to carbohydrates. Fats have a high calorie value of 9 calories per gram and should be limited in the daily diet.

Flexibility -The range of motion of the human body and the ease of movement of the joints.

Flushing – Exercise adds blood to the muscle being worked. Doing higher repetitions and reducing the time between exercises causes an increase in the blood flow and thus the size of the muscle. Also known as pumping up.

Forced reps – Also known as "cheating." When the last few repetitions of an exercise become difficult to do, in strict form, a training partner assists with the weight so a few additional reps can be forced out. A technique sometimes used to blast pass "sticking points."

Free radicals – Mutations in the cells that can cause cellular damage and contribute to disease and aging, due to interaction with DNA. The antioxidants Vitamins A, C, and E are believed to aid in combating the negative effects.

Giant sets – A high endurance workout where you select 4-5 exercises for one specific body part and complete in a non-stop circuit. Rest and perform additional sets, but only do one body part per workout in this manner.

Glycemic index –An indicator of the ability of different foods that contain carbohydrates to elevate the blood glucose levels within two hours.

Hoffman Formula – A formula devised to compare lifters of various weight classes to determine the overall best. Each bodyweight is given a specific coefficient that is multiplied by their total weight lifted. This formula was revised by Herb Glossbrenner in 2004. There is a second coefficient multiplied when comparing Masters category lifters.

Hydration - Keeping the body supplied with adequate water and liquids.

Instinctive training – The principle of knowing which body part to exercise and not by a pre-arranged routine. Not recommended for the novice.

Intensity - Maximizing physical workouts by reducing the rest time between sets, increasing the repetitions, or increasing the weight lifted during exercise.

Isolation – Specific training on one body part. Good for thickening and bulking up a lagging muscle group.

Isometrics - A type of strength training where a muscle is worked or exerted against an immoveable force with no visible joint movement.

Isotonics – A type of training where the muscles are moved against a partial moveable object or force.

Kinesiology - The scientific study of the human body, it's movement and how it functions.

Large muscles – These include the larger support muscles which include the back, thighs, and abdominals.

Ligaments – A band of strong connective tissue that connects bone to bone. (ex. Anterior cruciate ligament of the knee)

Limitations - Knowing what your body is capable of without inducing injury.

Malone-Meltzer Formula – A formula designed to compare powerlifters of various weight classes to determine the best overall lifter in the meet. Similar and achieves the same purpose as the Hoffman-Glossbrenner Formula.

Mesomorph - One of the three body types that has a leaner more ideal appearance.

Muscle density – Sometimes referred to as "extended sets." This system combines a basic power exercise like a bench press with a lighter shaping exercise like dumbbell flyes.

Muscle priority – Concept of working your weakest muscle or muscle group first in your workout while you are the freshest.

Muscles - Refer to the anatomy charts in Chapter 1.

Pilates - An exercise system developed in the 1920s focused on improving flexibility, strength, and body awareness without building bulk. Specific spring resistance equipment is utilized with an emphasis on developing "core" strength and spinal alignment.

Peak contraction- After completing an exercise adding reps to cramp or create a burning sensation that can add sharper definition to the muscle.

Plyometric – a type of training that incorporates many types of jumping, but all jumping is not necessarily plyometric. This concept was first developed by the Russian track coaches in the 1980s by having athletes jump onto boxes of various heights, which required the muscles to exert maximum force in a short time. This dynamic system of training to increase speed and power has found new popularity in the training programs of today.

Progressive sets - Adding weight to each successive set of an exercise.

Protein - A complete protein contains all of the 10 essential amino acids, which are necessary for maximum muscular growth, building new tissue and repair. Found in both animal and vegetable forms.

Pumping up – See flushing.

Quality training – Getting the greatest amount of work completed in the allotted training session.

Repetitions - The number of times you perform an exercise in a given set. An example would be to perform one set of arm curls 10 times or repetitions.

Resistance training – Commonly refers to weight training of some sort

335

Rhythm - The pace you conduct your training.

Rupture - A complete tear of a ligament, tendon or muscle.

Sets - The number of times you perform a repetition in an exercise equals one set.

Single rep training – Not recommended unless you are a competitive weight or power lifter. Any person over 50 needs to forget about their ego and maxing out.

Small Muscles - These include the arms, (biceps, triceps) calves, and deltoids.

Split routine - Working different muscles on each day versus the entire body.

Sprain - Injuries to the ligaments, which stabilizes the joints of the body. The sprains may be classified as a 1, 2 or 3 based on severity.

Sticking points – A plateau that is reached when trying to improve the amount of weight you are capable of training with.

Strain - An injury to a muscles or the tendons, which attaches the muscles to the bones.

Super sets - Working antagonistic or opposing muscles in a non-stop motion. Ex. Performing a bicep exercise followed immediately with a triceps exercise or a leg curl followed with leg extensions.

Target heart rate –Your resting heart rate can be taken in the morning or at night by counting the pulse on your wrist for 10 seconds and multiplying by six. During a period of activity do the same and that will be your maximum heart rate. It is recommended that any aerobic exercise period stay within 50-

85% of that range for best results. Another method of estimating your maximum heart rate is to subtract your age from 220.

Tears - Same as a complete rupture of a ligament, tendon or muscle.

Tempo -The pace you move through your exercise program.

Tendons - Connective tissue that attaches the muscles to the bones. The Achilles tendon is the largest and thickest in the body.

Triglycerides - A combination of glycerol and the three fatty acids. (stearic, oleic, palmitic) Most animal and vegetable fats are triglycerides

Made in the USA
Las Vegas, NV
25 September 2024